OXF

MENO AI

MW01004258

PLATO (c.427–347 BCE), ... pro-
found and lasting influence upon Western intellectual tradition. Born
into a wealthy and prominent family, he grew up during the conflict
between Athens and the Peloponnesian states which engulfed the Greek
world from 431 to 404 BCE. Following its turbulent aftermath, he was
deeply affected by the condemnation and execution of his revered master
Socrates (469–399) on charges of irreligion and corrupting the young. In
revulsion from political activity, Plato devoted his life to the pursuit of
philosophy and to composing memoirs of Socratic enquiry cast in dialogue form. He was strongly influenced by the Pythagorean thinkers of
southern Italy and Sicily, which he is said to have visited when he was
about 40. Some time after returning to Athens, he founded the Academy,
an early ancestor of the modern university, devoted to philosophical and
mathematical enquiry, and to the education of future rulers or
'philosopher-kings'. The Academy's most celebrated member was the
young Aristotle (384–322), who studied there for the last twenty years
of Plato's life. Their works mark the highest peak of philosophical
achievement in antiquity, and both continue to rank among the greatest
philosophers of all time.

Plato is the earliest Western philosopher from whose output complete
works have been preserved. At least twenty-five of his dialogues are
extant, ranging from fewer than twenty to more than three hundred
pages in length. For their combination of dramatic realism, poetic beauty,
intellectual vitality, and emotional power they are unique in Western
literature.

ROBIN WATERFIELD has been a university lecturer (at Newcastle upon
Tyne and St Andrews), and an editor and publisher. Currently, however,
he is a self-employed writer, whose books range from philosophy and
history to children's fiction. He has previously translated, for Oxford
World's Classics, Plato's *Republic*, *Symposium*, *Gorgias*, and *Phaedrus*,
Aristotle's *Physics*, Herodotus' *Histories*, Plutarch's *Greek Lives* and
Roman Lives, Euripides' *Orestes and Other Plays* and *Heracles and Other
Plays*, Xenophon's *The Expedition of Cyrus*, and *The First Philosophers:
The Presocratics and the Sophists*.

OXFORD WORLD'S CLASSICS

*For over 100 years Oxford World's Classics have brought
readers closer to the world's great literature. Now with over 700
titles—from the 4,000-year-old myths of Mesopotamia to the
twentieth century's greatest novels—the series makes available
lesser-known as well as celebrated writing.*

*The pocket-sized hardbacks of the early years contained
introductions by Virginia Woolf, T. S. Eliot, Graham Greene,
and other literary figures which enriched the experience of reading.
Today the series is recognized for its fine scholarship and
reliability in texts that span world literature, drama and poetry,
religion, philosophy and politics. Each edition includes perceptive
commentary and essential background information to meet the
changing needs of readers.*

OXFORD WORLD'S CLASSICS

PLATO

Meno and Other Dialogues

Charmides, Laches, Lysis, Meno

Translated with an Introduction and Notes by
ROBIN WATERFIELD

OXFORD
UNIVERSITY PRESS

OXFORD
UNIVERSITY PRESS

Great Clarendon Street, Oxford OX2 6DP

Oxford University Press is a department of the University of Oxford.
It furthers the University's objective of excellence in research, scholarship,
and education by publishing worldwide in

Oxford New York

Auckland Cape Town Dar es Salaam Hong Kong Karachi
Kuala Lumpur Madrid Melbourne Mexico City Nairobi
New Delhi Shanghai Taipei Toronto

With offices in

Argentina Austria Brazil Chile Czech Republic France Greece
Guatemala Hungary Italy Japan South Korea Poland Portugal
Singapore Switzerland Thailand Turkey Ukraine Vietnam

Oxford is a registered trade mark of Oxford University Press
in the UK and in certain other countries

Published in the United States
by Oxford University Press Inc., New York

First published as an Oxford World's Classics paperback 2005
Reissued 2009

British Library Cataloguing in Publication Data

Data available

Library of Congress Cataloging in Publication Data

Plato.
[Dialogues. English. Selections]
Meno and other dialogues / Plato ; translated with an introduction
and notes by Robin Waterfield.
p.cm.—(Oxford world's classics)
Includes bibliographical references (p.   ) and index.
1. Philosophy. I. Waterfield, Robin, 1952–   . II. Title.
III. Oxford world's classics (Oxford University Press)
B358 .W38 2005   184—dc22   2004030366

ISBN 978-0-19-955566-6

5

Typeset in Ehrhardt
by RefineCatch Ltd, Bungay, Suffolk
Printed in Great Britain by
Clays Ltd, St Ives plc

CONTENTS

INTRODUCTION

One plausible view of Socrates is that he did not really have a philosophy, in the sense of a body of doctrine, so much as a method of philosophical enquiry. This volume contains four Platonic dialogues. Three of them are usually taken to be canonical 'dialogues of search'—that is, dialogues in which Plato portrays Socrates using his method of enquiry—while the fourth, *Meno*, shows Socrates above all working through issues thrown up by his method of enquiry. And it is usually thought that the three dialogues of search (*Charmides, Laches,* and *Lysis*)[1] belong to Plato's earliest period of writing, when he was concerned mainly to portray his mentor at work, while *Meno* belongs on the borderline of his middle period, when he was beginning to reflect upon aspects of his Socratic inheritance. Thus, while the first part of *Meno* (up to 79e) looks very like a dialogue of search, tackling the question 'What is excellence?',[2] the bulk of the dialogue raises fruitful questions which are designed to overcome difficulties raised by the search.

Socrates' method of enquiry is also known as the elenchus. The word is a transliteration of a Greek word at whose heart is the idea of 'challenge' or of 'testing'. In Plato's *Apology of Socrates*—his largely fictitious version of the defence speech Socrates delivered before the Athenians at his trial in 399 BCE—Socrates explains that, in response to the famous Delphic oracle which declared that there was no one wiser than Socrates, he began to question people, to see if they really knew what they thought they knew.

---

[1] Other Platonic dialogues of search: *Euthyphro, Hippias Major*, the first book of *Republic* (which many scholars believe to have been written separately, before the bulk of the dialogue). The much later dialogue *Theaetetus* is also written as a dialogue of search.

[2] This word will recur, so I had better say from the start that it is my preferred translation of the Greek *aretē*. *Aretē* is what makes a person or a thing perform its function well, and so it means, for instance, 'courage' in Homeric contexts, or 'virtue' in Socratic contexts; but it is also what makes you stand out, or excel. No translation is entirely satisfactory, yet it is one of the key words in fifth-century debate and in Plato's Socratic dialogues.

He challenged them, then, and invariably found that they had no more than superficial knowledge, or beliefs inherited from somewhere but not fully thought out, and not part of a coherent system of beliefs; they did not have anything which had the stability and certainty one would expect from knowledge. And so 'elenchus' in the sense of 'challenge' very often took on the aggressive sense of 'refutation', and the dialogues of search tend to end in *aporia* ('having no resources', 'having no way to progress', 'being in an impasse', 'being stuck'), as Socrates traps his interlocutors into infuriating self-contradiction. An impasse is more precise than 'confusion', as the word is often translated; it refers to the state of mental frustration which results when you have followed a train of thought as far as it can go, and it has failed to take you where you wanted or expected, and you can see nowhere else to go. Socrates clearly believed that *aporia* was good for the soul (e.g. *Charmides* 166c; without this belief, an aporetic conversation would just seem futile), and at *Gorgias* 458a Plato has Socrates even say that it is better to be refuted than to refute others. Our basic and worst sin, he thought, is believing that we know something when we really do not, and *aporia*, unlike plain ignorance, is a state where we are compelled to be aware of our ignorance and will hopefully be motivated to do something about it (though, oddly, few of the characters in the aporetic dialogues evince much interest in continuing their education).

So we are shown characters in the dialogues who believe they can define a virtue (an aspect of excellence), but are reduced to *aporia*. As long as they can be reduced to *aporia*, this shows that they did not really know what they were talking about. This applies even to Nicias in *Laches* or Critias in *Charmides*, whose definitions are Socratic and possibly correct, but are only accidentally correct, because they have heard them from someone else, not thought them up, thought them through, and made them known. The possession of a belief is in itself more or less useless: it remains a mere slogan unless one can defend it.[3] Equally, the

---

[3] See G. Rudebusch, 'Plato's Aporetic Style', *Southern Journal of Philosophy*, 27 (1989), 539–47; repr. in N. D. Smith (ed.), *Plato: Critical Assessments*, vol. 1: *General Issues of Interpretation* (London: Routledge, 1998), 349–56; repr. in G. Rudebusch, *Socrates, Pleasure, and Value* (New York: Oxford University Press, 1999), 9–17.

imparting of information by a teacher is more or less useless without understanding. Hence Socrates did not teach, but explored the contexts of his interlocutors' answers, even if that meant creating *aporia* in them. Later in his life, Plato looked back on Socratic enquiry and picked out as its chief features that, through cross-examination, it points up inconsistencies in a person's beliefs, and thereby makes people angry with themselves and more tolerant of others, purges the soul of the conceit of knowledge, and leaves the soul believing that it knows only what it does actually know (*Sophist* 230a–d).

The Dialogues of Search

The dialogues of search need some introduction, because there are aspects of them that can seem puzzling. They all end inconclusively: what has been the point? *Charmides* and *Lysis* are particularly odd, in that sometimes Plato seems to fall into little more than silly word games. The arguments Plato put into Socrates' mouth are sometimes bad, in the sense that they are formally fallacious, but these were still the early days of rational argumentation and the mistakes are often quite subtle. In any case, Plato was more concerned to show Socrates puzzling over critical issues, and to leave readers some room to work things out for themselves. The point of the arguments is to change people's lives, to make us better people, in the sense that, especially where moral issues are concerned, thinking something through and identifying underlying assumptions are always preferable to the unthinking and uncritical acceptance of society's injunctions. From this point of view, Plato was more interested in the process and in the conclusions than he was in providing formally valid arguments. Formal validity helped him only because it was persuasive, and he was concerned above all to persuade *individuals*—the kinds of people we see interacting with Socrates in the dialogues—which often gives the arguments an *ad hominem* feel.

The moral nature of these three dialogues is clear in the first place from their subject matter. *Charmides* investigates the nature of self-control, *Laches* does the same for courage, and *Lysis* explores the concept of friendship. Some readers might meet a moment's puzzlement here: why was friendship considered worthy of philosophical investigation? The goal of all Plato's dialogues, and his teaching in the school he set up (the Academy), was to get his audience to improve the quality of their lives—to live the good life, to fulfil themselves as human beings, to attain happiness, to live as godlike a life as is humanly possible. For Plato, these were just different ways of saying the same thing. Without friends, one's life would not just be emptier, but would hardly be a human life at all. Interaction with other people is part of what it is to be a human being, living in the real world, and friendly interaction improves the quality of one's life. So friendship has been investigated not just by Plato, but by a number of philosophers from all eras.[4] Moreover, the ancient Greeks invariably took friendship to be based on reciprocity: you are my friend if you scratch my back, and you expect me to do the same for you. This made friendship far more volatile and uncertain than we normally take it to be nowadays—and so, given the assumption that friendship improves the quality of life, it was more urgent for Plato to explore it.

The aspects of excellence examined in the other two dialogues were standard members of any ancient Greek list of cardinal virtues. Courage has been regarded as a virtue at all periods of human history. Of course, it is particularly relevant in a society such as that of ancient Athens, which was more or less constantly at war until membership of various empires sidelined it, but (as Plato was quick to point out) courage is important even outside of any military context: it takes courage to stand up to injustice and aggression in all walks of life, to face threats, and to preserve one's integrity in situations which would damage it.

Self-control, by contrast, is one of the quiet virtues, to do with co-operation rather than competition. The Greek word *sōph-*

[4] There is an excellent anthology: M. Pakaluk (ed.), *Other Selves: Philosophers on Friendship* (Indianapolis: Hackett, 1991). Pakaluk omits the interesting (but not philosophically central) Socratic discussions of friendship in Xenophon, *Memoirs of Socrates* 2.4–6.

rosynē means, originally, 'being of sound mind' (and so Plato implicitly defines it as mental health at *Charmides* 157a) and referred primarily to self-knowledge in the sense of knowing one's proper place in society. It covered a range from self-reliance and moderate self-restraint in the face of one's emotions and bodily appetites, through discretion, prudence, politeness, and good manners, to the kind of humility and self-effacement that patriarchal Greeks required of their womenfolk and the younger generation. In a political context, it had overtones of aristocratic conservatism; in a philosophical context (such as that of Heraclitus, Fragment 112), it could even mean the ability to see things as they are, without imposing one's own views.[5] All these shades of meaning play a part in *Charmides*, as Plato struggles to find some common core which underlies them, points out how difficult it is to understand the concept on traditional lines, and perhaps paves the way for a new understanding.

It is peculiarly appropriate to the moral nature of these three dialogues, and to the *ad hominem* nature of the argumentation, that Plato devotes so much care to characterization and scene-setting.[6] In *Laches*, half the dialogue has passed before Socrates gets down to investigating courage; in *Charmides* and *Lysis* the characterization not just of Socrates, but of the teenagers who are Socrates' interlocutors, is brilliantly and deftly handled, often with great charm and subtlety. The upper-class men and boys we find Socrates talking to in these dialogues are typical of his interlocutors; the other main category of interlocutor, not represented in this volume, consisted of professionals such as Sophists. These three dialogues of search are remarkable not just for the similarity of their structure and their portrait of Socrates at work, but for the artistry of their composition. Scene-setting and vivid interludes, brilliantly executed, occupy several pages in each dialogue, and it is clear that Plato cared about such things—though perhaps not so much as a way of communicating or supporting

[5] See especially H. North, *Sophrosyne: Self-knowledge and Self-restraint in Greek Literature* (Ithaca, NY: Cornell University Press, 1966).

[6] For the dramatic dates of the dialogues, see the notes to *Charmides* 153a, *Laches* 182a (second note), *Lysis* 211e (second note), and *Meno* 76e (third note).

some philosophical point, but as a way of flexing his artistic muscles.[7]

Another common feature to these three dialogues is the focus on young boys (the homoerotic aspect has been briefly covered in the Explanatory Notes). Although this is by no means universal in the dialogues—Socrates converses with people of all ages—in this respect Plato was surely giving us a faithful portrait of the historical Socrates. For almost all of Socrates' life, his native city was involved in a cold war, which often reached boiling point, with its great rival, Peloponnesian Sparta. The aristocratic youths who were Socrates' interlocutors in these dialogues would form the next generation of power-possessing politicians. It must have seemed crucial to Socrates that they should not unthinkingly accept the moral prescriptions of earlier generations, but should have reflected upon underlying principles, which could then be translated into prescriptions appropriate for the new world into which post-war Athens would emerge.

Charmides

Self-control forms the background to this dialogue, as well as its overt topic. Faced with a dialogue in which Socrates converses with Critias and Charmides, Plato's readers would immediately have been reminded of the subsequent careers of these two aristocratic members of Plato's own family (see the Index of Names). As prominent members of the brutal and bloody oligarchic regime which briefly ruled Athens in 404–403 BCE, they could hardly be said to have practised self-restraint,[8] as normally understood, though paradoxically, as opponents of Athenian democracy, the politically conservative overtones of *sōphrosynē* would have appealed to them. Socrates is distanced from them, not just by the fact that he disagrees with what they say, but by his display

[7] There is a broad division in Platonic scholarship at the moment between those who focus more on the arguments, those who focus more on the drama, and of course those who try to combine both approaches.

[8] Xenophon accuses Critias not just of being the most violent of the oligarchs, but of an intemperate private life too (*Memoirs of Socrates* 1.2). But then Xenophon is expressly defending Socrates against the charge of having helped to mould Critias' character.

of self-control at, especially, 155d–e: he does not allow his desire for Charmides' body to distract him from the task at hand, improving Charmides' soul.

Once they get down to discussing self-control, Charmides first proposes that it is a kind of unhurriedness (159b). Socrates' refutation of this idea is typical of many arguments in the dialogues. He points to several counter-examples, enough to show that Charmides' idea does not satisfy the criterion that a good definition should be universal: it should not be too narrow (it should not exclude things rightly held to fall under the concept in question) nor too broad (it should not include things rightly held not to fall under the concept in question). Socrates' approach is to gain Charmides' admission that self-control, whatever it may be, must be a good thing; the counter-examples, then, are simply cases (chosen from those familiar to Charmides' own experience) where unhurriedness is not or not always a good thing.

Charmides next moves from external behaviour to the internal state that might prompt such behaviour, and proposes that self-control is modesty (160e), but Socrates disposes of this by means of a single counter-example, gleaned from the authority of Homer: modesty is not always good, and therefore, given the assumption that self-control is always good, the two cannot be the same. These two definitions, and the next, were well entrenched in the everyday meanings of *sōphrosynē*, but Socrates is not necessarily claiming that the common understanding of *sōphrosynē* was entirely wrong; the elenchus is pointedly personal, and so we can take Plato to be claiming only that Charmides has failed to defend the common understanding, or that these ideas do not encompass all there is to say about self-control.

At this point Critias enters the conversation. In all three of the dialogues of search translated here, the entry of a new interlocutor indicates a rise in the level of sophistication of the search. And so Charmides' third definition (voiced by him, but attributed slyly to Critias at 161b–c and overtly at 162c–d) is that self-control is 'doing what pertains to oneself' (161b). There can be no doubt that Plato was attracted towards this definition: it became the definition of social justice in the later dialogue *Republic* (433a).

Here too it is placed in a social context, and Socrates refutes it by pointing out that in any such context people are involved to some extent in other people's business: teachers teach others, artisans make things for others, and so on. A society in which people did only what pertained to themselves, without any interaction with others, would hardly be a good society; but self-control must be something good, and so the definition is taken to be refuted.

Critias now enters the discussion in person (162c), prompted by the teasing of Charmides and Socrates. He proposes to reveal the idea underlying the definition of self-control as doing what pertains to oneself. This is important: it explains why Plato does not have Socrates subject his ideas to the same kind of blunt critique that Charmides' first two definitions received. Plato was attracted to the idea that self-control is doing what pertains to oneself, but he wanted to see it refined until it was unassailable, and so could stand as the definition of self-control. So the conversation with Critias can be seen as consisting of successive attempts to refine the definition.

Socrates first tries to substitute 'making' for 'doing' in the definition, but Critias rightly resists this move (162e–163c). He does so, however, in a peculiarly snobbish fashion, by sneering at artisans for 'making' things and commending the 'doing' of things as admirable. This allows Socrates to force a refinement of the definition: it is not 'doing what pertains to oneself', but 'the doing of good things' that is self-control (163e). This is a pretty desperate first attempt at refinement, but rather than demolishing it or considering what the vague phrase 'good things' might mean, Socrates simply uses it as an excuse to introduce the topic of knowledge, which will dominate the rest of the dialogue. The introduction of knowledge is significant because, as we will see more fully in *Laches*, Socrates appears to think that every aspect of excellence is or involves knowledge.

Someone may do good, or act beneficially, without knowing that he is doing so; therefore, Socrates claims, Critias' definition of self-control as doing good implies that self-controlled people do not know that they are self-controlled (164a–c). Socrates could have pulled this rabbit out of the hat whatever Critias had said, but Critias alters his definition of self-control to 'knowledge of

oneself'. Socrates tries to argue (as elsewhere in the early dialogues) that all branches of knowledge have a product, but Critias
rightly resists this move (165e–166c). By the time this piece of
Platonic self-criticism is over,[9] 'knowledge of oneself' has become
'knowledge of itself'—that is, knowledge of knowledge (166e),
which is the definition with which the remainder of the dialogue
is occupied.

Socrates tries to generate an impasse by pointing out that, if
there is such a thing as knowledge of knowledge, it is an oddity:
there is no such thing as sight of sight, or desire of desire. Critias
could simply respond that it may be a unique case, but Plato only
allows him to end up just as puzzled as Socrates (169c). All this is
Plato's way of getting us to think about knowledge of knowledge,
to remember that it is a familiar human experience that we can
not just know things, but be aware that we know things. On such
occasions the human psyche is split, so to speak, into higher and
lower levels, with the higher level overseeing the lower; in fact the
Greek word *sōphronistēs*, cognate with self-control, meant 'supervisor'. It is surely essential to self-control that a person has the
ability to stand back from whatever emotion or desire is moving
her, or is about to move her, in order to resist it. This must be
what Plato is driving at.

Over the subsequent pages, 'knowledge of knowledge' is inter-
preted in several different ways. First, it is taken to be 'knowing
what one does and does not know'. Intuitively, this is a reasonable
notion of *sōphrosynē*, which involved knowing one's limitations.
But Socrates gradually whittles away at the idea that knowledge
of knowledge has any true content: he first reduces it to 'knowing
that one does and does not know', and then to a kind of vague
awareness that one knows *something*, or at best a kind of general
supervisory knowledge, which ensures the smooth operation of
all other branches of knowledge. The chief assumption governing
the discussion is that all types of knowledge are the same, each
having just one domain and one product. On this assumption,
knowledge of knowledge is just that, knowledge of knowledge,

---

[9] It is self-criticism if Plato accepts Critias' point that not all 'crafts' have a
product. He does seem to accept it—'You're right,' he has Socrates say—and the
point recurs at *Statesman* 258d–e.

and cannot involve knowledge of anything else: it is not knowledge of health or knowledge of knowledge-of-health.

Moreover, on this assumption, knowledge of knowledge (if it can do anything) can *only* guarantee the smooth operation of the various other branches of knowledge; it cannot guarantee that such branches of knowledge will lead to happiness, because that will be a *different* branch of knowledge, namely knowledge of good and bad (174b–175a). Knowledge of knowledge, therefore, may make one efficient, but it makes no real contribution towards human life or happiness. It cannot be the same as self-control, then, because self-control must enhance one's life. Put another way, Plato seems to be pointing to the difficulty of understanding how knowledge of knowledge, understood as a purely cognitive state, can be equated with an aspect of moral excellence.

The final assumption controlling the argument, then, is that the possession of any excellence is bound to be beneficial,[10] and more specifically to contribute towards our happiness. The precise relation between excellence and happiness is a thorny topic in Socratic studies, but at any rate Socrates saw a very close link between the two, such that either excellence is both necessary and sufficient for happiness, or is at least necessary.[11] And the link is generated by the close connection between excellence and knowledge: in a famous argument (found in two minimally different versions, at *Euthydemus* 278e–282a and *Meno* 87d–89a), Plato has Socrates argue that it is always knowledge which guarantees success and therefore happiness. It is the fact that each aspect of excellence is some kind of knowledge that guarantees that it contributes towards human happiness. *Charmides* makes this more precise: it is knowledge of good and bad that is a necessary and sufficient condition for happiness. There is even the suggestion

[10] This is easier in Greek than in English: in Greek, 'excellence' (or 'virtue') is the abstract noun for 'goodness', and 'beneficial' means 'good for'—so of course the possession of goodness is bound to be good. Greek moralists, however, could cast self-control, *qua* a 'quiet' virtue, as not always helpful, e.g. when forceful action is needed.

[11] For the bearing on this debate of a passage in *Lysis*, see G. Lesses, 'Plato's *Lysis* and Irwin's Socrates', *International Studies in Philosophy*, 18 (1986), 33–43 (repr. in Prior (ed.), vol. 4, 252–62). For a short introduction to the issues, see A. Gómez-Lobo, *The Foundations of Socratic Ethics* (Indianapolis: Hackett, 1994). See also the note on *Meno* 87d.

that people with this kind of knowledge should, in an ideal world, have political power—and so the irony of having Charmides and Critias as interlocutors comes full circle: Charmides was generally held to be self-controlled, and Critias used the virtue as a political slogan; they both came to hold political power in Athens, but they were not truly self-controlled, because they lacked knowledge of good and bad.

The dialogue ends in the usual *aporia*—the interlocutors fail to arrive at a definition of self-control which survives Socrates' challenges—but several features of the discussion stand out as those which come closest to satisfying our intuitions about self-control. First, Plato makes it absolutely clear that he finds the notion of self-control as 'doing what pertains to oneself' highly promising: the entire latter half of the dialogue is devoted to trying to explicate this idea; it is just that neither Charmides nor Critias found a way to defend it. Second, the idea that self-control involves layers or levels of awareness and executive control within the human psyche must be right. Third, a little reflection on human happiness might have brought Socrates and Critias closer to the realization that self-control (or any of the virtues) involves not just an inner state (say, knowledge of knowledge), but external activity: if Critias had said that self-control was knowing what you do and do not know (i.e. knowing one's limitations) *and acting accordingly*, Socrates might have found it hard to challenge him. Since in other dialogues Plato is aware that excellence involves both an inner state and external action, he may even be expecting his readers to pick up on the strange omission and supplement the text accordingly.

Laches

The interaction between the five protagonists that occupies the first half of the dialogue leads naturally towards an enquiry into courage. Lysimachus and Melesias want to hear the opinion of Laches and Nicias about the value for their sons of an education in combat. In the late 420s (the time when the dialogue is set: see the second note to 182a), Nicias and Laches were at the height of their power in Athens, but they were to lose their lives in campaigns that helped to seal Athens' defeat in the Peloponnesian War, and Nicias, at any rate, gained a reputation for prevarication, if not outright cowardice. For Plato's fourth-century readers, then, there was no little irony in the choice of protagonists for this dialogue. Anyway, Socrates argues that what Laches and Nicias would have to say would be useful only if they were experts in education. The function of education is always to improve the pupil's soul, and therefore Laches and Nicias should demonstrate that they are experts in excellence. That is too grandiose a topic, however, and so they propose to focus on the 'part' of excellence which is presumably relevant to combat, and that is courage.

Laches first suggests that courage is remaining at one's post in battle (190e), but this restricts courage to the battlefield alone, whereas there are plenty of other situations in which courage can be displayed. Socrates wants to know what is common to courage in all situations (191e). Laches suggests, more plausibly, that it is 'mental persistence' (192b), but Socrates argues, first, that unintelligent persistence may be bad, and, second, that sometimes unintelligent persistence may be more courageous than intelligent persistence. Since everyone assumes that courage is a good thing and stupidity is a bad thing, Laches' definition fails. The first definition failed because it was too narrow (it failed to accommodate many cases of courage); the second failed because it was too broad (it failed to separate off unintelligent persistence). Laches may have failed, but he has allowed Socrates to introduce the idea that some kind of knowledge or intelligence is essential to courage, and it is the purpose of the rest of the dialogue to explore what kind of knowledge that might be.

So Nicias now enters the fray, with the explicitly Socratic idea that courage is a kind of knowledge (194c–d)—specifically, knowledge of what is and is not threatening in every situation requiring courage (194e–195a). As in *Charmides*, we move from traditional, Homeric ideas about the virtue in question to something more sophisticated, more theoretical, and more tinged with the learning current in Athens in the last quarter of the fifth century. After some preliminary sparring between Laches and Nicias, who have become rivals for Socrates' approval, Socrates initiates a more objective examination of this idea (196d). A threat lies in the future, so Nicias' definition implies that courage involves knowledge of the future. There is no branch or kind of knowledge, however, where knowing the future is different from knowing the past or present. Courage must therefore be knowledge of what is good and bad for oneself at any time, but that looks more like a definition of excellence as a whole, not just a part of it (199d–e; compare *Charmides* 174b–c). And so they have failed to define courage.

Laches is a more straightforward work than *Charmides*. We do not have to dig deep to uncover some positive lessons from the apparently negative course of the dialogue. Minor points of some importance include the distinction of morally neutral kinds of knowledge from those with moral relevance (195c–d) and the distinction between courage and fearlessness (196e–197d), both of which remain unchallenged. Most important, however, is the Socratic notion that goodness and knowledge always go together. It is not just that this idea informs the most serious part of the enquiry, but also that the conclusion it entails is endorsed by Plato's Socrates in other dialogues. In the dialogue *Protagoras*, Plato has Socrates argue precisely that every aspect of excellence is the same as every other, because they are all knowledge of good and bad, or at least that all the aspects of excellence are mutually entailing (see *Protagoras* 332a–333b, 349e–350c).[12] In other words, Nicias' definition of courage as knowledge of what is good and bad for oneself can stand; the reader has only to understand that Nicias' argument fails *only if* courage is taken to be merely an aspect of excellence. The main passage which has been taken to tell against this view of the purpose of the dialogue is 192b–193d,

[12] Opinions differ as to the precise details of the doctrine. See the papers reprinted in the section entitled 'The Unity of the Virtues' in Prior (ed.), vol. 4, and J. Cooper, 'The Unity of Virtue', *Social Philosophy and Policy*, 15 (1998), 233–74 (repr. in id., *Reason and Emotion: Essays on Ancient Moral Psychology and Ethical Theory* (Princeton: Princeton University Press, 1999), 76–117). On whether *Laches* qualifies Socratic intellectualism, see D. Devereux, 'The Unity of the Virtues in Plato's *Protagoras* and *Laches*', *Philosophical Review*, 101 (1992), 765–89 (repr. in Prior (ed.), vol. 4, 124–43); T. Penner, 'What Laches and Nicias Miss—and Whether Socrates Thinks Courage Merely a Part of Virtue', *Ancient Philosophy*, 12 (1992), 1–27; J. Gericke, 'Courage and the Unity of the Virtues in Plato's *Laches*', *South African Journal of Philosophy*, 13 (1994), 21–6.

where Socrates argues that sometimes unintelligent or at least uninformed action is more courageous than intelligent action. But this does not really tell against the intellectualist definition of courage: it simply awaits the distinction between courage and fearlessness (196e–197d). What appears to be unintelligent courage is actually fearlessness or recklessness, not courage. And then we should note that at *Meno* 88b boldness plus knowledge seems to be a candidate for courage. Perhaps Plato means us to read the entire latter part of the dialogue as an attempt to find what kind of knowledge needs to be added to a disposition such as Laches' 'persistence', so that we arrive at a definition of courage as 'persistence based on knowledge of what is good and bad'.

Socratic 'intellectualism' or 'rationalism'—the idea that excellence is knowledge—also manifests in certain paradoxical views attributed by Plato to him. Above all, Plato's Socrates held (1) that no one deliberately does wrong, and in fact that it is better to have wrong done to one than to do it oneself; (2) that no one wants anything bad, only good, and that any pursuit of anything bad is therefore involuntary.[13] The most paradoxical consequences of the paradoxes are that they appear to deny two things: (*a*) that a criminal or anyone does wrong deliberately; (*b*) that anyone can suffer from *akrasia*—weakness of will—such as knowing that I should not have that sixth glass of wine, but having it anyway. But deliberate criminality and weakness of the will are common occurrences. Nevertheless, Socrates did not think he was being paradoxical; he thought he was stating plain facts.

The denial of deliberate criminality is not a denial of the existence of crime as a social phenomenon; rather, it is an assertion that if the criminal *knew* what he was doing, he would not do wrong at all. All people aim at happiness or pleasure. The

---

[13] On the paradoxes, see G. Santas, 'The Socratic Paradoxes', *Philosophical Review*, 73 (1964), 147–64 (repr. in Sesonske and Fleming (eds.), 49–64, and in Santas, *Socrates*, 183–94); G. Nakhnikian, 'The First Socratic Paradox', *Journal of the History of Philosophy*, 11 (1973), 1–17 (repr. in Day (ed.), 129–51); H. Segvic, 'No One Errs Willingly: The Meaning of Socratic Intellectualism', *Oxford Studies in Ancient Philosophy*, 19 (2000), 1–45. Further reading is recommended in the note to *Meno* 77e. For the background to the paradoxes, see M. J. O'Brien, *The Socratic Paradoxes and the Greek Mind* (Chapel Hill: University of North Carolina Press, 1967).

criminal's mistake is that he supposes that his happiness lies in committing crimes. In fact, though, happiness is a function of the soul, not of the possession of material goods. And doing wrong harms the soul (even if it may benefit the body), so that the soul is not really being made happy by crime. Hence in *Gorgias* Plato goes so far as to argue that it is better to have wrong done to you than to do wrong yourself. Thus the criminal thinks he is acting in his own interest, but is not; he is acting from false belief, not from knowledge. If he acted from knowledge, he would not be a criminal.

The paradox of the denial of weakness of the will can be resolved in much the same way. If I really had knowledge of what was good and bad for me, I would not fail to act on it;[14] therefore the fact that I do have that sixth glass of wine shows that I do not really have knowledge. Wanting something that is (in actual fact) bad for me is a clear sign of lack of knowledge: we want only things that are good for us, but sometimes we foolishly mistake bad things for the good things we want. The difference between a man of knowledge and a fool is not that a fool wants bad things—that is impossible, according to Plato's Socrates—but that he mistakes what things are bad for him. In this context, in *Protagoras*, Plato has Socrates talk of a calculus of happiness. The person of knowledge weighs up pleasures and pains. He knows that the present pleasure of that extra glass of wine is going to be vastly outweighed by pain the next morning (or even sooner). And so he avoids the sixth glass (and probably stops at two, anyway).

This nest of ideas connects with the doctrine of the unity of the virtues. All virtue or excellence, as *Laches* suggests, is or involves knowledge of what is good and bad for me. Virtues are necessarily beneficial to the virtuous person, and it is the element of knowledge in them that makes them beneficial. So a person of knowledge, such as Socrates, stops after two glasses of wine, and is praised for his self-control; he refrains from criminal action, and is praised for his justice; he can be courageous, and so on. In all these situations, he is acting only from knowledge of what is

---

[14] Plato ignores what has been called the 'decision–action gap': there is a gap between deciding to do something and actually doing it.

good and bad for him, and from this point of view the common distinction between the virtues or aspects of excellence is meaningless. The knowledge involved in excellence, then, is self-knowledge, and this is the point of Socrates' frequent recommendation to 'look after one's soul' (e.g. Plato, *Charmides* 156e–157a, *Laches* 185d–e, *Apology* 29d–30a).[15]

Lysis

Lysis is a discussion of friendship—or rather, it is a discussion of *philia*. 'Friendship' is often an adequate translation of *philia*, but the Greek term was used to describe not just a human relationship, but being fond of certain pursuits or things: 'philosophy', for instance, is literally 'love of knowledge'. Where human relationships are concerned, *philia* is not just friendship, but drifts into 'love' (passionate or otherwise), 'affection', and even 'loyalty', since the Greeks were always pragmatic about friendship: it was defined as much by ties of mutual obligation as it was by any feeling or emotion, and often carried distinctly political connotations, in that your 'friends' were those who helped you in your political career and who expected to be repaid once you had gained a position of influence.[16] Hence in *Lysis* Plato has Socrates link friendship with need or lack (215a–b, 221d–e), and the background to several of the arguments is a broadly instrumentalist view of friendship. The semantic situation is enormously complicated by the fact that *philos*, the adjective cognate with *philia*, could bear an active sense, a passive sense, or both at once. That is, the same word could mean 'friendly towards' or 'liking', 'a friend of' or 'dear to' or 'liked', or 'friend' in the sense that two people are each other's friends.

---

[15] All this sounds very egoistical, and in a sense it is, but it is not immoral egoism, because Plato assumes that inner morality and external moral behaviour are inseparable. It is good for the agent to behave morally towards others. My soul is harmed by any wrong I do to others.

[16] The best brief account is D. Konstan, *Friendship in the Classical World* (Cambridge: Cambridge University Press, 1997), but for more on the political aspects see the essays by L. Foxhall and M. Schofield in P. Cartledge *et al.* (eds.), *Kosmos: Essays in Order, Conflict and Community in Classical Athens* (Cambridge: Cambridge University Press, 1998).

Plato has fun and games with these ambiguities (see the Explanatory Notes for examples).

As with *Charmides* and *Laches*, the scene-setting of *Lysis* is peculiarly relevant to the subsequent discussion. There is a lot of banter at the start about how Hippothales is in love with Lysis. The term translated 'love' here is not *philia*, but *erōs*, which was the word for 'passionate love' or even 'lust', and especially for what an older man felt for an attractive teenage boy. We have at least two models of affection in the characters of the dialogue: Hippothales' one-sided love for Lysis, and the friendship between Lysis and Menexenus. We also hear in the early stages of the dialogue of the *philia* felt by parents for their children (207d ff.), which is oddly said to depend on the children's usefulness to their parents. This would be the case only if the relationship between parents and children consisted solely in the parents' allowing or disallowing their offspring to do certain things.

Some interesting points emerge from this discussion about parental *philia*. A friend, it is implied, wants the best for his friend. He wants him to be happy, or to be free to do what he likes (short of harming himself in any way). But this freedom is granted only to those with knowledge, because it is knowledge that makes someone useful to others, and it is knowledge that guarantees that someone will not be harmed but benefited. It follows—though this is not explicitly brought out—that a true friend will educate his friend if he can, to give him the knowledge that brings happiness. There is no doubt that Plato means us to see Socrates' attitude towards his young associates as a model of this educational friendship, and the implication that a man of knowledge will be everyone's friend (210c–d) is a nice tribute to Socrates. Socrates embodies wisdom or knowledge; we have *philia* for what we lack; if we are aware of our lack of knowledge, we will want knowledge, which is to say that we will be philosophers. Socrates made his young associates philosophers.

There is one respect in which *Lysis* differs from *Charmides* and *Laches* (and other dialogues of search): Socrates himself comes up with all the ideas about friendship which are then examined. The dialogue, then, is not 'maieutic'—Socrates does not act as a 'mid-wife' for the birth of others' ideas.[17] We do not need to exaggerate this difference, however: there is no reason to think that Socrates did not use the elenchus to examine his own views (see Plato, *Apology* 21b; both Critias in *Charmides* and Nicias in *Laches* are mouthpieces for Socratic or quasi-Socratic views; and Plato came later to define thinking as an internal dialogue[18]). In any case, the arguments progress in a standard dialectical fashion: even though it is Socrates who proposes definitions or ideas for discussion, he does not examine them until he has gained a measure of agree-ment from his interlocutor. It is true that the dialogue does not start with a question of the form 'What is F?', as do both *Char-mides* (159a) and *Laches* (190d),[19] but this is a mere formality: the investigation of friendship is in all important respects parallel to those of other dialogues which search for a definition. The topic is 'what it is to be a friend' (216c, 223b), even though the first question was not 'What is a friend?', but 'Who is whose friend?' (212b). Plato is looking for the cause of friendship, with his usual definitional aims: so that he can understand the concept and iden-tify genuine cases.

By 216c, we want to say, 'So far, so good.' Plato has set out to examine friendship as a human relationship, explored the ambigu-ities inherent in the term (211d–213c, a flawed but very system-atic passage), and come across difficulties in two contradictory but initially plausible notions: that people who are similar are friends (214a–215c), and that people who are opposites are friends (215c–216b). The argument has been guided above all by the instrumentalist and egoist principle that friendship is a kind of lack or need; friendship is based on reciprocity and mutual utility and perceived value. But the dialogue now takes a curious dog-leg. Instead of talking about friendship as a relationship between two humans, much of the subsequent discussion is con-cerned with the nature of the befriended object, whether that is a

[17] For Socrates as a 'midwife' of ideas, see Plato, *Theaetetus* 150b–d, with M. Burnyeat, 'Socratic Midwifery, Platonic Inspiration', *Bulletin of the Institute of Clas-sical Studies*, 24 (1977), 7–16 (repr. in Benson (ed.), 53–65).

[18] *Theaetetus* 189e, *Sophist* 263e–264a, *Philebus* 38e; see also *Republic* 534b.

[19] This difference is stressed by D. Sedley, 'Is the *Lysis* a Dialogue of Definition?', *Phronesis*, 34 (1989), 107–8.

person or something inanimate. *Philia* changes from being a mutual relationship to attraction towards something. A lot of the puzzlement some readers feel is due to the fact that we think of friendship as a mutual relationship, whereas Plato spends much of the dialogue exploring one-sided attraction. This is because he sees human friendship as a species of desire or attraction, which is the more general concept.

Given that the previous discussion has already excluded the possibilities that good is attracted towards good, or bad towards bad, or good towards bad, or like towards like, we are left with the possibility 'that what is neither good nor bad may be the friend of [i.e. attracted to] what is good' (216e–217a). These are the terms of the ensuing discussion. Plato first argues (217a–218c) that it is the presence of something bad that attracts what is neither good nor bad towards the good. That is, for instance, illness (bad) causes a body (in itself, neither good nor bad) to be attracted to health (good). The thing that is neither good nor bad cannot be totally or essentially corrupted by the presence of the bad thing, because then it would be bad, not neither good nor bad, and bad things cannot be friends of good things; but something bad must be non-essentially or contingently present to it. This is the first occurrence in philosophical literature of the critical distinction between essential and non-essential properties.

Again, the argument rests on the egoist assumption that a person is attracted towards something because of the good it can do him. This attitude towards friendship has been harshly criticized —should we not value friends for their own sake (whatever that may mean), not for what they can do for us?—but Plato is exploring the foundation of friendship. It is not clear that he is wrong that the foundation of friendship is some kind of need, and he still leaves room for affection and a less self-centred type of relationship to develop on the utilitarian foundation: one of his examples of 'friendship', for instance, is the love of parents for a baby (212e–213a). Moreover, the criticism anachronistically applies a post-Romantic conception of friendship to the ancient Greeks, for whom the *value* of friends was uppermost.

The interlocutors rest on their laurels only momentarily, however, before Socrates introduces a complication. After summarizing the previous argument in somewhat different terms (218d–219b), he draws out from it, as an implication, the notion that anything attractive is found attractive only as a means to some further attractive end (219b–c). This process will necessarily either go on *ad infinitum*, or end with a 'primary lovable object, the final end which makes everything else that is lovable lovable' (219d). And if there is such a primary lovable object, the model of 'friendship' they arrived at before—that it is the presence of something bad that attracts what is neither good nor bad towards the good—needs qualification, because only the primary lovable object is a true friend (object of desire), while everything else is a subordinate or second-rate friend, a friend not in itself but only as a means to a further end (219d–220b). Plato thinks that we should now be in a position to see what is essential to friendship or attraction.

The qualification that Plato insists upon, somewhat tortuously (220b–221d), is to eliminate as non-essential the idea that it is the presence of badness which makes something lovable or attractive. In actual fact, he says, it is just desire or lack which makes something attractive. He makes this move, I think, because he wants the primary lovable object to be attractive *in itself*, not because of the presence of something bad; so there is a hint here of the possibility of altruistic friendship, in which something is found attractive not just for the good it can do the person who finds it attractive. Desire is then analysed, with alarming abruptness (221e), as desire for something close to oneself. Since closeness is a symmetrical relationship (if A is close to B, B is also close to A), then if A loves, likes, desires, or befriends B, B must also do the same for A (222a). We have turned back along the dog-leg to friendship as a personal and reciprocal human relationship, but more importantly this idea conflicts with principles earlier taken to be stable, especially that bad people cannot be friends (222b–d). And so the dialogue ends with the usual *aporia*—and as usual the *aporia* is caused by Plato's own terminological confusion and his insistence on trying to find just one common core to a multi-faceted concept.

It is possible to spot one or two propositions that remain unrefuted in the course of the dialogue, and so to claim that Plato means us to deduce that, for instance, what is good in a person is attracted towards what is good in another person, and that this is the basis of their friendship. Then we can note that, at *Phaedrus* 255b, for instance, Plato readily agrees with this proposition: 'It is fated', he says, 'that bad men can never be friends and that good men can never fail to be friends' (see also *Laws* 837a). In the context of mutual affection between good people, Plato remains convinced that the principle 'like is friend to like' is valid (*Gorgias* 510b, *Phaedrus* 240c), despite its rejection in *Lysis*. So if we reinstate the principle, then what is neither entirely good nor entirely bad (i.e. a person) may be the friend of what is neither entirely good nor entirely bad (another person), to which it is similar, in those respects in which the two parties are good. And we can say that the basis of their friendship is that they should be useful to each other (benefit each other, bring out the good in each other), because this instrumentalist assumption is nowhere questioned and guides several of the arguments. All desire is for the good; something perceived as good (whether or not it actually is) is always the object of desire. When a person's desire for the good is channelled through a relationship with another person, that is human friendship.[20] The dialogue is not an incoherent muddle, shifting from the reciprocal to the passive sense of 'friendship' and simultaneously from a reciprocal human relationship to one-sided attraction: it is a study of attraction, bracketed by an investigation of the human relationship as a type of attraction.

It also seems clear, on surveying the course of the arguments, that what really interested Plato was what we may call the non-obvious, subliminal, or even metaphysical aspects of attraction. When we find something attractive, what is it about it that we are *really* attracted to, and why? Does this differ from what we say or think we are attracted to? Plato's main suggestions here are that we are attracted to something either because of some imperfection in ourselves (as a body is attracted towards a doctor because of its illness) or because of some psychic need which is as natural

---

[20] This is fully compatible with the view of friendship which can be extracted from *Republic*: see G. X. Santas, 'Plato on Friendship and Familial Love in the *Lysis* and the *Republic*', *Philosophical Inquiry*, 6 (1984), 1–12 (also chapter 4 of his *Plato and Freud: Two Theories of Love* (Oxford: Basil Blackwell, 1988)).

as physical thirst and hunger. *Lysis* is an essay in psychology as much as a logical investigation, and it is precisely this interest in the hidden aspects of love that Plato was to take to even more rarefied heights in *Symposium* and *Phaedrus*. In these dialogues the 'primary lovable object', so barely hinted at in *Lysis* that we cannot even say what it is, is fleshed out as the domain of those metaphysical entities which are usually called 'Forms': the Form of Beauty is the true object of love, and all other lovable objects are pale reflections.

The Socratic Elenchus

Several questions arise from our survey of these three dialogues, and we may as well start with one of the trickiest. Each dialogue ends in *aporia*: the interlocutors fail to come up with definitions that satisfy the elenchus. Can the Socratic elenchus do more than point up inconsistencies or other forms of deficiency in others' views? Is it purely destructive, or can it be constructive?[21]

The structure and nature of the standard elenchus is pretty straightforward. Essentially, one of the speakers (usually not Socrates) offers a definition of a moral concept. Socrates then shows how this definition D (or its consequences) clashes with some other proposition P (or its consequences).[22] Faced with a choice of rejecting D or P, the proposer of the original definition invariably chooses to reject D.[23] He prefers P to D because the ideas represented by P are, as the summary of the dialogues above shows, invariably general propositions taken to be self-evident, such as 'Courage is a good thing' or 'Excellence is beneficial'. The interlocutor weighs up the evidence in favour of D and the evidence in favour of P, and rejects D.

[21] I acknowledge that my use of the singular 'elenchus' disguises the fact that Socrates uses a variety of argumentative and other techniques to achieve his ends. I use the term as a convenient way to refer to Socratic argumentation, which was always testing, and because I focus on one common form of argument, usually called 'the standard elenchus', which is the kind of argumentation that was particularly distinctive of Socrates. For a corrective to this simplification, see Brickhouse and Smith in Scott (ed.), 145–57.
[22] Often, the train of consequences is not given in full, but obvious stages are missed out. Moreover, P is usually assumed to be true, rather than argued for.
[23] There are rare exceptions: *Charmides* 164c–d, *Laches* 197a–b.

This is the bare, logical skeleton of the elenchus. It is not so much a refutation of D as it is a testing of D, by indirect means, and though Socrates may sometimes conclude that D is wrong (e.g. *Charmides* 161b), he may also say no more than words to the effect that 'D is not necessarily right' (e.g. *Charmides* 160c). Even when he says that D is wrong, he may be saying no more than that D is conditionally wrong: it is wrong if P is accepted. This is important: logically, it is clear that the elenchus can do no more than test for consistency, and it is in the first instance not a refutation of D, but a refutation of the interlocutor's belief in D and a test of his ability to defend D. At *Charmides* 162d Plato has Critias protest that Charmides' failure to defend the third definition of the dialogue shows no more than that Charmides put up a bad defence; it does not show that the proposition is inherently wrong.

The elenchus is not just a logical tool; each elenctic conversation hinges too much on the views and even the character of the interlocutor to attain objectivity. Then again, Socrates often distorts or alters D, or fails to get the interlocutor's secure assent to all the consequences of either or both of D and P. In short, Plato finds a number of ways to blur the potentially clean logical edges of the elenchus. The personal character of the elenchus is inescapable and is enhanced by a factor called the 'sincere assent' constraint.[24] If the elenchus is to purge an interlocutor of the conceit of knowledge, which is what Plato takes it to do (as at least one of its primary purposes), then the interlocutor must be present (so at *Meno* 71d Socrates refuses to engage with the absent Gorgias) and must believe in D, because otherwise the argument will not show that he thought he knew something when he did not, and he must give his assent to P and to the consequences of P which prove to be D's downfall.

But Plato does not have Socrates consistently insist on sincere assent: he waives the constraint from time to time, or allows interlocutors to get away with qualified assent, or professes himself

---

[24] On which see (apart from items in the main bibliography, especially Beversluis, *Cross-Examining Socrates*, ch. 2), T. Irwin, ' "Say What You Believe" ', in T. Irwin and M. Nussbaum (eds.), *Virtue, Love, and Form: Essays in Memory of Gregory Vlastos* (Edmonton: Academic Printing & Publishing, 1993), 1–16.

interested only in the ideas, not the people. In this volume, for instance, we meet the constraint at *Meno* 83d and *Charmides* 166d–e, but nowhere else. This suggests that Plato did think that the elenchus could or should be a tool for examining ideas, not just people, and there is plenty of other evidence to support this view, starting with the explicit assertion of this at *Charmides* 161c: 'We're not remotely interested in considering whose idea it is, just in whether or not it's true' (see also 166c–e). Then again, in several dialogues (e.g. *Euthyphro* 11e, *Hippias Major* 293d) the conversation does not end with the *aporia* of the interlocutor: Socrates himself makes a suggestion to keep things going. Likewise, several times in *Meno* (within the passage 74b–76e) and elsewhere (in the dialogues translated in this volume at *Laches* 192a–b), Socrates provides model definitions to help his interlocutor along. It is true that in all these cases Socrates and his interlocutors end up in *aporia* anyway, but that is not the point: the point is that they tried; they did not just stop as soon as refutation had occurred. In short, Plato has Socrates take a genuine interest in examining ideas for their own sake, even if they come from him or from some external source such as a poet. The elenchus is above all a method of enquiry, not just a means of puncturing someone's conceit.

Those who believe that the elenchus can only be destructive point above all to the fact that this is all we are shown in the dialogues: we are consistently shown interlocutors reaching a state of puzzlement, but no more. Plato's Socrates clearly believes in the positive, cathartic effects of *aporia*, but those positive effects are not a direct result of the elenchus; the elenchus is no more than a preliminary. 'In order to make men virtuous, you must make them know what virtue is. And in order to make them know what virtue is, you must remove their false opinion that they already know. And in order to remove this false opinion, you must subject them to elenchus.'[25]

---

[25] Robinson, 15. Benson is currently the main proponent of the non-constructionist interpretation of the elenchus, whose forefather was Carneades in the second century BCE. Other views are represented by various items in the main bibliography, and the starting-point, as usual, is the essays reprinted in Prior (ed.), vol. 3.

However, there is overwhelming evidence that Plato did think the elenchus could have constructive results, and could do so directly, not just as a preliminary. In a later dialogue, at *Theaetetus* 149a, Plato has Socrates say that the interpretation of the elenchus as purely destructive is a sign of ignorance; he can also use it to elicit ideas from people. At *Charmides* 166d Socrates boldly claims that the elenchus can reveal 'the nature of each and every existing thing', and a passage a little later in *Charmides* also supports the idea that the elenchus can have a constructive purpose. If, as scholars agree, the definition of *sōphrosynē* as 'knowledge of knowledge and of lack of knowledge' (166e) is meant to be, at least in part, a description of the effect of the Socratic elenchus, it is important to note that it is not just the ability to uncover lack of knowledge, but also of actual knowledge: the elenchus does not just prick bubbles of conceit,[26] but reveals when someone does genuinely know something. What survives the elenchus may be taken to be true, as Plato says at *Gorgias* 479e, 505e, 508e–509a, and at *Crito* 46b, 48d–e, and 49d–e; this is also implied by *Sophist* 230a–d (paraphrased on p. ix). *Charmides* 175d is just one of several passages where Plato has Socrates say that he expects the elenchus to come up with the truth.

How, then, does something survive the elenchus? In order to challenge D, Socrates produces another idea, P, which directly or indirectly contradicts D. In accepting P, or at any rate preferring P to D, the interlocutor is accepting that P is right, or is more likely to be right than D.[27] In other words, these more general propositions not only regulate the discussion, but also serve as the parameters for possible constructive accounts: in order to survive the elenchus, a proposition must be consistent with P. Even if the dialogues fail to take us past *aporia*, they do show how a constructive discussion should proceed, and in *Gorgias* (a later, more reflective work), Plato gives several examples of elenctic arguments throwing up ideas which are taken to be true.

But how can Socrates claim to be searching for truth when all

---

[26] Hence it is often contrasted with arguing just for the sake of winning, as at *Laches* 196b–c.

[27] H. May (in McPherran (ed.), 37–50) usefully spells out the notion of something being 'more likely to be right' or 'more nearly right' in the Socratic dialogues.

he can reasonably expect to do is test for consistency? As Irwin trenchantly puts it: 'Whatever Socrates may think, the formal structure of the elenchus allows him to test consistency, not to discover truth. If I survive an elenchus with my original beliefs intact, I have some reason to believe they are consistent; but they may be consistently crazy.'[28] The way out of this puzzle is to recognize (as a number of scholars have done) that Plato's Socrates seems to believe that there are two kinds or degrees of truth.[29] On the one hand, there is the knowledge which experts have; on the other hand, there is correctable or fallible knowledge, as exemplified in everyday speech, for instance, when a non-doctor says, 'I know it's unhealthy to smoke.' An expert can be reasonably certain that he has grasped the truth of some matter. Correctable knowledge, however, is what Plato's Socrates believes the elenchus can produce. It is correctable in the sense that further bouts of the elenchus on the same issue may improve one's knowledge. To the extent that Socrates himself knows anything (as he occasionally claims to) or steers arguments in particular directions (which presupposes hunches, at the very least), he may claim to have correctable knowledge. At the same time, his constant disavowal of knowledge is sincere: he is a genuine participant in the search for more certain knowledge.[30]

In short, then, the truth which Socrates searches for by means of the elenchus is the kind of truth which accompanies consistency. If a consistent set of beliefs, which incorporates notions (all those Ps) which are reasonably held to be true, survives repeated elenchi, it has a better chance of being true than an inconsistent set. Consistency is close to being the mark of a set of true beliefs, Plato's Socrates believes (and he would not be the last coherence

[28] Irwin, *Plato's Moral Theory*, 41.

[29] Aristotle too equivocates in the same way on 'knowledge' in his description of Socratic argumentation at *Sophistical Refutations* 172a.

[30] Plato frequently has Socrates disavow moral knowledge. In this volume, see *Charmides* 165b–c, 166c–d, 169a; *Laches* 186c, 200e; *Lysis* 223b; *Meno* 71a–b, 80d. I take the disclaimer to be sincere and restricted to infallible moral knowledge; it is not the disavowal of *all* knowledge, nor of the possession of certain convictions which may even be true beliefs. The papers reprinted in the section 'Socratic Ignorance' in Prior (ed.), vol. 1, provide the starting-point for further reading.

theorist to do so);[31] and we may go along with him to the extent of agreeing that consistency is both rare and rationally compelling. Nevertheless, Plato is aware that this kind of truth falls short of absolute truth, which he attributes to genuine experts.

The elenchus is not a monolithic enterprise; it is complex, hard to pin down, and constantly surprising. It punctures interlocutors' conceit of knowledge as a preliminary to replacing false beliefs, challenges the moral views by which they have guided their lives, throws up propositions on which any more defensible views should be founded, and constantly seeks the clarification of ideas and the attainment of beliefs which serve to explain broad moral issues and to allow people to live more moral lives in the future.

Socrates' Search for Definitions

Each of the three dialogues paraphrased above is motivated by the search for the definition of a moral concept. Why was definition important for Socrates, and what did he expect of it?[32] In Socrates' time, disputable terms (such as moral terms, above all) were not settled. Are they ever? But there was not even a dictionary or encyclopedia to which one could refer, and people used these terms in very different ways, depending on their social status (a lot of Socrates' interlocutors, who were always aristocrats, betray their snobbishness), or on how much of the new learning they had imbibed, or on what various poets had said about the concept in question, and so on. Socrates saw his job as settling definitions once and for all, in a rational manner, as a legacy to the future, so that people could then know what these terms meant. Hence he rightly kept emphasizing that one needs first to know what a thing is before trying to determine its

---

[31] For a short introduction to the issues, see A. R. White, *Truth* (London: Macmillan, 1970).

[32] See the essays in Prior (ed.), vol. 3; Robinson; L. Grimm, *Definition in Plato's Meno* (Oslo: Oslo University Press, 1962); G. Nakhnikian, 'Elenctic Definitions', in Vlastos (ed.), 125–57; Beversluis, 'Socratic Definition'; Crombie in Day (ed.), 172–207; Wolfsdorf, 'Understanding the "What-is-F?" Question' and 'Socrates' Pursuit of Definitions'.

properties: one *does* need a standard to refer to in the case of dispute, and if one also adheres to the principle of univocality, that standard will be single.[33]

It is important to notice that, in his search for definitions, Socrates is not committed to a view which became known in the scholarly literature as the 'Socratic fallacy'—that one cannot know *anything* about a concept until one can define the concept and until one knows what it is in itself. On this view, for instance, *Lysis* 223b was taken to be saying that, despite being friends, Socrates and his companions could not even know if they were friends unless they could define friendship. This position is obviously absurd in itself, and it is not true to the relevant texts. Here, for instance, Plato is saying no more than that friends have the best chance of knowing what friendship is. Other alleged versions of the fallacy occur in our dialogues at *Meno* 71a–b and 100b, *Charmides* 159a, 176a–b, *Laches* 190b–c, and *Lysis* 212a. But a close look at these passages (and at *Euthyphro* 6d–e, 15c–e, *Hippias Major* 286c–d, 304d–e, *Republic* 354b–c, *Gorgias* 448e, 463c) shows that, in committing Socrates to the epistemic priority of definition, Plato committed him only to a nest of reasonable points of view: (1) in order to determine whether or not F has such-and-such a disputable property, it is necessary to know first what F is (e.g. it helps to know what excellence is in order to decide whether or not it is teachable); (2) there are certain things only an expert knows about F, and expertise requires knowing the essence of F or being able to define F; the rest of us, while falling short of expertise, may still have true beliefs about F; (3) in certain

---

[33] The principle of univocality is the somewhat odd assumption that terms are not ambiguous—that the Greek language, in having a single term for something, reflected reality. Of course Plato recognized the ambiguity of many terms, but for some reason he has his Socrates take for granted, and take as the foundation of his enquiries, the principle of univocality. Particularly prominent cases of the assumption in this volume can be found at *Laches* 191e and *Meno* 72a–c and 74d. *Meno* 73a is interesting, as the only time in the dialogues that the assumption of univocality is questioned and defended (though *Laches* 192b–c comes close), and we are not meant to take it as a serious worry, since it comes from Meno not Socrates. The assumption is that there is a character F which makes all instances have F-ness; that this character F is what F is; and that this character F is not identical with its instances, but is something that can be shared among instances.

cases, theoretical knowledge is preferable to experiential knowledge.[34]

So Socrates asks for a definition of a term, and his interlocutors attempt to answer him to his satisfaction. There are a number of things wrong, Socrates thinks, with the answers he usually gets, and he expresses his dissatisfaction with their first attempts by saying that what he wanted was a definition of F in itself, not a catalogue of F's properties, nor a list of kinds of F behaviour, nor anything else. But it is extremely difficult to know what Plato was asking for when he asked for a definition of F *in itself* as opposed to naming any of its attributes. Was he, as some commentators think, trying to introduce a new entity into our conceptual treasury—an entity F which is ontologically distinct from all the things and kinds of things characterized as F? Or was he simply using the term 'F' as a convenient way of referring to a universal, the common characteristic of all F things, without implying any or much metaphysical baggage? It seems most likely that Socrates was not a metaphysician (that the theory of Forms was a Platonic development) and that he conceived of the universal as an inherent property of each and every particular F or kind of F: 'The definiendum of a Socratic definition of F-ness or the F is probably an attribute, which (a) is one and the same in all things that are F, (b) is that by reason of which all F things are F, (c) is that by which all F things do not differ but are the same, and (d) is that which in all F things we call "F-ness" or "the F".'[35]

But there are still difficulties. If we define 'human being' as 'animated featherless biped', that will enable us to identify human beings, but we have named attributes of human beings. One of the perennial problems with definitions is that it is very hard to avoid employing terms in the definition which in turn beg for their own

---

[34] The controversy can be tracked through the papers reprinted in the section 'Socratic Definition' in vol. 3 of Prior (ed.). Additional important papers: M. Burnyeat, 'Examples in Epistemology: Socrates, Theaetetus and G. E. Moore', *Philosophy*, 52 (1977), 381–98; G. Vlastos, 'Is the "Socratic Fallacy" Socratic?', *Ancient Philosophy*, 10 (1990), 1–16 (repr. in id., *Socratic Studies*, 67–86); W. Prior, 'Plato and the "Socratic Fallacy" ', *Phronesis*, 43 (1998), 97–113; D. Wolfsdorf, 'The Socratic Fallacy and the Epistemological Priority of Definitional Knowledge', *Apeiron*, 37 (2004), 35–67.

[35] Santas, *Socrates*, 108.

definitions. An infinite regress ensues. Plato shows himself aware of this problem and would allow what we may call working definitions or conceptual analyses (*Meno* 75b–c; see also the note to *Laches* 192b). They may not perfectly state the essence of excellence (or whatever), but they allow us to identify cases of excellence, and that is a good start.

Now, there are different kinds of definition. Above all, a 'nominal' or 'dictionary' definition tells us how people or a privileged group of people use or should use a term, whereas a 'real' or 'essential' definition tells us about the thing itself, not just about verbal usage (though that may be covered as well, with all the possibility of confusion that may be implied by saying that Plato was looking for two different kinds of definition at once).

It seems clear that Plato was not after just a nominal definition. A true definition, he held, must have enormous explanatory power; it must cover each and every instance of the concept being defined, and it must cover only the concept being defined. It must allow us to identify cases of the concept in question, to understand what makes them such cases, and to deduce further properties of the concept (as in *Meno* the definition of excellence is supposed to tell us whether excellence is teachable). It must also be such that, every time one uses the term being defined, one could replace it with the definition, but not in the way that a mere synonym would: it must reveal something about the essence of the concept being defined, about what self-control (or whatever) really is, and what makes a self-controlled person self-controlled. It must not simply pick out contingent attributes of the concept: self-control may indeed on occasion be akin to modesty or unhurriedness, but it is not always, and so defining self-control in these terms does not illuminate its essence. It must not implicitly employ the term to be defined in the definition: Laches' first definition of courage, for instance, is (in brief) resistance. But if courage is resistance, then in answer to the question 'What is courage?' he is saying no more than courage is the ability to act courageously. In short, it must articulate the structure of reality, or at least of as much of reality as is encapsulated by the term in question. It seems reasonable to think that Plato was striving towards what would later be called definition *per genus et differentiam*: in this way F is related to members of the same family, and we also hear what makes it specifically different. So Plato has Socrates qualify Laches' generic definition of courage as 'persistence' by specifying that perhaps 'intelligent persistence' stands a better chance as a definition, or he qualifies Meno's definition of excellence as 'rulership' by specifying that it must be 'just rulership', or at *Meno* 76a he offers a model definition of shape as 'the limit of a solid'.

The rigour of these requirements on a good definition has important moral and methodological consequences. It is precisely because Socrates' expectations are so stringent and perhaps unrealistic that he can tie his interlocutors up into knots and reduce them to *aporia*. A core assumption of the elenchus is that knowledge presupposes the ability to give an account: if I know F, I can say what F is. Moroever, if someone possesses an aspect of excellence, one may reasonably expect him to be able to give an account of it, or to know it (*Charmides* 158d–159a, *Laches* 193d–e, *Lysis* 223b). Hence Socrates converses with Charmides about self-control because Charmides is held to possess self-control; he converses with generals about courage, and he converses with friends about friendship. But what happens? They are incapable of producing satisfactory definitions. They thought they knew what F was, but end up being uncertain of this—and even doubting that they possess the quality, because they lack a way of safely identifying whatever it is that they possess as an instance of the quality in question. They are therefore impelled—or so Plato piously hoped (*Meno* 84a–c)[36]—to start again, to find some way of possessing the aspect of excellence and of knowing for sure that they do so.

Meno

As already remarked, *Meno* begins as a dialogue of search. Meno asks whether excellence (virtue) is teachable or a natural endow-

---

[36] The short pseudo-Platonic dialogue *Cleitophon* interestingly has the interlocutor criticize Socrates for doing no more than encouraging people to change their lives, and for failing to tell them in practical terms how to build on the foundation provided by the elenchus. See S. R. Slings, *Plato: Clitophon* (Cambridge: Cambridge University Press, 1999).

ment,[37] and Socrates, true to the principle of the epistemic priority of definition (p. xxxiv), converts the question to 'What is excellence?' Meno's attempts at definitions are all unsatisfactory. First (71e–72a), he does not even answer the question. Instead of addressing the question 'What is excellence?', he acts as if the question had been 'What different kinds of excellence are there?': he lists examples of excellence, and Socrates deploys the assumption of univocality to ask what is common to them all. Meno then suggests that it is the ability to rule (73c), but Socrates argues that this definition is simultaneously too broad and too narrow. First, there are counter-examples (is a slave excellent if he has the ability to rule his master?), and second, if the ability to rule bears any relationship to excellence, it does so only because a good or excellent ruler makes use of justice (in other words, it is not merely a question of what one does, but how one does it). But justice is only one aspect of excellence, so that does not bring us any closer to understanding what excellence is as a whole or in itself. Finally, Meno suggests that excellence is the ability to procure good things for oneself (78c, a modification of 77b), but if the ability to procure good things is to stand a chance as a definition of excellence, it needs a qualification that names at least one aspect of excellence (e.g. 'procuring things justly, not unjustly'), and so the definition fails for the same reason as the previous one, and is meaninglessly circular.

By 80a, then, the dialogue has reached the usual state of *aporia*. Unlike *Charmides, Laches*, and *Lysis*, however, *Meno* does not stop there. At 80a–d, wriggling with embarrassment at his failure in the first part of the dialogue, Meno tries to regain the advantage first by blaming Socrates for his own failure (a not unparalleled ploy from a Socratic interlocutor), and then by challenging Socrates with an apparent paradox. What is the point of trying to define anything—of asking 'What is F?' about anything—when you necessarily either already know it or you do not? If you already know it, you do not need to undertake the search (this is the 'paradox of enquiry'); if you do not know it, how will you recognize it when you find it (this is the 'paradox of recognition')?

---

[37] This is the topic also of Plato's *Protagoras*, and compare *Laches* 190d–e.

Plato could perhaps have given Socrates easy responses. He could argue against the paradox of enquiry that one knows that one is looking for 'excellence' (or whatever it is that is named in the question which initiates the search) without knowing what actual thing corresponds to the word in inverted commas, or in other words that there are stronger and weaker senses of 'know': we need to be able only to identify a subject in order to make it a topic for enquiry. And against the paradox of recognition he could argue that he will recognize his quarry when he reaches it because it will enable him to identify what is common to all instances and kinds of excellence. He could even have constructed an answer along the lines of *Charmides*—that it is possible to know in some sense both what one knows and what one does not know. Instead, however, Plato takes the paradox to strike at the very heart of the Socratic enterprise of definition. In asking 'What is F?', Socrates assumes an answer is possible, and that F can be known.[38] Plato interprets Meno's paradox as asking how we can know anything (or at least anything non-empirical, because Meno's paradox does not rule out empirical knowledge, only the kind of knowledge Socrates was after with his 'What is F?' question).

Plato's answer—an answer of astonishing daring—is that everything we know, everything we seem to 'learn', is a truth to which we already have access. The paradox claimed that we either do or do not have knowledge, and that in either case enquiry (or at least the kind of enquiry where the quarry has been set in advance) is superfluous; Plato's response is to claim that there is middle ground—that we may know something latently without knowing it consciously. The soul is immortal, and at some unspecified time or times in the past it has acquired knowledge of

---

[38] Weiss denies this, stressing that philosophy for Socrates was an ongoing, never-ending quest. Knowledge will never be attained. This leads her to a controversial interpretation of the dialogue: since at face value the theory of recollection is a theory of the recovery of knowledge, Weiss has to deny that the theory is more than a fantastic myth, a 'sham doctrine' (see also W. S. Cobb, 'Anamnesis: Platonic Doctrine or Sophistic Absurdity?', *Dialogue*, 12 (1973), 604–28); since the episode with the slave is supposed to illustrate the process of recollection, she has to deny that it is more than a geometry lesson; since Plato says at 98a that true belief can be converted into knowledge (and this is said to be relevant to the slave too), Weiss has to deny the obvious meaning of these words.

everything.[39] As the experiment with the slave (82b–85b) is supposed to show, the correct process of questioning (by oneself or by an external agent) elicits recollection of the relevant truths. At first, this may be insecure, but repeated questioning (85c) will lead a person to understand why things are as they are, and convert insecure knowledge (which is another way of saying 'true belief') into certain knowledge (97a–98b).

The experiment with the slave is explicitly a version of a typical Socratic elenchus, and what is more Plato provides us with his own commentary on the proceedings. The conversation is interrupted in order for Socrates to explain what has been going on, and what will happen next. The questioning of the slave is said to produce distinct stages in his progress. First, his false ideas are proved wrong, with the result that he succumbs to *aporia* (82e, 84a). Second, latent true beliefs are aroused within him; they are based at least partly on clues given by the negative first stage (85b–c). Third (though we are not shown this stage) his true belief could be converted into knowledge (85c). Socrates' confidence, throughout the dialogues of search, that he will eventually elicit a true belief from his interlocutor is justified, we are told, because the true beliefs are in there, inside the interlocutors: that is the point of the theory of recollection. These innate true beliefs are what allow an interlocutor instantly to recognize the greater evidential value of P over D. The elenchus can then build on these true beliefs to elicit further true beliefs, because of the kinship of all nature (81d). Socrates, then, would reject Irwin's logical point (p. xxxii) that it is possible to be consistently crazy or wrong: he believes that we innately have true beliefs which, under dialectical questioning, will lead us to reject false or immoral ideas.[40]

The paradox of enquiry has been defused: there is a point to the elenchus. There is a point to searching for what one does not know, because the search—the questioning—puts one into contact with innate truths. Plato does not have Socrates directly

---

[39] Plato's psychological assumptions, as revealed by this passage, are fascinatingly uncovered by B. Shanon, '*Meno*—A Cognitive Psychological View', *British Journal for the Philosophy of Science*, 35 (1984), 129–47.

[40] The most powerful expression of this comes in *Gorgias*, where, several times during the conversation with Polus, Socrates claims that Polus already subconsciously agrees with Socrates, despite his denials.

address the paradox of recognition; presumably such recognition is gained by pitting the knowledge, framed as a definition, against test cases. The definitional formula that encapsulates the knowledge may need refinement as a result of this process, but that too is part of the process of converting true belief into knowledge.

Socrates' interest in establishing definitions was to come up with something stable in the face of the uncertainty generated by various traditions. These traditions, which count as 'teaching', give us the contents of our conscious mind. These contents are our beliefs, which may be more or less organized into a coherent system and which may be true or false; but they are not pieces of knowledge. Knowledge lies latent beneath them, and needs recovering. Then we will have a stable epistemological state and we can come up with definitions or standards to refer to. So the recovery of knowledge is simultaneously the 'acquiring' of definitions. Not everyone will do this, presumably. Whereas everyone has some contact with their latent knowledge, because Plato is adamant that *all* learning is recollection, not everyone will convert their beliefs to knowledge. Perhaps only philosophers do so, and the means of their doing so is by questioning themselves, or being questioned by Socrates. No wonder Plato's Socrates saw himself as the gods' gift to Athens (*Apology* 30a).

Of course, in the case of the slave, Socrates steered the discussion: he was not ignorant of the answer, and he fed the slave leading questions to guide him towards finding the answer for himself (in so far as that is possible). Where both or all interlocutors are ignorant (remember that Socrates usually professes ignorance about any important matter), the way to proceed is to make assumptions (86d–87b). Now, those who believe that the Socratic elenchus was designed purely for negative purposes, for refutation, proclaim the introduction of the 'hypothetical method' in *Meno* as a new departure—a method of enquiry that will allow Plato to aim for positive results. But since (as we have seen earlier in this Introduction) the elenchus is not merely destructive in its effects, and since Plato has explicitly used assumptions earlier (as at *Charmides* 169d), this must be wrong.

In fact, the 'hypothetical method' is another way—in addition to the theory of recollection, that is—in which Plato reflects in

Meno on his Socratic legacy. The hypothetical method is little more than a formalization of the practice of the elenchus, in its constructive rather than aporetic mode.[41] Just as a geometrician asks what has to be the case for something else to be the case, so Socrates (here in *Meno*) asks from what proposition it will follow that excellence is teachable, and traces this back to the logically prior proposition that excellence is knowledge, and this proposition in turn is traced back to the supposedly prior proposition that excellence is good (87d). The original assumption is tested not just by seeing what its consequences are, but by seeing whether it stems from propositions to which all the parties agree, and which may even be true. But this is exactly the practice of the elenchus: an assumption (a proposed definition) is tested in the same ways. Laches' proposed definition of courage as 'mental persistence', for instance (192b), is tested by referring back: if mental persistence is to be courage, then courage may be a bad thing, since mental persistence is not always a good thing. Do we agree that courage is a bad thing? No—so let's start again with a different assumption, one that squares with what we have gained from this, that courage must be good. The same word that is translated 'assumption' or 'hypothesis' is used at *Charmides* 163a for the thesis that self-control is doing what pertains to oneself and at 160d for the 'higher' hypothesis that self-control is admirable; at *Euthyphro* 9d the word is used again for one of the trial definitions proposed for piety. Neither *Euthyphro* nor *Hippias Major* end with the *aporia* of the interlocutor: in both cases Socrates himself proposes a new definition or idea for examination, and since Socrates professes ignorance of all such matters, we may fairly take his proposals to be provisional or hypothetical. A hypothesis is simply a proposition that is put forward in order to be tested, and that is what happens throughout the Socratic dialogues.

[41] Plato also offers outlines of the hypothetical method in *Phaedo* and *Republic*. In no case is there a serious clash with Socratic practice. On *Phaedo* and Socratic practice, see my paper 'Truth and the Elenchus in Plato', in P. Huby and G. Neal (eds.), *The Criterion of Truth* (Liverpool: Liverpool University Press, 1989), 39–56. On the method in general, see Bluck, 85–108; I. Mueller, 'Mathematical Method and Philosophical Truth', in R. Kraut (ed.), *The Cambridge Companion to Plato* (Cambridge: Cambridge University Press, 1992), 170–99; S. Menn, 'Plato and the Method of Analysis', *Phronesis*, 47 (2002), 193–223.

In *Meno*, then, Plato suggests that the way out of the *aporia* that often frustrates moral enquiry is to find a logically prior proposition, which can then be investigated in the same way (see, in brief, the movement of *Meno* 73a–c). If the interlocutors still fail to agree, the process can be repeated until a point of agreement is reached. That point of agreement may well serve as a definition—albeit necessarily a provisional one—of the concept in question, and Plato tantalizingly dangles the possibility that this process is related to the way to convert true belief into knowledge, by working out the chain of causes that make something the case (98a): the logical process of working back to a point of agreement may well be the same process as that which converts true belief into knowledge, by making true beliefs less provisional and more anchored. Working back to 'higher' (more general) hypotheses is meant to cover the 'different ways' of looking at a topic (85c) which will convert one's view of it from true belief to knowledge. This shows that by the time he wrote *Meno* Plato was aware that Socrates had been operating with two degrees or kinds of knowledge (see p. xxxii): fallible knowledge (here called true belief) and expert knowledge, which is what one increasingly approximates to by working out reasons (98a).

Meno also allows us to clear up another puzzle too. Plato's Socrates, we know, tries to elicit knowledge from his interlocutors in the form of a definition, but the ability to state even a true definition is not enough on its own to count as or signify knowledge. If it were, Nicias' definition of courage as knowledge of good and bad would make him a man of knowledge, and so perhaps would Critias' definition of self-control as doing what pertains to oneself. The ability to state a true definition is necessary for knowledge, but it is not sufficient. When Socrates tests a definition by means of the elenchus, he is concerned to turn the interlocutor's belief (true belief, if the definition is true) into knowledge (see, perhaps, *Laches* 194c). Now we see from *Meno* that it is working out the chain of causes that converts true belief into knowledge. I have already suggested that the 'method of hypothesis' is a formalization of the practice of the elenchus and is the same as 'working out the reason', in that it anchors the belief with a chain of reasons or higher hypotheses and so converts it into knowledge; and now we have reached the same conclusion from another angle.

When the enquiry into the teachability of excellence resumes, then, they make the following assumptions: (1) if excellence is a kind of knowledge, it is teachable, and otherwise it is not; (2) excellence is good for one. The latter assumption allows Socrates slyly to reintroduce the issue of the nature of excellence (apparently banished at 86d–e, and constantly resisted by Meno throughout the dialogue) and to argue that excellence is knowledge or a kind of knowledge (87d–89a); therefore, *ex hypothesi*, it is teachable (89b–c). We are not stymied, then, by our inability to define concepts; we can make assumptions or hypotheses and carry on—and one of those assumptions may in any case serve as a definition. We should note, however, that since 'teachable' has been redescribed by the theory of recollection, according to which innate knowledge is recovered by questioning, then to say that excellence is teachable is to say that excellence is both innate and teachable. The stark either–or option with which Meno began the dialogue has been mitigated.

In *Meno* the first set of assumptions led to the conclusion that excellence was teachable, but Socrates now makes a further assumption, that if it is teachable, there must be teachers of it (which is to say that the proposition that excellence is teachable is traced back to the logically prior proposition that excellence has teachers). He then argues at length that there are no teachers of excellence (89d–96c), and that therefore excellence is not teachable. If it is not teachable, people must become good by some other route, and the final suggestion is that excellence is true belief, which is just as good as knowledge for all practical purposes (97a–98c). But true belief, Plato claims, is neither a natural endowment nor a product of teaching, and therefore it is not within our control. The dialogue concludes with the evidently ironic suggestion (99d–100a) that excellence is a miracle, 'a dispensation awarded by the gods'.[42]

[42] An almost lone voice denying the irony of this conclusion is M. Reuter, 'Is Goodness Really a Gift from God? Another Look at the Conclusion of Plato's *Meno*', *Phoenix*, 55 (2001), 77–97.

What is going on? Not only does this contradict the earlier conclusion that excellence is teachable, but it also contradicts a constant aspect of Socratic thought, the intellectualist assumption that excellence is knowledge, which, as we have seen, is operative in *Laches* and *Charmides* (and other dialogues). Partly, Plato is concerned to demonstrate the importance of hypotheses, and their danger: different hypotheses lead to radically divergent conclusions. But, apart from methodology, can we also extract any doctrinal conclusions from the dialogue? Is Plato casting doubt on the Socratic idea that excellence is knowledge?

We cannot give absolutely secure answers to these questions, and it seems very likely that Plato himself was uncertain whether or not excellence was teachable, or at least was unwilling to commit himself to its being *just* teachable (as opposed to a natural endowment or whatever else). It is *implied* by Socratic thought that it is, but whenever Plato addressed the question directly, he leaves things open. In *Protagoras* he had Socrates argue first that excellence is not teachable, and then that it is; in *Meno* this order is reversed. But as long as we are not looking for certainty, we can draw some conclusions.

The elimination of the proposition that excellence is knowledge was achieved by arguing that excellence is not teachable because it is not taught. But Plato holds out the possibility at 99e–100a that one day excellence might be taught by a Teiresias-like figure (Socrates? Plato?), which implies that excellence is knowledge after all. Plato has not abandoned the idea that excellence is knowledge, but he has upgraded it to an ideal. Moreover, since abandoning the attempt to define excellence at 86d, nothing about excellence is taken to be known and everything is hypothetical: if there are no teachers, it is not knowledge—but there may be teachers one day. Even the conclusion may be understood to be provisional, since Plato says that it awaits confirmation (100b); in other words, if excellence is not knowledge and does not come as a natural endowment, it may be true belief and therefore given by the gods. Alternatively, we may understand the conclusion to be referring to ordinary, everyday excellence: even if this is equated with true belief and is due to divine dispensation, ideal excellence is still knowledge.[43] Plato may also have intended us to reflect—as the dialogue prompts us—on teaching: conventional excellence may indeed be teachable by a Sophist or a father, but true excellence, true knowledge, is attainable only through recollection.

[43] The distinction between conventional excellence and knowledge-based excellence is developed by Plato at *Phaedo* 68c–69c.

NOTE ON THE TEXTS

In the case of all four of the dialogues in this volume, I have translated the Oxford Classical Text of J. Burnet, *Platonis Opera*, volume 3 (Oxford: Oxford University Press, 1903), except for the passages listed in the Textual Notes (pp. 184–5), which have been marked in the translations with an obelus (†). Asterisks refer to the Explanatory Notes (pp. 144–83).

The numbers and letters which appear in the margins of the translation are the standard means of precise reference to passages in Plato. They refer to the pages and sections of pages of the edition of Plato by Stephanus, or Henri Estienne (Geneva, 1578). This edition was published in three volumes, each with separate pagination. Each page was divided into two columns, with the Greek text on the right and a Latin translation on the left. The column with the Greek text was divided into (usually) five sections labelled 'a' to 'e' by Stephanus.

SELECT BIBLIOGRAPHY

There has been a lot of very high-quality work on Plato's Socrates in the last thirty or forty years, and as a result I have mentioned more books and papers in this volume than is usual (while, of course, restricting myself to those I consider best). They are not all listed here, however: this bibliography lists works of general relevance to Plato's Socrates, and works of general or central relevance to each of the four dialogues translated. Books and articles with narrower focuses have been restricted to footnotes in the Introduction or mentioned *in situ* in the Explanatory Notes.

Plato's Socrates in General

Benson, H. H., *Socratic Wisdom: The Model of Knowledge in Plato's Early Dialogues* (New York: Oxford University Press, 2000).

Beversluis, J., *Cross-Examining Socrates: A Defense of the Interlocutors in Plato's Early Dialogues* (Cambridge: Cambridge University Press, 2000).

Brickhouse, T. C., and Smith, N. D., *Plato's Socrates* (Oxford: Oxford University Press, 1994).

Dancy, R. M., *Plato's Introduction of Forms* (Cambridge: Cambridge University Press, 2004).

Gulley, N., *The Philosophy of Socrates* (London: Macmillan, 1968).

Guthrie, W. K. C., *A History of Greek Philosophy*, vol. 4: *Plato: The Man and His Dialogues, Earlier Period* (Cambridge: Cambridge University Press, 1975).

Irwin, T., *Plato's Moral Theory* (Oxford: Oxford University Press, 1977).

—— *Plato's Ethics* (Oxford: Oxford University Press, 1995).

Kahn, C. H., *Plato and the Socratic Dialogue* (Cambridge: Cambridge University Press, 1996).

Kraut, R., *Socrates and the State* (Princeton: Princeton University Press, 1984).

Mackenzie, M. M., 'Impasse and Explanation from the *Lysis* to the *Phaedo*', *Archiv für Geschichte der Philosophie*, 70 (1988), 15–45.

McPherran, M. L., *The Religion of Socrates* (University Park, Pa.: Pennsylvania State University Press, 1996).

Penner, T., 'Socrates and the Early Dialogues', in R. Kraut (ed.), *The Cambridge Companion to Plato* (Cambridge: Cambridge University Press, 1992), 121–69.

Prior, W. J., 'Socrates Metaphysician', *Oxford Studies in Ancient Philosophy*, 27 (2004), 1–14.

Santas, G. X., *Socrates: Philosophy in Plato's Early Dialogues* (London: Routledge & Kegan Paul, 1979).

Seeskin, K., *Dialogue and Discovery: A Study in Socratic Method* (Albany: State University of New York Press, 1987).

Teloh, H., *Socratic Education in Plato's Early Dialogues* (Notre Dame, Ind.: University of Notre Dame Press, 1986).

Vlastos, G., *Socrates: Ironist and Moral Philosopher* (Cambridge: Cambridge University Press, 1991).

White, N. P., *Plato on Knowledge and Reality* (Indianapolis: Hackett, 1976).

Wolfsdorf, D., 'Interpreting Plato's Early Dialogues', *Oxford Studies in Ancient Philosophy*, 27 (2004), 15–40.

Collections of Essays

Each of these books contains a number of essays with relevance to Plato's Socrates in general, or to one or more of the dialogues translated in this volume. To save space, I have not listed these essays elsewhere in this bibliography, even though the collections contain some of the best and most important work.

Benson, H. H. (ed.), *Essays on the Philosophy of Socrates* (New York: Oxford University Press, 1992).

Boudouris, K. J. (ed.), *The Philosophy of Socrates*, 2 vols. (Athens: International Center for Greek Philosophy and Culture, 1991, 1992).

Brown, M. (ed.), *Plato's Meno: Text and Essays* (Indianapolis: Bobbs-Merrill, 1971).

Day, J. M. (trans. and ed.), *Plato's Meno in Focus* (London: Routledge, 1994).

Gower, B. S., and Stokes, M. C. (eds.), *Socratic Questions: The Philosophy of Socrates and its Significance* (London: Routledge, 1992).

McPherran, M. L. (ed.), *Wisdom, Ignorance and Virtue: New Essays in Socratic Studies* (Edmonton: Academic Printing & Publishing, 1997 = *Apeiron*, 30/4).

Nehamas, A., *Virtues of Authenticity: Essays on Plato and Socrates* (Princeton: Princeton University Press, 1999).

Prior, W. J. (ed.), *Socrates: Critical Assessments*, 4 vols. (London: Routledge, 1996).

Robinson, T. M., and Brisson, L. (eds.), *Plato: Euthydemus, Lysis, Charmides* (Sankt Augustin: Academia, 2000).

Scott, G. A. (ed.), *Does Socrates Have a Method? Rethinking the Elenchus in Plato's Dialogues and Beyond* (University Park, Pa.: Pennsylvania State University Press, 2002).

Sesonske, A., and Fleming, N. (eds.), *Plato's Meno: Text and Criticism* (Belmont, Calif.: Wadsworth, 1965).

Smith, N. D., and Woodruff, P. B. (eds.), *Reason and Religion in Socratic Philosophy* (New York: Oxford University Press, 2000).

Vlastos, G. (ed.), *The Philosophy of Socrates: A Collection of Critical Essays* (New York: Doubleday, 1971).

—— *Socratic Studies* (Cambridge: Cambridge University Press, 1994).

Socratic Elenchus and Definition

Adams, D., 'Elenchos and Evidence', *Ancient Philosophy*, 18 (1998), 287–307.

Beversluis, J., 'Socratic Definition', *American Philosophical Quarterly*, 11 (1974), 331–6.

Bolton, R., 'Aristotle's Account of the Socratic Elenchus', *Oxford Studies in Ancient Philosophy*, 11 (1993), 121–52.

Irwin, T., 'Common Sense and Socratic Method', in J. Gentzler (ed.), *Method in Ancient Philosophy* (Oxford: Oxford University Press, 1998), 29–66.

Polansky, R., 'Professor Vlastos' Analysis of Socratic Elenchus', *Oxford Studies in Ancient Philosophy*, 3 (1985), 247–59.

Robinson, R., *Plato's Earlier Dialectic* (2nd edn., London: Oxford University Press, 1953).

Scaltsas, T., 'Socratic Moral Realism: An Alternative Justification', *Oxford Studies in Ancient Philosophy*, 7 (1989), 129–50.

Wolfsdorf, D., 'Understanding the "What-is-F?" Question', *Apeiron*, 36 (2003), 175–88.

—— 'Socrates' Pursuit of Definitions', *Phronesis*, 48 (2003), 271–312.

The Four Dialogues: Editions, Translations, and Commentaries

Allen, R. E., *The Dialogues of Plato*, vol. 1 (New Haven: Yale University Press, 1984).

Benson, H. H., *Plato: Charmides* (Project Archelogos: www.archelogos.com/xml/toc/toc-charmides.htm).

Bluck, R. S., *Plato's Meno* (Cambridge: Cambridge University Press, 1964).

Bolotin, D., *Plato's Dialogue on Friendship* (Ithaca, NY: Cornell University Press, 1979).

Guthrie, W. K. C., *Plato: Protagoras and Meno* (Harmondsworth: Penguin, 1956).

Klein, J., *A Commentary on Plato's Meno* (Chapel Hill: University of North Carolina Press, 1965).

Robinson, D. B., and Herrmann, F.-G., *Plato: Lysis* (Project Archelogos: www.archelogos.com/xml/toc/toc-lysis.htm).

Saunders, T. J. (ed.), *Plato: Early Socratic Dialogues* (Harmondsworth: Penguin, 1987).

Schmid, W. T., *On Manly Courage: A Study of Plato's Laches* (Carbondale: Southern Illinois University Press, 1992).

—— *Plato's Charmides and the Socratic Ideal of Rationality* (Albany: State University of New York Press, 1998).

Sharples, R. W., *Plato: Meno* (Warminster: Aris & Phillips, 1985).

Sprague, R. K., *Plato: Laches and Charmides* (Indianapolis: Bobbs-Merrill, 1973).

Sternfeld, R., and Zyskind, H., *Plato's Meno: A Philosophy of Man as Acquisitive* (Carbondale: Southern Illinois University Press, 1978).

Thomas, J. E., *Musings on the Meno* (The Hague: Nijhoff, 1980).

Weiss, R., *Virtue in the Cave: Moral Inquiry in Plato's Meno* (New York: Oxford University Press, 2001).

Charmides

Dyson, M., 'Some Problems concerning Knowledge in Plato's *Charmides*', *Phronesis*, 19 (1974), 102–11.

Ketchum, R. J., 'Plato on the Uselessness of Epistemology: *Charmides* 166e–172a', *Apeiron*, 24 (1991), 81–98.

Morris, T. F., 'Temperance and What One Needs in the *Charmides*', *Diálogos* (Puerto Rico), 28 (1993), 55–72.

Santas, G. X., 'Socrates at Work on Virtue and Knowledge in Plato's *Charmides*', in E. N. Lee *et al.* (eds.), *Exegesis and Argument* (Assen: Van Gorcum, 1973), 105–32.

Laches

Devereux, D., 'Courage and Wisdom in Plato's *Laches*', *Journal of the History of Philosophy*, 15 (1977), 129–41.

Emlyn-Jones, C., 'Dramatic Structure and Cultural Context in Plato's *Laches*', *Classical Quarterly*, 49 (1999), 123–38.

Gould, C. S., 'Socratic Intellectualism and the Problem of Courage: An Interpretation of Plato's *Laches*', *History of Philosophy Quarterly*, 4 (1987), 265–79.

Hobbs, A., *Plato and the Hero: Courage, Manliness and the Impersonal Good* (Cambridge: Cambridge University Press, 2000).

Kahn, C. H., 'Plato's Methodology in the *Laches*', *Revue internationale de philosophie*, 156–7 (1986), 7–21.

O'Brien, M. J., 'The Unity of the *Laches*', *Yale Classical Studies*, 18 (1963), 133–43; repr. in J. P. Anton and G. L. Kustas (eds.), *Essays in Ancient Greek Philosophy* (Albany: State University of New York Press, 1971), 303–15.

Stokes, M. C., *Plato's Socratic Conversations* (London: Athlone, 1986).

Lysis

Adams, D., 'The *Lysis* Puzzles', *History of Philosophy Quarterly*, 9 (1992), 3–17.

—— 'A Socratic Theory of Friendship', *International Philosophical Quarterly*, 35 (1995), 269–82.

Annas, J., 'Plato and Aristotle on Friendship and Altruism', *Mind*, 86 (1977), 532–54.

Glidden, D. K., 'The *Lysis* on Loving One's Own', *Classical Quarterly*, 31 (1981), 39–59.

Mooney, T., 'Plato's Theory of Love in the *Lysis*: A Defence', *Irish Philosophical Journal*, 7 (1990), 131–59.

Morris, T. F., 'Plato's *Lysis*', *Philosophy Research Archives*, 11 (1985), 269–79.

Pangle, L. S., 'Friendship and Human Neediness in Plato's *Lysis*', *Ancient Philosophy*, 21 (2001), 305–23.

Price, A. W., *Love and Friendship in Plato and Aristotle* (Oxford: Oxford University Press, 1989).

Reshotko, N., 'Plato's *Lysis*: A Socratic Treatise on Desire and Attraction', *Apeiron*, 30 (1997), 1–18.

Robinson, D. B., 'Plato's *Lysis*: The Structural Problem', *Illinois Classical Studies*, 11 (1986), 63–83.

Versenyi, L., 'Plato's *Lysis*', *Phronesis*, 20 (1975), 185–98.

Vlastos, G., 'The Individual as an Object of Love in Plato', in id., *Platonic Studies* (2nd edn., Princeton: Princeton University Press, 1981), 3–42.

Meno

Bedu-Addo, J. T., 'Sense-experience and Recollection in Plato's *Meno*', *American Journal of Philology*, 104 (1983), 228–48.

—— 'Recollection and the Argument "from a Hypothesis" in Plato's *Meno*', *Journal of Hellenic Studies*, 104 (1984), 1–14.

Benson, H. H., 'Meno, the Slave-boy and the Elenchus', *Phronesis*, 35 (1990), 128–58.

—— and Wolfsdorf, D., 'The Method of Hypothesis in the *Meno*', *Proceedings of the Boston Area Colloquium in Ancient Philosophy*, 18 (2002), 95–143.

Desjardins, R., 'Knowledge and Virtue: Paradox in Plato's *Meno*', *Review of Metaphysics*, 39 (1985), 261–81.

Devereux, D. T., 'Nature and Teaching in Plato's *Meno*', *Phronesis*, 23 (1978), 118–26.

Dimas, P., 'True Belief in the *Meno*', *Oxford Studies in Ancient Philosophy*, 14 (1996), 1–32.

Ebert, T., 'Plato's Theory of Recollection Reconsidered: An Interpretation of *Meno* 80a–86c', *Man and World*, 6 (1973), 163–81.

Fine, G., 'Inquiry in the *Meno*', in R. Kraut (ed.), *The Cambridge Companion to Plato* (Cambridge: Cambridge University Press, 1992), 200–26; repr. in id., *Plato on Knowledge and Forms: Selected Essays* (Oxford: Oxford University Press, 2003), 44–65.

Franklin, L., 'The Structure of Dialectic in the *Meno*', *Phronesis*, 46 (2001), 413–39.

Gentzler, J., and Cicovacki, P., 'Recollection and "The Problem of the Socratic Elenchus"', *Proceedings of the Boston Area Colloquium in Ancient Philosophy*, 10 (1994), 257–311.

Klein, S., 'Socratic Dialectic in the *Meno*', *Southern Journal of Philosophy*, 24 (1986), 351–64.

Morgan, M. L., 'How Does Plato Solve the Paradox of Inquiry in the *Meno*?', in J. P. Anton and A. Preus (eds.), *Essays in Ancient Greek Philosophy*, vol. 3: *Plato* (Albany: State University of New York Press, 1989), 169–81.

Scott, D., 'Platonic Recollection', in G. Fine (ed.), *Plato*, vol. 1: *Metaphysics and Epistemology* (Oxford: Oxford University Press, 1999), 93–124.

Williams, T., 'Two Aspects of Platonic Recollection', *Apeiron*, 35 (2002), 131–52.

SELECT BIBLIOGRAPHY

Further Reading in Oxford World's Classics

Plato, *Defence of Socrates, Euthyphro, Crito*, trans. David Gallop.
—— *Gorgias*, trans. Robin Waterfield.
—— *Phaedo*, trans. David Gallop.
—— *Phaedrus*, trans. Robin Waterfield.
—— *Protagoras*, trans. C. C. W. Taylor.
—— *Republic*, trans. Robin Waterfield.
—— *Selected Myths*, ed. Catalin Partenie.
—— *Symposium*, trans. Robin Waterfield.

CHARMIDES

SOCRATES [*addressing an unnamed friend**]: We came back yester- 153a
day evening from the army at Potidaea.* I'd been away for a while,
so I was delighted to be back and I visited my old haunts, especially Taureas' wrestling-ground, opposite the shrine of the
Queen.* When I went inside, I found a great many people there,
most of whom, but not quite all, were known to me. Nobody was
expecting to see me, so greetings were shouted out to me from b
the distance here and there at my entry, and that madman
Chaerephon leapt up from the group of people he was with and
ran over to me. He took hold of my hand and said, 'Socrates, how
did you manage to survive the battle?' I should say that a few days
before we left the region there'd been a battle at Potidaea, news of
which had only just reached Athens.

'Safe and sound,' I replied, 'as you can see.'

'The report we received here,' he went on, 'was that it was a
hard-fought battle and that lots of our acquaintances were killed.' c

'That's not far off the truth,' I said.

'Were you involved in the fighting?' he asked.

'I was.'*

'Come and sit here,' he said, 'and tell us about it. We've not yet
had a full and detailed report.' While he was saying this he took
me over and sat me down next to Critias the son of Callaeschrus.

After I'd sat down, I said hello to Critias and everyone else, and
then answered all their questions – everyone asked something d
different – and gave them the news from the front. Once we'd
exhausted that topic of conversation, it was my turn and I asked
them for news from here. I wanted to know what was happening
at the moment in the field of education,* and whether there were
any young men who had come to stand out from the rest for their
intelligence or beauty or both. Critias looked towards the door- 154a
way, because he'd spotted several boys coming inside – they were
exchanging insults and were followed by a sizeable crowd of
people – and he said: 'I don't think you're going to have to wait
long to find out which boys are beautiful, Socrates. This lot

coming in now are the advance guard, the admirers of the one who is widely held—at the moment, anyway—to be the most beautiful boy in town. It must mean that the boy himself isn't far away now, on his way here.'*

'Who is he,' I asked, 'and who's his father?'

'I'm sure you must know him,' Critias said, 'but he hadn't yet

b reached puberty by the time you left. He's my cousin Charmides, the son of my uncle Glaucon.'

'Yes, by Zeus, I know him,' I said. 'He was quite promising even then, when he was still a young boy, but I imagine that by now he must have matured a lot.'

'You won't have long to wait to see what he's like and how he's matured,' said Critias, and as he was saying this Charmides came in.

Now, my friend, you can't be guided by me: where beauty is concerned, I'm nothing but a white line,* in the sense that just about every boy in his prime looks beautiful to me. On that occasion, however, this particular boy struck me as truly remarkable,

c for his height as well as his beauty,* and I got the impression that everyone else was in love with him, because they became all flustered and agitated when he came in. And he was followed by another crowd of admirers too. Now, although this reaction was hardly surprising among us men, I was watching the boys too, and I noticed that none of them, not even the youngest, was looking elsewhere: they were all gazing at him as if he were a statue.*

d 'So what do you think of the boy, Socrates?' Chaerephon called out to me. 'Isn't he good-looking?'

'Extraordinarily so,' I said.

'But if he can be induced to strip,'* he went on, 'he has such a fantastic body that you won't even notice his features.'

Everyone else expressed their agreement with Chaerephon on this, and I said: 'By Heracles,* the man you're describing is a paragon—or at least he is if he has just one other tiny feature too.'

'What's that?' Critias asked.

e 'If he's got an attractive soul,'* I said, 'as he should, Critias, since he's a member of your family.'

'As it happens,' he said, 'he's very beautiful and good in this respect too.'

4

'So why don't we strip this part of him too,'* I said, 'and examine it before we look at his body? At any rate, at his age, I'm sure he won't mind joining in a conversation.'

'He certainly won't,' said Critias. 'You should know that he's fond of intellectual pursuits and is generally held—by others too, 155a not just himself—to be quite a good poet as well.'

'Critias, my friend,' I said, 'this admirable gift goes way back in your family, since you're related to Solon. But why don't you call the lad over and let me examine him? Even if he were younger than he is, it wouldn't be unseemly for him to talk to us as long as you're present, since you're his guardian as well as his cousin.'*

'That's a good idea,' he said. 'We'll get him over here.' With these words he said to his attendant: 'Slave, tell Charmides to join b us. Tell him I want to introduce him to a healer who can help with the ailment he told me about the day before yesterday.' And Critias turned to me and said: 'He told me the other day that he's been suffering from headaches when he gets up in the mornings. What's to stop you pretending to him that you know a medicine for the head?'*

'Nothing,' I said. 'All he has to do is come over here.'

'Well, he will,' he said.

And that's exactly what happened. His arrival caused a lot of laughter, because each of us who were sitting down immediately c began to push his neighbour, to make room for Charmides to sit next to himself, until we forced the man sitting at one end to stand up and dumped the one at the other end on the ground to the side. Charmides sat down between Critias and me—and I immediately lost my bearings, my friend. Previously, I'd been sure that I'd find it very easy to talk to him, but this rash confidence had just been knocked out of me. Critias told him that I was the one who knew the treatment; Charmides looked at me with an indescribable expression in his eyes and was on the point d of launching a question at me; the entire crowd of visitors to the wrestling-ground was gathering all around us—and at just this moment, my noble friend, I saw inside his clothes. I was on fire! I was in ecstasy! I realized what a true expert on love Cydias was, when in speaking of a beautiful boy he warned that 'one should beware of going as a fawn into the presence of a lion, and being

5

e seized as a portion of meat'. I certainly felt as though I'd been caught by some such creature. Still, when he asked me if I knew the medicine for his head, I stammered an affirmative reply.

'And what is it?' he asked.

I said that it was a particular herb, but that there was an incantation that went with it; if one chanted the spell and treated the patient with the herb at the same time, I explained, the medicine was absolutely effective, but without the incantation the herb was useless.

156a 'So I'll get the wording of the spell from you,' he said.

'With or without my consent?' I asked.

'With your consent, Socrates,' he answered with a laugh.

'All right,' I said. 'And are you sure you've got my name right?'

'Yes,' he said, 'unless I'm quite wrong. Boys my age quite often mention you, and I also remember you and Critias here passing time together when I was young.'

'Good for you!' I said. 'Now I'll be less likely to keep the
b wording of the spell secret from you. I was just wondering how I could explain its power. You see, Charmides, it isn't just capable of curing the head, but . . . well, in the past you too have probably heard what good healers say when someone comes to them with painful eyes. They say, as you know, that they can't set about curing just the eyes, but have to treat the head too at the same time, if the eyes are to get better. They also insist that one would
c have to be deeply stupid to think that the head can be treated on its own, without the whole body. In keeping with this principle, they focus on the whole body and set about prescribing courses of treatment designed to treat and cure the part along with the whole.* You've heard them saying this, haven't you? You know that this is what happens?'

'Yes,' he said.

'And do you think they're right? Are you happy with the principle?'

'Absolutely,' he said.

d My morale was restored by his approval, my confidence gradually recovered, and I felt a fresh burst of energy. 'Well, Charmides,' I said, 'the same goes for the incantation too. I learnt it from a Thracian healer, a priest of Zalmoxis, while I was serving

6

with the army up north. These healers are also said to make people immortal. Anyway, this Thracian told me that the Greeks were right to make the claim I mentioned a short while ago, and he said: "But our lord and master, the divine Zalmoxis, tells us that just as one should not undertake to cure the eyes without also e curing the head, nor the head without the body, so one should not set about treating the body without the soul. This is exactly why most ailments are beyond the capabilities of Greek healers: they neglect the whole when that is what they should be paying attention to, because if the whole is in a bad state it's impossible for any part of it to be in a good state." He said that the soul is the origin and source of everything that happens, good or bad, to the body and to every individual, just as the head is the origin and source of the eyes, and that therefore one should take care of the soul first 157a and foremost, if the head and every other part of the body are to be in a good condition.

'He went on to say, my dear Charmides, that the way to treat the soul was with certain spells, consisting of fair words—that is, he said, the kind of words which are responsible for implanting self-control in souls. Once self-control has been implanted in the soul and is a feature of it, he said that it was easy to cure the head and the rest of the body. As he was teaching me about the herb b and the spells, he said, "Make sure that no one gets you to treat his head with this herb unless he has first let you treat his soul with the incantation. The error of doing otherwise is very widespread these days: people separate self-control and bodily health and try to be healers in one or the other." And he gave me very strict instructions against letting anyone, no matter how rich or well-born or beautiful, persuade me to use any alternative approach to healing. Now, I shall obey his instructions: I gave him c my solemn word, so I have no choice but to do so. As for you, if you're willing to go along with the Thracian's instructions and let me first charm your soul with his incantations, I'll go on to treat your head with the herb; otherwise, there's nothing we can do for you, my dear Charmides.'

After I'd finished speaking, Critias said: 'The boy's headache will turn out to have been an unexpected piece of good fortune* for him, Socrates, if the problem with his head forces him to d improve his mind. But I should tell you that Charmides is generally held to stand out from his contemporaries not just for his looks and physique, but also for precisely that quality for which you say you have the spell. You were talking about self-control, weren't you?'

'Yes,' I said.

'Then you should know,' he went on, 'that he's generally held to display far more self-control than anyone else alive today, as well as yielding to no one in any other quality, taking his age into account.'

'In actual fact, Charmides,' I said, 'it's only right that you
e should stand out from everyone else in all these respects. After all, I doubt whether anyone else in this city of ours could easily show which two families in Athens, other than those from which you come, might reasonably be expected to produce from their union a more admirable and better person. On your father's side, members of the family of Critias the son of Dropides have been celebrated over the years by a great many poets, including Anacreon and Solon, for their outstanding beauty, goodness, and what is
158a thought of as prosperity. And the same goes for your mother's side: no man in Asia, we hear, gained more of a reputation for his beauty and stature than your uncle Pyrilampes, whenever he went to the court of the Persian king or on some other diplomatic mission in Asia. The members of your mother's family were all on a par with your father's family in every respect. Since you're the product of two such outstanding families, it's hardly surprising that you're unrivalled in everything.

b 'Now, to judge by what I can see of your body, my dear boy, I don't think you fall short of your ancestors in *any* respect. If you're also as adequately endowed with self-control and so on as our friend here suggests, Charmides, then when your mother gave birth to you she gave birth to one truly blessed. Anyway, this is how things stand: if Critias here is right and you do possess self-control and display it well enough, you no longer have the
c slightest need of Zalmoxis' spells, nor those of Abaris the Hyperborean, and I'd have to give you the herb for your head straight away. On the other hand, if I find that you aren't yet quite perfect in these respects, I must chant the spell before I give you the

8

medicine. So why don't you tell me yourself whether you agree with Critias here? Do you claim to be already adequately endowed with self-control, or would you say that you've still got some way to go?'

At first Charmides blushed, which made him look even more attractive, since his embarrassment suited his age, but then he gave quite a refined answer. He said that, in the present circumstances, it wasn't easy to answer either yes or no to the question. 'After all,' he said, 'if I say that I'm not self-controlled, there are d two problems: first, it's a strange thing for a person to say about himself and, second, I'd make not only Critias here out to be a liar, but also a lot of other people, who according to him take me to be self-controlled. On the other hand, if I say that I'm self-controlled and pay myself that compliment, it will come across as offensive. So I don't know what reply to give you.'*

'That seems a reasonable reply to me, Charmides,' I said. 'I think the two of us should consider together whether or not you possess the quality I'm asking about. Then *you* won't be forced to e say anything you don't want to say, and *I* won't turn to healing without having given the issue proper consideration. So, if you've no objection, I'm prepared to look into the matter with your help. If you don't like the idea, we can just drop it.'

'No,' he said, 'I've absolutely no objection. So as far as that's concerned, do please proceed with the investigation however you think best.'

'Well,' I said, 'I think I know the best way to conduct the investigation into this issue. Clearly, if you do possess self-control, you can form some thoughts about it. After all, as one of your attributes—if it is one of your attributes—it must make 159a itself perceptible to you, and on this basis some thoughts would arise in you about what self-control is, or at least what sort of thing it is. Don't you think so?'

'Yes, I do,' he said.

'And since you know how to speak Greek,' I went on, 'you must surely be able to express in words these thoughts of yours about what you take it to be.'

'I suppose so,' he said.

'So,' I said, 'tell us what you think self-control is. That way, we'll be able to guess whether or not it's a quality you possess.'

b   At first, he hesitated and was rather reluctant to reply, but then he said that, in his opinion, self-control was doing things politely and unhurriedly—walking in the streets, talking with people, and doing everything else in the same way. 'In short,' he concluded, 'I think that the quality you're asking about is a kind of unhurriedness.'

'I wonder whether you're right in this,' I said. 'Unhurried people are certainly called self-controlled, Charmides, so let's see

c   if there's any truth to this. Tell me, for a start, don't you think that self-control is an admirable quality?'

'Yes,' he said.

'Now, at school is it more admirable to write equally well-formed letters rapidly or unhurriedly?'

'Rapidly.'

'And what about reading? Quickly or slowly?'

'Quickly.'

'And it's far more admirable to play the lyre quickly and to wrestle vigorously than to do so unhurriedly and slowly, isn't it?'*

'Yes.'

'And doesn't the same go for boxing and the pankration?'*

'Yes.'

'What about running and jumping and all physical activities?

d   Isn't vigorous and rapid execution the mark of an admirable person, and laborious and unhurried execution deplorable?'

'It seems so.'

'So it seems to us, then,' I said, 'that where the body is concerned, at any rate, great speed and vigour are more admirable than unhurriedness. Yes?'

'Yes.'

'But self-control is an admirable thing, isn't it?'

'Yes.'

'So where the body is concerned, at any rate, speed, not unhurriedness, would be the more self-controlled way to do things, since self-control is admirable.'

'It looks that way,' he said.

e   'Well, now,' I said, 'which is more admirable, being good or bad at one's lessons?'

'Being good at them.'

'But isn't it the case that those who are good at their lessons learn quickly, while those who are bad at them learn unhurriedly and slowly?'

'Yes.'

'And where teaching is concerned, isn't it more admirable to teach someone quickly and energetically rather than unhurriedly and slowly?'

'Yes.'

'What about recollection and remembering? Is it more admirable to be able to remember things unhurriedly and slowly or energetically and quickly?'

'Energetically and quickly,' he said.

'And isn't cleverness a kind of mental vigour, rather than 160a having anything to do with unhurriedness?'

'True.'

'What about understanding what someone is saying, whether it's at school or at the music-teacher's or anywhere else? The most admirable way to go about it is as quickly as possible, isn't it, not as unhurriedly as possible?'

'Yes.'

'And when undertaking any kind of mental enquiry, such as deliberating, it's not, as far as I can see, the man who deliberates and reaches his goal in a totally unhurried and laborious fashion who's generally held to deserve praise, but the one who does so with as much fluency and speed as possible.'   b

'That's true,' he said.

'So in every mental activity undertaken by human beings, as well as in all our physical activities, Charmides,' I said, 'doesn't it turn out that speed and vigour are more admirable than slowness and unhurriedness?'

'It does look that way,' he said.

'From what we've been saying, then, it follows that self-control can't be a kind of unhurriedness, and a self-controlled life can't be an unhurried life, since a self-controlled life has to be admirable.* There are in fact two possibilities. First, there are either no or extremely few areas of life where unhurried behaviour turns c out to be more admirable than quick and forceful behaviour.

Alternatively, my friend, if there are at the most as many unhurried actions which happen to be more admirable as there are vigorous and fast ones, it still wouldn't follow that self-control was unhurried action rather than energetic and rapid action, whether one was walking or talking or anything else. Nor would it follow that an unhurried life was more self-controlled than a
d hurried one, since our assumption in the argument has been that self-control is something admirable, and fast actions have turned out to be just as admirable as unhurried ones.'

'I think you're right, Socrates,' he said.

'So why don't you try again, Charmides?' I said. 'Think more carefully this time, and look inside yourself. Consider what kind of person the presence in you of self-control makes you and what kind of quality it must be in order to make you that kind of person, and once you've reckoned everything up tell us, clearly
e and courageously, what you take it to be.'

After a short period of resolute self-examination, he said: 'Well, I think self-control makes a person feel shame and embarrassment, and so that self-control is the same as modesty.'

'All right,' I said. 'Now, didn't we just agree that self-control is something admirable?'

'Yes, of course,' he said.

'And men who are self-controlled are also good men, aren't they?'

'Yes.'

'Well, can something be good if it doesn't make men good?'

'Certainly not.'

'It turns out, then, that self-control is not just admirable, but also good.'

161a 'Yes, I think so.'

'Well,' I went on, 'don't you think that Homer was right to say that "Modesty ill suits a man in need"?'*

'I do,' he said.

'Then modesty both is and is not a good thing.'

'It seems so.'

'And self-control is a good thing if it makes those who have it good and doesn't make them bad.'

'Yes, I think you're right.'

12

'It follows, then, that self-control cannot be modesty, if self-control really is something good, and modesty is no more good b than bad.'

'Well, I think you're right on this, Socrates,' he said. 'But here's another idea about self-control, which I've just remembered. Tell what you think about it. I once heard someone saying that self-control was doing what pertains to oneself. What do you think about this? Was the person who told me it right or wrong, do you think?'

'Damn you!' I said. 'It was Critias here or one of his fellow intellectuals who told you this.' c

'He didn't get it from me,' Critias said, 'so I suppose it was from someone else.'

'Does it matter who I heard it from, Socrates?' asked Charmides.

'Not at all,' I said. 'We're not remotely interested in considering whose idea it is, just in whether or not it's true.'

'Now you're on the mark,' he said.

'By Zeus, yes,' I said. 'But I wonder whether we'll be able to find out whether or not it's true, because it sounds like a riddle.'

'In what respect?' he asked.

'Because,' I said, 'presumably his spoken words—the state- d ment that self-control is doing what pertains to oneself—didn't really communicate his meaning. Or do you think that a teacher is doing nothing when he's writing or reading?'

'No,' he said, 'I think he's doing something.'

'So do you think that the teacher writes and reads only his own name or also teaches you boys? Or, to take another example, didn't you spend just as much time writing the names of your enemies, of yourselves, and of your friends?'

'Yes, we wrote them all equally.'

'And when you were doing that, were you interfering in other people's business? Did doing that make you lose your self-control?' e

'Of course not.'

'But you weren't doing what pertained to yourselves—or at least you weren't if writing and reading are to be classified as doing something.'

'Well, they certainly are.'

'And consider healing, my friend, and building and weaving and the production of any professionally produced object you care to mention, thanks to any branch of expertise you care to mention: each of them is, presumably, to be classified as doing something.'

'Yes.'

'Well,' I said, 'do you think a community would be well run if there was a regulation to the effect that each person should weave and wash his own clothes, and make his own shoes, oil flask, strigil, and so on and so forth, without having anything to do with 162a anyone else's property, but with each person making his own things and doing what pertains to himself?'

'No, I don't think it would,' he said.

'But surely,' I said, 'if a community is regulated along self-controlled lines it is regulated well.'

'Of course,' he said.

'It follows, then,' I said, 'that self-control can't be doing what pertains to oneself in these and similar situations.'*

'I suppose you're right.'

'As I said not long ago, then, it looks as though the person who claimed that self-control was doing what pertains to oneself was being enigmatic, because I don't imagine he was as simple-b minded as he seems. Or was it perhaps some idiot that you got this idea from, Charmides?'

'No, far from it. In fact he had the reputation of being extremely knowledgeable.'

'His overriding concern, then, in my opinion, was to present the idea as a riddle, in the sense that it's hard to understand what doing what pertains to oneself might mean.'

'You may be right,' he said.

'So what might doing what pertains to oneself be? Can you explain it?'

'By Zeus, no,' he said. 'I don't know what it means. Maybe even the man who proposed the idea didn't know what he meant. Why not? It's possible.' And he accompanied these words with a smile and a glance at Critias.

c   Now, it had been clear for quite some time that Critias was

14

raring to go and was anxious to shine in front of Charmides and the rest of the assembled company. He'd been struggling to restrain himself before, but this was too much for him. I'm absolutely certain that my suspicion was right—that it was from Critias that Charmides had heard the answer he'd given to my question about what self-control was—and so, because Charmides wanted Critias rather than himself to justify the answer, he'd been trying to provoke him to take part himself, and had been making sure that he knew he'd been challenged. d And so Critias had reached the end of his tether. I thought he was angry with Charmides, much as a playwright might be with an actor who spoiled his work. The upshot was that Critias looked straight at Charmides and said: 'Is that what you think, Charmides? Do you really think that if *you* don't know the thinking behind the idea that self-control is doing what pertains to oneself, the author of the idea doesn't either?'

'Critias, my dear friend,' I said, 'it's hardly surprising that one so young should be ignorant. But you're older, and you've taken e an interest in the issues, so it's likely that you know what's going on. If you agree with what Charmides here has said about what self-control is, and if you're prepared to take over the argument, I for one would feel a lot better if you joined me in my investigation of whether or not what he said is true.'

'I definitely agree with it,' he said. 'I'll take over.'

'You're doing the right thing,' I said. 'So tell me, do you agree with what I was asking just now, that all artisans make something?'*

'Yes.'

'Do you think they make only their own things, or other 163a people's things as well?'

'Other people's too.'

'Do they display self-control in making not only their own things?'

'Why not?' he asked.

'Don't look to me for a reason why not,' I said. 'But it might be a problem for the person who takes self-control to be doing what pertains to oneself, if he then says that there's no reason for

15

denying self-control even to those who do what pertains to other people.'

'Yes,' he said, 'I suppose I've admitted that those who *do* what pertains to other people are self-controlled, if I've agreed that those who *make* what pertains to other people are.'

b   'Tell me,' I said, 'aren't "making" and "doing" the same in your vocabulary?'

'Certainly not,' he said. 'Nor, for instance, are "producing" and "making" either. I learnt this from Hesiod, who said that production was no disgrace.* Do you really think that if he'd been describing the kinds of activities you were talking about a moment ago as "productions"—as "producing" and "doing"— he'd have said that there was no disgrace in being a cobbler or a salt-fish seller or a prostitute? You can't seriously believe that, Socrates. No, Hesiod too, in my opinion, was distinguishing "making" from "doing" and "producing". He thought that a

c thing which is "made" may sometimes be disgraceful, when there is nothing admirable about it, but that a "product" is never disgraceful at all. He used the term "products" for things which are made so as to be admirable and useful, and the making of such things he called both "production" and "doing". We have to take him to believe that only admirable and beneficial things are one's own, whereas harmful things always belong to others. And the upshot is that we're bound to think that Hesiod, just like any other intelligent person, was describing as self-controlled someone who does what pertains to himself.'

d   'Critias,' I said, 'I grasped your position more or less perfectly straight away, because I've heard Prodicus distinguishing endlessly between this term and that. You reserved the term "good" for things which belong and pertain to oneself, and the term "doing" for the making of good things. I'll let you classify any term however you like, as long as you explain the reference of any term you use. So please start again and provide us with a clearer

e definition. Are you saying that the doing of good things—or the making of them or whatever term you like to use—is self-control?'

'Yes, I am,' he said.

'So someone who does bad things is not self-controlled, only someone who does good things?'

'Don't you agree, my friend?' he said.

'That's irrelevant,' I said. 'At the moment, we're not investigating what I think, but the meaning of this assertion of yours.'

'Well,' he said, 'this is my position: anyone who makes bad things rather than good things is not self-controlled; anyone who makes good things rather than bad things is self-controlled. And so I state my definition clearly for you: self-control is the doing of good things.'

'And it may very well be true,' I said. 'Nevertheless, I'm aston- 164a ished to find you believing that self-controlled people don't know that they're self-controlled.'

'But I don't believe that,' he protested.

'Didn't I hear you say a short while ago,' I said, 'that there was no reason why artisans should not be self-controlled even when they're making other people's things?'

'Yes, I said that,' he admitted. 'What of it?'

'Nothing. But tell me: do you think that a healer, in making someone healthy, is doing something that is beneficial both for b himself and for the person he's curing?'*

'Yes, I do.'

'And is the healer in this situation acting properly?'

'Yes.'

'And someone who acts properly is self-controlled, isn't he?'

'Yes, he is.'

'Does it follow that the healer must also recognize when his curing is beneficial and when it isn't? And the same goes for every artisan: is he bound to recognize when he'll benefit from the productive work he's doing and when he won't?'

'Probably not.'

'Sometimes, then,' I said, 'a healer does something without recognizing whether he's acted beneficially or harmfully. But c according to you, if he's acted beneficially, he's acted with self-control. Isn't that what you were saying?'

'Yes.'

'So doesn't it look as though sometimes, in acting beneficially, he acts with self-control and is self-controlled, but doesn't know that he is self-controlled?'

'But that could never happen, Socrates,' he said. 'In fact, if you think it follows as a necessary consequence of anything I've agreed to earlier, I'd rather take back a concession or two. It d wouldn't embarrass me to admit that I was wrong, and I'd rather do that than ever agree that a self-controlled person could fail to know himself, since I'd almost be prepared to say that knowing oneself is exactly what self-control is. I agree with whoever it was who dedicated the inscription to that effect at Delphi, and I think it was set up as an alternative greeting from the god to those entering his shrine instead of "Be well and happy".* It's as if e saying "Be well and happy" isn't an appropriate form of greeting—as if it's more important to recommend self-control to one another than that—and so the god doesn't greet those who enter his shrine with the form of address we normally use. This, I think, was the intention of the man who dedicated the inscription: essentially, he's claiming that what the god is saying to anyone who enters the shrine is "Be self-controlled". Like a professional diviner, however, he's more ambiguous than that, because although "Know yourself" and "Be self-controlled" are 165a the same (as the inscription claims, with my agreement), they might be taken to be different. In fact, I think the people who dedicated the later inscriptions, "Nothing in excess" and "Financial pledges lead to ruin", *did* take them to be different: they thought that "Know yourself" was a piece of advice, not the god's greeting to visitors to the shrine, and so they set up their inscriptions out of a desire to dedicate pieces of advice that were just as useful. Anyway, Socrates, here's the reason I've brought all this b up: I grant you everything that's gone before—it may be that you were closer to the mark in what you were saying, or it may be that I was, but in any case nothing we were saying was particularly clear or certain—but I'm prepared to justify this position of mine, unless you agree that self-control is knowing oneself.'

'Well, Critias,' I said, 'you're treating me as though I were claiming to know the answers to my questions and as though I'd agree with you if I chose to. But it's not like that: I just investigate each proposition as it comes along, with you as my partner in the search, because I don't have any knowledge myself.* Once the investigation is complete, I'll gladly tell you whether or not I c agree with you, but please wait until I've finished.'

'Go ahead, then,' he said.

'All right, here goes,' I said. 'If self-control is knowing something, it obviously must be a kind of knowledge and it must be knowledge of something. Yes?'

'Yes, it's knowledge of oneself,' he said.

'And what about the art of healing?' I asked. 'Is it knowledge of health?'

'Yes.'

'Now,' I said, 'if you were to ask me: "If the healing art is knowledge of health, what good is it? What is its product?" I'd reply that it's enormously beneficial, because its product is d health, which is something desirable for us human beings. Are you happy with this answer?'

'Yes, I am.'

'And if you were to ask me what I'd identify as the product of building, which is knowledge of building houses, I'd reply that its product was houses.* And I'd give similar answers to questions about all the other arts and crafts. Since you claim that self-control is knowledge of oneself, you ought to be able to answer the equivalent question. So suppose you were asked: "Critias, if self-control is knowledge of oneself, what is its product and does its e product deserve to be called desirable?" Let's hear what your answer would be.'

'Socrates,' he said, 'you're going about the investigation in the wrong way. Self-control differs from other branches of knowledge (which also differ from one another, anyway). But you're conducting the investigation on the basis of an assumption that they're all similar. I mean, tell me: what product is there of arithmetic or geometry which is equivalent to a house in the case of building, or to clothes in the case of weaving, or to the many equivalent products that one could point to in the case of many arts and crafts? Can even you show me an equivalent product of 166a arithmetic and geometry? Of course you can't.'

'You're right,' I said. 'But there *is* something I can show you, and that is what each of these branches of knowledge is knowledge of, which in each case is something different from the branch of knowledge itself. For example, arithmetic is, I'd say, the knowledge of the quantity of even and odd numbers in themselves and of the relations between even and odd numbers. Yes?'

'Yes,' he said.

'Odd and even numbers being different from arithmetic itself?'

'Of course.'

b 'Or, to take another example, weighing is the knowledge† of the weight of things that are heavier and lighter, but heavy and light weights are different from weighing itself? Do you agree?'

'Yes.'

'Tell me, then: what is self-control the knowledge of, which is different from self-control itself?'

'This is just what I was getting at, Socrates,'* he said. 'You reach the point in your investigation of seeing how self-control differs from all other kinds of knowledge, but then you try to see how it resembles them. But self-control isn't like that: all the c other branches of knowledge involve knowledge of something else, not of themselves, and self-control alone is knowledge of all other cases of knowledge and of itself. There's no way you can have missed this, so I think that instead you're doing what you recently promised not to do:* you're trying to test *me*, instead of focusing on the topic of our discussion.'

'How can you do this?' I said. 'If I'm doing my best to challenge you, how can you think I have any reason for doing so other than what would also make me check to see whether something *I* d was saying was right—that is, out of fear that I might on some occasion have failed to notice that I don't actually know something I think I know? This is what I'm doing now too: I'm looking at the argument, above all for my own good, but perhaps also for the good of the rest of my friends. But maybe you don't think that the clarification of the nature of each and every existing thing is something that benefits almost everyone in the world.'

'No, Socrates,' he said, 'I think it does.'

'Don't get downhearted, then, my friend,' I said. 'Give your honest answer to every question that's put to you, and don't e worry whether it's Critias or Socrates who's being tested. Just focus on the argument and see what happens when it's tested.'

'I'll do that,' he said. 'I think what you've said is fair.'

'Tell us, then,' I said, 'what, in your opinion, self-control is.'

'All right,' he said. 'I maintain that it's the only kind of knowledge which knows itself and all other cases of knowledge.'

'If it's knowledge of knowledge,' I asked, 'would it also be knowledge of lack of knowledge?'*

'Yes,' he said.

'Only a self-controlled man, then, will know himself and will 167a be capable of looking to see what he actually knows and what he doesn't know. By the same token only a self-controlled man will be capable of examining others to see what a person knows and thinks he knows (assuming that he does have knowledge), and whether there are things which he thinks he knows, but doesn't really. And no one else will be capable of doing this.* This is what it is to be self-controlled, what self-control is, and what knowing oneself is: it is knowing what one knows and what one doesn't know. Is this your position?'

'Yes, it is,' he said.

'Let's make more or less a fresh start, then,' I said, 'with a third libation to Zeus the Saviour.* Let's consider first whether or not b it's possible to know that one knows and doesn't know what one knows and doesn't know. After that, if it really *is* possible, we should consider what good such knowledge would do us.'

'Yes, that's the right procedure,' he said.

'All right, then, Critias,' I said. 'Now, I wonder whether you find yourself to be less baffled than I am about all this. I'm stuck, you see. Shall I tell you what's puzzling me?'

'By all means,' he said.

'If what you're saying is true,' I said, 'what it all boils down to, surely, is that there's one special kind of knowledge which is knowledge of nothing but itself and all other cases of knowledge, and that this same knowledge is also knowledge of lack of know- c ledge. Is that right?'

'Yes.'

'But we're committing ourselves here to an extraordinary assertion, my friend. If you try to find the same phenomenon elsewhere, you'll see how impossible it is, I think.'

'Why? What do you mean by "elsewhere"?'

'Here. I wonder whether you think there's a kind of seeing which isn't the seeing of those things which all other cases of seeing are of, but is the seeing of itself and of all other cases of seeing, and at the same time of cases of lack of seeing as well. Despite being seeing, it doesn't see colour at all, rather than itself and all other cases of seeing. Do you think that such a kind of seeing exists?'

d

'By Zeus, no, I don't!'

'What about hearing?† Is there a kind of hearing that doesn't hear any sound, but hears itself and all other cases of hearing and not hearing?'

'No, I don't think that kind of hearing exists either.'

'Taking all the senses together, then, have a look and see whether you think there's a kind of perception which is perception of cases of perception and of itself, but never perceives anything which the other senses perceive?'

'No, I don't think there is.'

e

'Well, do you think there's a kind of desire which doesn't desire any pleasure, but desires itself and all other cases of desire?'

'Of course I don't.'

'Nor, I imagine, is there a kind of wanting which wants nothing good, but wants itself and all other cases of wanting.'*

'No, there isn't.'

'And would you say that there was a kind of love which is such that it isn't love of anything beautiful,* but of itself and all other cases of loving?'

'No,' he said, 'I wouldn't.'

'And have you ever come across a kind of fear which fears itself and all other cases of fear, but doesn't fear anything threatening at all?'*

168a

'No, I haven't.'

'Or any thinking which thinks of other cases of thinking and of itself, but doesn't think of any of the things which other cases of thinking think of?'

'Of course not.'

'But apparently we're saying there's a kind of knowledge which is such that it isn't knowledge of any field of study, but is knowledge of itself and of all other cases of knowledge.'

'Yes, that's what we're saying.'

'So it's an anomaly, isn't it, if it turns out to exist? But let's not yet insist that it doesn't exist; let's carry on trying to see whether it does.'

'Good idea.'　　　　　　　　　　　　　　　　　　　　　　　　　b

'All right, then. Knowledge, in itself,† is knowledge of something, isn't it? It does have the property of being of something?'

'Yes.'

'And we also say that something greater has the same property: it is greater than something, isn't it?'*

'Yes, it is.'

'In fact, if it's to be greater, it's greater than something smaller.'

'Necessarily.'

'So if we were to find something which is greater than greater things and than itself (rather than being greater than any of the things which all other greater things are greater than), I imagine that it absolutely must have the property, if it's to be greater than c itself, of also being smaller than itself. Do you agree?'

'Yes, it certainly must, Socrates,' he said.

'Likewise, if there's something which is double all other doubles and itself, it and all other doubles must be half of it, for it to be double, because any double is double of a half.'

'True.'

'Something which is more than itself will also be less than itself, then, something heavier will also be lighter, something older will also be younger, and so on and so forth: anything whose property is relative to itself will also have the attribute to which its d property is relative, won't it? To illustrate what I'm getting at, consider hearing: we say that hearing is the hearing of noise, don't we?'

'Yes.'

'So if it's to hear itself, what it will hear of itself is noise, which must be a feature of it. Otherwise it wouldn't be a case of hearing.'

'Yes, that's absolutely right.'

'And the same goes for sight, my friend: if it's to see itself, it must possess some colour, because it's impossible for sight ever to see anything which has no colour.'　　　　　　　　　　　　　　　　e

'No, that's right.'

'Do you see, then, Critias, that in every case we've covered, we've found it either completely impossible or highly unlikely that they could ever possess their own properties relative to themselves? We found it completely impossible for size and number, didn't we?'

'Yes, indeed.'

'And in a whole raft of cases including hearing and sight—and let's add the idea that change could change itself, or that heat could burn itself—the idea would generally be found unlikely, even if not by everyone. What we need, my friend, is some great man to determine satisfactorily in all cases whether nothing that exists is so constituted as to possess its own property relative to itself rather than to something else, or whether some things do, but others don't; and, if there are certain things which are relative to themselves, he would also have to determine whether the knowledge we're calling self-control falls into that category. Now, I'm not at all sure that I'm capable of settling these questions on my own, and that's why I can't be certain whether the existence of knowledge of knowledge is possible. Moreover, even if it really *is* possible, I find myself unable to accept that it's self-control until I've considered whether or not such a thing would do us any good (because my guess is that self-control is something that is beneficial and good). So, since it's your position that self-control is knowledge of knowledge and also of lack of knowledge, Critias, it's up to you to show, first, that what I've just said is possible, and second, that in addition to being possible, it's also beneficial. If you can do that, you might prove to my satisfaction that you're right about what self-control is.'

Critias heard me out. He could see that I was stuck, and I got the impression that, thanks to my puzzlement, he too found himself, against his will, in the snares of perplexity—much as people who see others yawning in their presence find themselves yawning too. Given his high reputation in every walk of life, this was making him feel uncomfortable in front of the assembled company. He was reluctant to admit that he couldn't settle the issues I was raising, and at the same time his attempt to cover up

24

his puzzlement was making what he was saying confused and d confusing. I wanted the discussion to make progress, so I said: 'If you like, Critias, why don't we agree that knowledge of knowledge is possible and postpone our consideration of whether or not this is right? So, assuming that it really *is* possible, how does it make a person more likely to know what he knows and what he doesn't know—which was, you'll remember, how we explained what knowing oneself and being self-controlled was, didn't we?'

'Yes, we did, Socrates,' he said, 'and I think it makes sense. After all, if someone possesses self-knowledge, knowledge which e knows itself, he'd resemble what he possesses. Anyone who possesses speed, for example, is fast, anyone who possesses beauty is beautiful, anyone who possesses knowledge is knowledgeable, and presumably, therefore, anyone who possesses self-knowledge is knowledgeable of himself.'

'I've got no problem with the idea that when a person possesses self-knowledge he'll know himself,' I said, 'but why does the possession of self-knowledge necessarily make a person know what he knows and what he doesn't know?'

'Because the one thing is the same as the other, Socrates.' 170a

'You may be right,' I said, 'but I seem to be no better off: I still don't understand how knowing what one knows and what one doesn't know can be self-control.'

'What do you mean?' he asked.

'Here's what I mean,' I said. 'If there is such a thing as knowledge of knowledge, will it be able to do more than distinguish cases of knowledge from cases of lack of knowledge?'

'No, just that.'

'Well, are knowledge and lack of knowledge of health, and knowledge and lack of knowledge of justice,† the same as know- b ledge of knowledge?'

'Of course not.'

'Because they are, respectively, the art of healing and the art of conducting public affairs, while the other is just plain knowledge.'

'Of course.'

'So if a person doesn't know health and justice, but knows only knowledge, because this is all he has knowledge of, in all

25

likelihood he'd know that he knows something—that he possesses some kind of knowledge. And he'd be able to recognize this wherever it occurred, not just in his own case, wouldn't he?'

'Yes.'

c 'But how will this knowledge help him to know *what* he knows? I mean, it's not self-control but the art of healing that enables him to know what is healthy, and it's not self-control but music that enables him to know what is harmonious, and it's not self-control but building that enables him to know how to build houses, and so on for every branch of knowledge. Yes?'

'I suppose so.'

'If self-control is nothing more than knowledge of instances of knowledge, how will it enable him to know that he knows what is healthy or how to build houses?'

'It can't.'

'Anyone who's ignorant in this respect, then, won't know *what* he knows, but only *that* he knows.'

'It looks that way.'

d 'It follows, apparently, that self-control isn't knowing what one knows and what one doesn't know, but is only knowing that one knows and that one doesn't know.'

'That's probably so.'

'It also follows that a person with this knowledge won't be able to test the truth of someone else's claim to know something and see whether or not this other person does have the knowledge he claims to have. All such a person will know, apparently, is *that* this other person has knowledge of some kind, but self-control won't enable him to know *what* this other person has knowledge of.'

'I suppose not.'

e 'So he won't be able to tell someone who falsely pretends to be a healer from someone who genuinely is a healer, or to do likewise for any technical expert. Let's look at it this way. If a self-controlled person (or indeed anyone else) is to distinguish a genuine from a spurious healer, won't he act as follows? Won't he talk to him† about the art of healing—naturally enough, because, as we said, all a doctor understands is good and bad health? Isn't this what he'll do?'

'Yes, that's right.'

'But a healer doesn't know the first thing about knowledge, because we attributed that to self-control alone.'*

'Yes, we did.'

'Nor does an expert healer know about the art of healing, then, since the art of healing is a branch of knowledge.'*

171a

'True.'

'So our self-controlled person will recognize that a healer has knowledge of some kind, and when he has to try to understand precisely what it is, surely he'll consider what it's knowledge *of*, won't he? I mean, isn't it precisely the objects of a branch of knowledge that we use to define each branch of knowledge as being not just knowledge, but knowledge of a particular kind?'

'Yes, that's how we do it.'

'And the art of healing is distinguished from all other branches of knowledge by being knowledge of good and bad health.'

'Yes.'

'So anyone who wants to look into the art of healing has to take into consideration those things which make it possible for him to b look into it. After all, I'm sure he wouldn't take external things into consideration, which don't help his investigation, would he?'

'Certainly not.'

'So the proper way to go about such an investigation is to use cases of good and bad health to look into the claims of a healer to be a skilled healer.'

'Apparently so.'

'So he'll use what the healer says or does in cases of good and bad health and try to see whether his words are correct and his actions appropriate. Yes?'

'There's no other way for him to go about his investigation.'

'Well, could anyone check up on either the words or the actions without knowledge of the art of healing?'

'Definitely not.'

'Only a healer could do so, then, it seems, and no one else—and c not a self-controlled person, because that would make him a healer as well as being self-controlled.'*

'True.'

'It clearly follows, then, that if self-control is nothing but knowledge of knowledge and of lack of knowledge, a self-controlled person will be incapable of distinguishing between a healer who knows his art and a quack who is pretending or who thinks that he knows the art. Nor will he be able to tell whether any other expert knows even the slightest thing, unless he's a specialist in the same field as the expert.'†

'I suppose so,' he said.

d 'So, Critias, how would we still benefit from self-control, if this is what it's like?' I asked. 'Our original hypothesis was that a self-controlled person knew what he knew and what he didn't know—which is to say that he knew that he knew what he knew, and knew that he didn't know what he didn't know—and that he was capable of examining anyone else who was in the same situation. If this were true, it would be enormously beneficial for us to be self-controlled, we may safely claim, because we'd live our lives free from error. Moreover, this would apply not only to us self-controlled ones, but to everyone else who

e was governed by us—to us because we wouldn't try to do anything we didn't know about, but instead would seek out the experts in that field and hand the job over to them, and to our subjects because we wouldn't let them do anything except what they would do well (that is, things they knew about).* In this way, with the help of self-control, a household would be well managed, a city would be well governed, and the same would go for everything else that was subject to self-control. For in a

172a regime from which error has been banished and which has accuracy at the helm, people are bound to do well and perform well in every activity. Isn't that what we were saying about self-control, Critias, when we were remarking on what a blessing it would be to know what one knows and what one doesn't know?'

'Yes, that's exactly it,' he said.

'But as things are,' I went on, 'you can see that our enquiry has at no point brought us at all close to uncovering the existence of any such knowledge.'

'Yes, I can,' he said.

b 'Anyway,' I said, 'at the moment we're finding self-control to be the knowledge of knowledge and of lack of knowledge. I wonder if this would be beneficial in the sense that it will be easier for anyone with such knowledge to learn a new subject and that everything will appear more vivid to him, because, in addition to whatever it is he's learning on any occasion, he also sees the branch of knowledge as a whole. Moreover, won't he be exceptionally good at questioning anyone else about the subjects he himself has learnt, while those who examine others without knowledge of knowledge will do so indecisively and inefficiently? Are these, my friend, the kinds of ways in which self-control will do us good? Are we looking at something that broad? Are we c looking for it to be broader than it actually is?'

'But self-control might be like that,' he said.

'You may be right,' I said, 'but it may also be that what we've come up with serves no practical purpose at all. My reason for saying this is that some extraordinary consequences emerge for self-control, if that's what it's like. Let's look at it this way, for instance—while agreeing, if you like, that it's possible to know knowledge and while retaining and granting our original assumption that self-control is knowing what one knows and does not know. With all these concessions in mind, let's take an even closer d look at whether such a thing could do us any good. You see, Critias, I don't think we were right to agree a short while ago that if self-control were something like this it would do us a great deal of good by taking charge of the management of household and community.'

'Why not?' he asked.

'Because,' I said, 'we too readily agreed that it would be immensely beneficial for people as a whole if each set of specialists stuck to their own field of expertise and left everything that was outside it to others—to those with the relevant knowledge.'

'There's something wrong with this?' he asked.   e

'I think so,' I said.

'That's a truly extraordinary thing to say, Socrates,' he said.

'By the Dog,* yes,' I said, 'I think it is too. That was what made me say just now that I could foresee some extraordinary consequences and that I was worried in case we weren't going about the investigation in the right way. In all honesty, you see, if this is really what self-control is like, I can't see that it does us any good 173a at all.'

'Why not?' he asked. 'Tell us. We too would like to know what you're getting at.'

'I may be wrong,' I said, 'but anyone who cares even a little bit for himself should examine the ideas that occur to him and not just let them go in an unmethodical fashion.'

'Quite right,' he said.

'Listen to my dream, then,' I said, 'and tell me whether you think it's come through the Gate of Horn or the Gate of Ivory.* If self-control, as we've defined it, were to have complete authority over us, everything would be done, surely, in conformity with the
b various branches of knowledge, no one could deceive us by claiming to be a helmsman when he wasn't really, and we would always be able to spot false claims to knowledge from people making themselves out to be healers or generals or something. Under these circumstances, wouldn't we be physically healthier than we are now? Wouldn't we survive dangers at sea and in war? Wouldn't all our belongings—our furniture and all our clothing
c and footwear, for instance—and objects from many other areas of life be made with professional skill because we'd be using genuine artisans and craftsmen? If you like, we can even concede that with self-control in charge of divination, understood as the knowledge of the future, impostors are debarred and true diviners are appointed to reveal the future for us. I understand that, in these circumstances, humans would act and live in conformity with
d knowledge, because self-control would be on the lookout for any lack of knowledge and would stop it insinuating itself into our lives and playing a part in our activities; but, my dear Critias, what we cannot yet grasp is whether in acting in conformity with knowledge we'd thrive and be happy.'

'Well,' he said, 'you won't easily find another way to ensure that we'd thrive, if you discount acting in conformity with knowledge.'

'All right,' I said, 'but could you please just clarify one further, trivial point for me? When you say "acting in conformity with knowledge", what is the knowledge that you're talking about *of*? Is it knowledge of shoemaking?'

e 'By Zeus, no. That's not what I mean.'

'Of metal-working, then?'

'Of course not.'

'Of working with wool or wood or something like that?'

'Certainly not.'

'As it turns out, then,' I said, 'we've moved on from saying that living in conformity with knowledge makes a man happy. I mean, the artisans we've just mentioned live in conformity with knowledge, but by your own admission aren't happy. You seem to be setting the happy man aside as one who lives in conformity with knowledge *of certain things*. Perhaps you mean the person I mentioned a short while ago, the one with perfect knowledge of the future, the diviner. Is this the one you mean, or someone 174a else?'

'Yes, I'd call him happy,' he said, 'but he's not the only one.'

'Who else?' I asked. 'Surely you don't mean the kind of person who knows the past and the present as well as the future, and is ignorant of nothing? I mean, let's suppose such a person exists. I'm sure you wouldn't say that there was anyone in the world whose conformity with knowledge was closer than his.'

'No, I certainly wouldn't.'

'But I still need to know *which* of his branches of knowledge makes him happy? Or do all of them equally make him happy?'

'No, not equally, of course,' he said.

'Which one contributes most towards his happiness? The one b that enables him to know *what* aspect of the present, past, and future? Is it the one that enables him to know backgammon?'

'What kind of a suggestion is that?' he said.

'The one which enables him to know arithmetic, then?'

'Of course not.'

'The one which enables him to know health?'

'That's more like it,' he said.

'But the one which is *most* like it is the one I'm after,' I said, 'which is the branch of knowledge that enables him to know *what*?'

'The one which enables him to know what is good and what is bad,' he said.

'Damn you!' I said. 'You've been leading me astray all this time! You've been concealing the fact that it isn't living in conformity with knowledge that causes us to thrive and be happy—or

31

c at least that it isn't the possession of all the other branches of knowledge, but just this one branch, which is concerned with good and bad. After all, Critias, what difference does it make if you detach this particular branch of knowledge from all the rest? The art of healing will still make us healthy, won't it? The art of shoemaking will still provide us with footwear and the art of weaving with clothes, won't they? Helmsmanship and generalship will still stop us dying at sea or in war, won't they?'

'Yes,' he said.

'But without this particular branch of knowledge, Critias, my
d friend, there's no chance that any of these products will turn out well and will do us good.'*

'That's right.'

'Apparently, then, this particular branch of knowledge isn't self-control but the branch of knowledge whose function is to do us good. I mean, it isn't the knowledge of cases of knowledge and of lack of knowledge, but of good and bad, and so if *it* does us good, self-control must be something different.'

'Why wouldn't self-control do us good?' he asked. 'If it really is knowledge of cases of knowledge, and if it presides over all
e other branches of knowledge, it follows that it would rule over knowledge of good as well, and so it would benefit us.'

'Would it make us healthy too,' I asked, 'or is that the job of the art of healing? Would it make the products of all the other arts and crafts, or are they produced by each of the various arts and crafts? Haven't we been asserting all along that it is knowledge only of knowledge and of lack of knowledge, not of anything else? Isn't that what it is?'

'Yes, I suppose so.'

'So it won't produce health?'

'No, definitely not.'

175a 'Because health is the product of a different branch of knowledge, isn't it?'

'Yes.'

'Then it won't produce benefit either, my friend, because just now we assigned that product to a different branch of knowledge, didn't we?'

'Yes.'

'If benefit isn't a product of self-control, then, how will self-control be beneficial?'

'Apparently it won't be, Socrates.'

'So, Critias, now you can see that my fears were well founded: I was quite right to tell myself off for going about the investigation into self-control in entirely the wrong way. I mean, if I were any good at conducting an efficient enquiry, we wouldn't have concluded that something which is acknowledged to be the best thing b in the world does no good at all. And now, wherever we turn, we're facing defeat: we're incapable of discovering which aspect of reality it was that the legislator named "self-control".* And we've failed even though in the course of the discussion we frequently made illogical concessions. For instance, we agreed that there was such a thing as knowledge of knowledge, when the argument disallowed and denied it,* and we also agreed to another proposition denied by the argument—that this know- c ledge knew the products of all other kinds and branches of knowledge*—because we wanted our self-controlled man to be in a position to know that he knows what he knows and that he doesn't know what he doesn't know. It was very magnanimous of us to agree to this without even considering how impossible it is for someone to know in any way whatsoever things which he doesn't know at all. After all, that's what this agreement of ours is claiming—that he knows what he doesn't know—even though I can hardly imagine a more irrational idea.*

'Nevertheless, although the enquiry found us to be easy-going d and compliant, it still failed to uncover the truth; in fact, it mocked the truth, in that it came to the utterly outrageous conclusion that self-control, as defined by our agreements and constructions, did us no good at all. I don't mind so much for myself,' I said, turning to Charmides, 'but it's *you* I'm worried about. It makes me really cross if you, who combine physical beauty with a perfectly self-controlled soul, will gain nothing from this self- e control of yours and if your possession of self-control does you no good in life. And I'm even more cross when I think of the incantation I learnt from the Thracian, since it now looks as though I went to all that time and trouble to learn a spell for something worthless. Anyway, I don't really think this is right: I think it's just that I'm a useless investigator. In my opinion, you see, self-control is a very good thing and you're lucky to have it. So why 176a don't you check to see whether you do have it? If you do, you have no need of my spell, and I'd advise you to regard me as a wrong-headed fool, incapable of conducting a reasoned examination of anything, and to think of yourself as happy to exactly the extent that you're self-controlled.'

'By Zeus, Socrates,' Charmides said, 'personally, I've no idea whether or not I possess self-control. How could I know such a thing, when by your own admission even you two cannot discover b what it is? But I think you may be quite wrong, Socrates: I think I badly need your spell. In fact, there's no reason why you shouldn't chant the spell over me every day, until you say I've had enough.'

'All right,' said Critias. 'But as far as I'm concerned, Charmides, your doing that will be convincing proof of your self-control—if you don't get sidetracked to the slightest extent, and let Socrates chant his spell over you.'

'Don't worry,' he said. 'I'll stick to this plan without getting sidetracked. After all, it would be shocking behaviour on my part c if I were to disobey you and not do what you tell me, when you're my guardian.'

'Well, yes,' he said, 'that is my advice to you.'

'Then that's what I'll do,' he said, 'starting today.'

'Hey!' I said. 'What scheme are you two coming up with?'

'Nothing,' Charmides said. 'We've already come up with it.'

'Are you going to leave me no choice?' I asked. 'Do I have any say in the matter?'

'You don't really have any choice,' he said, 'because Critias here is the one issuing the orders. And so you should start coming up with a plan of action yourself.'

d 'There's nothing left to plan about,' I replied, 'because if you undertake to do something and are prepared to override others' wishes, no one on earth will be able to resist you.'

'Then you'd better not resist me either,'* he said.

'I won't,' I said.

34

LACHES

LYSIMACHUS: So, Nicias and Laches, you've seen the man fighting in hoplite armour.* Melesias here and I didn't tell you at the
time why we asked you to join us in the audience for the display,
but we'll tell you now. After all, we think we should speak
openly to *you*. It's true that some people find such candour
ridiculous; if someone asks their advice they don't speak their b
minds, but guess at what the person who sought their advice
wants to hear. This makes them say something different from
what they really think. But in your case, we judged you capable
of forming an opinion and then of speaking your minds in a
straightforward fashion, and that is why we brought you along
for a conference about . . . well, we'll tell you what we want
your advice about. With apologies for such a long preamble,
here's the issue.

Each of us has a son—there they are. That one is the son of 179a
my friend Melesias here, named Thucydides after his grandfather, and the other one is mine. He too has his grandfather's
name:* we call him Aristeides after my father. We've decided to
do the best we can for them, rather than behaving like most
fathers, who let their sons do whatever they like once they've
become young adults. On the contrary, we think that now is the
time to start doing the best we can for them.

Now, we know that you've got sons as well, and we assumed
that you were prime examples of fathers who've taken an inter- b
estin what training would make your sons the best men possible. But if it turns out that you haven't paid attention to this
after all, we're here to remind you that you shouldn't neglect it
and to invite you to join us in taking an active interest in your
sons' welfare.

Nicias and Laches, I'd like to tell you how we came to decide
to look after our sons' welfare, even though it means my talking
for a little longer. I should explain that Melesias here and I take
our meals together, and we're joined by the boys. Now, as I said
at the beginning, we're going to speak openly to you. The point c

is that each of us is in a position to tell the boys about all the splendid achievements of our own fathers*—all the things they accomplished during times of war and peace in directing the affairs of both the allies* and this great city of ours—but neither of us can tell them of anything that we have achieved ourselves. This makes us feel ashamed before them, and we blame our fathers for letting us take things easy when we became young adults, while they were busy with other people's affairs.

d

We've explained precisely this point to the boys and told them that if they take no thought for themselves and don't do what we tell them, they'll turn out to be nonentities, whereas if they do take an interest in themselves they might become worthy of the great names they bear. They said they'd go along with our wishes, and so we're trying to find out what it is they should study or practise if they're to become the best men possible. Someone suggested this subject to us among others, and said that it was good for a young man to learn how to fight in hoplite armour. He recommended the man whose display you've just been watching and added that we should watch him in action. We decided that, in addition to coming and watching the man ourselves, we should also bring you along, not just to watch him with us, but also to advise us and, if you want, to help us take our sons in hand.

e

180a

That's what we wanted to tell you. So now it's up to you to advise us not only about this subject—about whether or not you think it worth studying—but also about any other project or activity you might like to recommend for a young man. And you'd better tell us also how you'd like to proceed with your part in their education.

NICIAS: Personally, Lysimachus and Melesias, I'm full of admiration for your scheme and I'll happily do what I can to help—as will Laches here too, I'm sure.

b LACHES: Yes, you're right, Nicias. Now, I thought that what Lysimachus was just saying was relevant not only to his and Melesias' fathers, but also to us and to everyone who's involved in the affairs of his community. They all end up in more or less exactly the situation he was describing: they neglect their private life as a whole, not just their sons, and fail to give much

thought to managing it.* So you're right about that, Lysimachus. I'm surprised, however, that you're inviting us to advise
you about the boys' education, but haven't called on Socrates
here to help you. It's not just that he belongs to the same deme c
as you;* he also frequents the places where one finds the kind of
admirable project or activity that you're trying to find for your
boys.

LYSIMACHUS: What's that, Laches? Do you mean that Socrates
here has taken an interest in this kind of thing?

LACHES: He certainly has, Lysimachus.

NICIAS: I can vouch for that too, just as well as Laches, from my
personal experience, because not long ago Socrates introduced
me to a music teacher for my son. It was Damon, who studied d
under Agathocles, and not only is he a highly accomplished
musician, but in all other respects too he's as good a teacher as
you could want for boys of this age.

LYSIMACHUS: Socrates and Nicias and Laches, you know that
people my age have lost touch with the younger generation,
because our advancing years make us spend most of our time at
home. But if you too have any good advice, Socrates, for your
fellow demesman here, you ought to give it—in fact, you're e
obliged to do so, because you're actually a friend of my family
through your father. He and I were always close, and to the day
he died we never fell out. But something just occurred to me
while our friends here were talking: the name 'Socrates' often
crops up in the boys' conversations at home as someone they
rate extremely highly, but I never asked them if they were
talking about Sophroniscus' son. Tell me, boys: is this the Soc- 181a
rates you keep mentioning?

LYSIMACHUS' SON: Yes, it is, father.

LYSIMACHUS: By Hera, Socrates, I'm glad to see that you're
doing that excellent man, your father, proud. And I'm
especially glad that there'll be close links between you and us.

LACHES: That's right, Lysimachus, you mustn't let him get away.
You should know that I've had the opportunity to see him
doing his native city proud, not just his father. He was with me b
during the retreat from Delium, and I can assure you that if the
rest of the troops had been prepared to conduct themselves as

he did, our city's pride would have remained intact and we wouldn't have suffered such an awful defeat on that occasion.*

LYSIMACHUS: Socrates, the compliments you're now receiving constitute high praise, coming as they do from men who command belief just when the topic is the qualities for which they are praising you. I can assure you, then, that when I hear your praises being sung like this, I'm happy to find you so well respected, and I want you to think of me as one of your most

c loyal friends. You should have visited us earlier of your own accord and considered us your friends: that would have been the right thing to do. But here we are now, and I want you to do just that from this day onward, now that we've made each other's acquaintance; I want you to spend time with us and get to know us and these lads of ours, so that you and they can keep our friendship intact. It will be your job to do that and ours to remind you of it in the future. But what do you all have to say about the issue we broached a short while ago? What's your view? Would this be a good project for the boys, to learn how to fight in hoplite armour?

d SOCRATES: Well, as far as that's concerned, Lysimachus, I shall offer you the best advice I can, and I shall also do my best to comply with all your other suggestions and invitations. But since I'm younger than these men here and have less experience in military matters, I really think I should listen first to what they have to say and learn from them. Afterwards, if I've got anything to add to what they've said, I shall try to explain what it is and to win both you and them round to my point of view. Well, Nicias, why doesn't one of you start us off?

NICIAS: That's all right with me, Socrates. In my opinion, there

e are a number of reasons why this is a useful subject for young men to learn. In the first place, it's a good idea for them to spend their time on this rather than on the things which young men tend to spend their time on when they aren't otherwise occupied. It's not just that it's no less effective and strenuous than other forms of exercise, and so it's bound to improve their

182a physique and physical fitness; it's also that this form of exercise, along with horsemanship, is particularly appropriate for a free man.* After all, the only people who are being trained for the contest in which we are engaged,* and for the conditions under which the contest is being held, are those who are being trained in the use of these implements of war.

In the second place, although this subject will also prove of some use on the actual battlefield, when one has to fight in a phalanx alongside large numbers of other people,* its greatest benefit will come when the phalanx has broken up and a man suddenly has to fight in single combat, either because he has set out in pursuit and is harrying someone who's defending himself, or because he's fleeing and is defending himself against the b assaults of an opponent. A man with this skill wouldn't suffer any harm from a single opponent, nor perhaps from more than one opponent; in any circumstances, this skill would give him the upper hand.

In the third place, an admirable skill such as this one motivates a man to acquire further admirable skills: everyone who knows how to fight in armour finds himself attracted towards the next subject, which is tactics, and once he has acquired this skill and devoted himself to it, he'll make his next objective c military leadership as a whole. So it should by now be clear that all the skills and activities which are related to tactics and leadership are admirable and very valuable for a man to learn and take up, and that the whole sequence of mastering these valuable skills is set in motion by the art of fighting in armour.

There's also one further point to add, a point of some importance: this branch of knowledge will make any man far bolder and more courageous in battle than he was before. And even though it may seem rather trivial to some people, let's not disdain to mention that it will also make a man better looking on those occasions when he ought to appear better looking and d when, moreover, his striking appearance will be more terrifying to his foes.

Anyway, Lysimachus, as I said, I do think one ought to get young men to learn this skill, and I've explained why I think so. But even so, if Laches has anything different to say, I'd be glad to hear it.

LACHES: Well, Nicias, it's not easy to dismiss any skill as pointless: expertise seems always to be a good thing. It follows, then,

e   that one ought to learn how to fight in armour, if it really is a
skill, as its teachers claim and Nicias thinks. On the other hand,
if it's not a skill—if the claims made for it are unsound—or if it
is in fact a skill, but not a very important one, what point would
there be in learning it? I'll tell you the consideration that makes
me say this. It's my personal belief that, if it were any use, it
wouldn't have been overlooked by the Spartans, whose sole
concern in life is to search out and take up any skill which, once

183a   mastered and practised, will give them the upper hand in war
over others. And if the Spartans had overlooked it, those who
offer to train others in it would still have noticed that there are
no Greeks who rate this kind of thing higher than the Spartans,
and it would have occurred to them that they would be held in
high regard in Sparta for it and would make more money there
than anywhere else, just as composers of tragedies are held in
high regard here in Athens.* That's why it's hardly surprising
that anyone who thinks he's good at composing tragedies
doesn't bother to take his shows on tour around other cities

b   outside Attica,* but rushes straight to Athens and displays his
compositions to the people here. But in my experience these
fighters in armour treat Sparta as if it were sacrosanct and
don't let even the tip of a toe touch the ground there; they skirt
its borders and prefer to put on their displays everywhere else,
and especially in those places where the inhabitants would be
the first to admit that there are plenty of people superior to
them in military matters.

c   Then again, Lysimachus, I personally have come across
quite a few of these men in action and I've seen what they're
like. So we can look at the matter from this point of view as
well. You see, almost as if it were deliberate, not a single one of
these trained fighters in armour has ever become renowned for
his actions on the field of battle, despite the fact that in every
other instance fame is the result of training and practice.
Apparently, however, these men have been quite remarkably
unlucky in this respect, compared with everyone else.

Take this man Stesilaus, for example, whom you and I

d   watched putting on a display in front of an enormous crowd
and whose self-aggrandizing boasts we heard. I once had a

better opportunity to watch him putting on a genuine, unfeigned display, though he didn't mean to. The ship on which he was serving as a marine rammed a cargo ship, and he launched himself into battle carrying a halberd which was as extraordinary a weapon as he is an extraordinary human being. None of the fellow's other exploits are particularly worth mentioning, but what happened with this clever invention of his, the combined spear and scythe, is remarkable. In the course of e the fighting, the halberd became tangled up in the ship's rigging and got stuck there.* Stesilaus was tugging away at it, in an attempt to free it, but he couldn't, and in the mean time his ship was passing the other ship. For a while, he ran along the deck of his ship, hanging on to the shaft of the halberd, but the time came when his ship was actually clearing the other one and his grip on the shaft meant that he was being pulled along after it. At that point he let the shaft run through his hands, until he was hanging on to the butt at the very end of it. The 184a crew of the cargo ship greeted his antics with laughter and clapping, and when a thrown stone landed on the deck at his feet and he let go of the shaft, even the crew of the trireme could no longer restrain their laughter at the sight of that strange halberd hanging from the rigging of the cargo ship.

Nicias may be right to say that there's something to it, but my personal experience of it is as I've described. As I said at the beginning, then, either it's a skill, but has only the kind of b trivial applications I've described, or it's not a skill, though there are people who insist on claiming that it is—but in either case it's not worth studying. In fact, I think that if a coward were to fancy himself an expert at it, it would increase his boldness and then it would be easier for people to see what he was like, and that if a brave man were to do so, people would watch him closely and would heap abuse upon him for every tiny mistake he made. You see, people resent it when you claim c to have this kind of skill, and this means that unless your bravery outstrips everyone else's to a remarkable degree, you're absolutely bound to be mocked for claiming expertise at it. That's more or less what *I* think about taking this subject seriously, Lysimachus, but as I said at the beginning, you shouldn't let Socrates here get away, but should ask his advice and try to find out what he thinks about the issue.

LYSIMACHUS: Well, I do ask your advice, Socrates, because our committee, so to speak, seems to me still to need someone to
d make the final decision.† If Laches and Nicias had agreed, there would be less need for such a person, but in fact, as you can see, they've cast their votes for contradictory positions. It would therefore be good to hear from you too, to find out which of them gets your vote as well.

SOCRATES: What, Lysimachus? Are you really intending to do something just because it has the support of the majority of us?

LYSIMACHUS: Yes, Socrates. What else can a man do?

SOCRATES: Is that what you'd do too, Melesias? If our committee
e was meeting to decide what kind of sport your son should take up, would you be guided by the majority of us, or by someone who had trained and practised under a good coach?

MELESIAS: By the man who'd had the good coach, Socrates, as is only reasonable.

SOCRATES: So you'd be more prepared to listen to him than to the four of us?

MELESIAS: Presumably.

SOCRATES: The reason being, I suppose, that a decision has to be made on the basis of expert knowledge rather than numbers, if it is to be a sound decision.

MELESIAS: Of course.

SOCRATES: So the first thing you should do now is find out
185a whether or not any of us has expert knowledge of the matter in question. If one of us does, you must listen to that single individual and ignore everyone else;* and if none of us does, you must look for someone else. Or do you and Lysimachus imagine that there's nothing very significant at stake here, rather than the most important of your possessions? I mean, sons may turn out good or they may turn out the opposite, and the condition of a father's household depends on how his sons turn out.

MELESIAS: You're right.

SOCRATES: So the topic demands a great deal of thoughtful attention.

MELESIAS: Yes.

SOCRATES: So, going back to what I was just saying, how would b
we set about trying to find out which of us had the most expertise in sports, if that was what we wanted to consider? Wouldn't
it be the one who had studied and practised, and who had had
good teachers in the subject?

MELESIAS: That's what I think, anyway.

SOCRATES: But the first step, don't you think, would be to try to
see in what subject we are looking for the person's teachers?

MELESIAS: What do you mean?

SOCRATES: Perhaps I can explain the point better like this. I
don't think we've started off by agreeing exactly what it is that
we're deliberating about when we're asking which of us is an
expert and has had teachers to make him so, and which of us c
hasn't.

NICIAS: But Socrates, aren't we looking into whether or not the
boys should study fighting in armour?

SOCRATES: Of course we are, Nicias, but when the issue is
whether a particular medicine should or should not be used to
treat the eyes, is one thinking at this point about the medicine
or the eyes, do you think?

NICIAS: The eyes.

SOCRATES: And when the issue is whether or not a horse should d
be introduced to the bridle, and when that should happen, isn't
one thinking at this point about the horse rather than the
bridle?

NICIAS: True.

SOCRATES: To sum up, then, when a person is considering A
only as a means to B, what he's really concerned about is B, for
the sake of which he was considering A; he isn't really concerned about the thing which he was looking into as a means to
something else.

NICIAS: That's bound to be the case.

SOCRATES: The same goes for our adviser too, then: what we
have to do is consider whether he's an expert in the care of that
thing for the sake of which we're considering what we're
considering.†

NICIAS: Yes.

e SOCRATES: So what we can say in the present instance is that we're considering a subject which is supposed to benefit the souls of the young men.*

NICIAS: Yes.

SOCRATES: So what we have to find out is whether one of us is an expert in care of the soul, is capable of taking proper care of it, and has had good teachers.

LACHES: Why, Socrates? There are people who acquire greater expertise in some fields without teachers than with them. I'm sure you've come across this phenomenon.

SOCRATES: Yes, I have, Laches. They're the kind of people whose claim to be skilled practitioners of an art or craft you'd refuse to trust, unless they were able to show you at least one well-

186a made product of their own skill.*

LACHES: Yes, you're right about that.

SOCRATES: So, Laches and Nicias, what we have to do, since Lysimachus and Melesias have invited us to act as an advisory committee on their sons, whose souls they're determined to improve as much as possible, is point out to them too, if we say we can, teachers who are, in the first place, evidently good men in their own right* and have demonstrably cared for the souls of many young men, and who, in the second place, were obviously

b our teachers. Alternatively, if one of us claims that, despite never actually having had a teacher, he still has personal accomplishments to tell us about, he has to come up with people—whether they're Athenians or foreigners, slave or free—who acknowledge that they have become good thanks to him. And if we can't do any of this, we had better recommend that they look elsewhere, because, where the sons of friends are concerned, we shouldn't run the risk of corrupting them and earning the utter condemnation of close friends.

As for me, Lysimachus and Melesias, I'll come right out and
c admit that I've not had a teacher in this subject, though I've been passionately interested in it ever since I was a young man. But I don't have the money to pay the Sophists, who were the only ones who were advertising their ability to make me a truly good person, and even now I'm still incapable of working out the method on my own. However, I wouldn't be surprised to

hear that Nicias or Laches has worked out or learnt the method, because their financial resources are better than mine, so that they might have studied with teachers, and because they're older, so that they could by now have worked it out by themselves. So I'm sure they have the ability to educate a per- d son. I mean, they'd never have so fearlessly spoken up about which activities are good and bad for a young man, unless they were confident that they had a good understanding of the subject.

However, although I basically trust them, I was surprised to find them disagreeing with each other, and this makes me want to ask you something in return, Lysimachus. You know how not long ago Laches told you not to let me get away, so that you could put your questions to me: well, I now urge you not to let Laches or Nicias get away, but to question them. 'Socrates', you should say, 'denies any understanding of the matter and e says that he isn't in a position to tell which of you is right, because he's never worked out for himself or learnt anything about this kind of matter. So why don't each of you, Laches and Nicias, tell us the master with whom you studied the upbringing of the young, and whether your knowledge of the subject comes from having learnt it from someone or from having worked it out by yourselves. If you learnt it, you had better each tell us who your teacher was and who else, besides him, is an expert in the same field. Then, if you're too busy 187a with political matters, we can go to these other experts and use money or favours or both to get them to take charge of our children as well as your own, to make sure that they don't bring shame upon their forebears by turning out bad. On the other hand, if you worked things out for yourselves, please could you give examples of people whom you have taken in hand and whose characters you have changed from bad to good. After all, if this is the first time you've undertaken an educational pro- ject, you'd better find a way to avoid putting your sons and your friends' children at risk, rather than the Carian, and to b avoid doing exactly what the proverb warns against, which is starting your pottery with a wine-jar.* So please could you tell us which of these alternatives applies and is relevant to you,

and which isn't.' That's what I think you should find out from
them, Lysimachus—and be sure not to let them escape.

LYSIMACHUS: My friends, I like the sound of what Socrates is
c saying, but it's up to you, Nicias and Laches, to make up your
own minds about whether or not you're prepared to face and to
answer this kind of question. It would obviously go down well
with Melesias here and me if you'd be willing to give thorough
replies to all Socrates' questions. After all, as I've been saying
right from the start, we invited you to act as our advisers
because we made the reasonable assumption that you'd taken
an interest in such matters, especially since your sons, like ours,
are almost old enough to be educated.* So, if you don't mind, do
d please join the discussion and help Socrates examine the issue
by exchanging your views with his. I mean, another one of his
good points was that what we're talking about here is of critical
importance to us.* Anyway, do please see whether you think this
is the way to proceed.

NICIAS: Lysimachus, apparently your knowledge of Socrates
really is limited to his father. I don't think you've ever actually
met him—unless perhaps as a child he accompanied his father
e and other fellow demesmen of yours and ended up close by you
in a shrine or at some other deme gathering. But you've obviously never come across the man since he's been grown up.

LYSIMACHUS: Yes, but what's your point, Nicias?

NICIAS: I don't think you appreciate what happens when you
come into close proximity with Socrates and strike up a conversation with him. Whatever the original topic of your conversation, eventually he's bound to head you off and to trap you into
188a trying to explain your own way of life and how you've lived up
to now. And once you're caught in the trap, Socrates won't let
you go until he's subjected every detail to a thorough, rigorous
test. I'm familiar with his ways and I know that such treatment
at his hands is inevitable. Besides, I'm sure to face it myself,
because I enjoy his company, Lysimachus, and I don't think
there's any harm in being reminded of flaws in our past or
b present behaviour. On the contrary, in the future you're bound
to be more thoughtful if you don't avoid this treatment but
submit to it, bearing in mind what Solon said,* and expect to go

on learning as long as you live, rather than imagining that old age arrives with wisdom in its train. Anyway, in my view being examined by Socrates isn't at all odd or unpleasant. No, I've been pretty sure for a while now that, with Socrates present, we and not our sons would be the focus of our discussion. So what I'm saying is that, speaking for myself, I've no objection to c spending time with Socrates however he likes; but you'd better see how Laches here feels about this kind of thing.

LACHES: Well, Nicias, my position on the spoken word is straightforward—or perhaps I should say that it changes key rather than being in a single key, because in different situations I can appear either to be enthusiastic about the spoken word or to be hostile to it. When I hear a man talking about excellence or about technical expertise of some kind, I'm inordinately pleased, if he's a real man and lives up to the words he's speaking, by the sight of speaker and words suiting and chiming with d one another. In fact, this kind of person seems to me to be a consummate musician, because he has perfected the tuning not of some recreational instrument such as a lyre, but truly lives† with his words and deeds in harmonious consistency. He has really tuned his life to the Doric mode rather than to the Ionic—and not to the Phrygian or the Lydian mode either, I think, but to the only mode that is truly Greek.* Anyway, I enjoy listening to this kind of man speaking and so warmly e do I welcome his words that anyone would take me to be an enthusiast for the spoken word, but I get upset by the opposite kind of person, and the better a speaker he appears to be, the more he upsets me and makes me seem, on the contrary, to be hostile to the spoken word.

Now, I may have no familiarity with Socrates' words, but I suppose I've experienced him in action,* and I found his conduct on that occasion to be the equivalent of words of high principle and utter candour. If this is what his speech is actu- 189a ally like, his wishes are mine too and I'd be absolutely delighted to be scrutinized by him. I won't be cross if there's a lesson in it for me, but I too agree with Solon, though with just one qualification: I'm willing to be taught plenty of lessons as I grow old, but only from good men. Let Solon agree with me that my

teacher is also to be a good man in his own right, and then I won't appear to be a dense pupil, because I won't be displeased with the conditions of my learning. On the other hand, I don't care in the slightest whether my teacher is younger than me or
b not yet famous or anything like that. So I offer myself to *you*, Socrates: you can teach me and challenge my views as you see fit, and in return learn what I know. I've felt this way about you ever since that day when you and I faced danger together and you let me glimpse your quality in the only kind of circumstances which make it possible to assess a man fairly. So do please say whatever you like, without taking our respective ages into consideration at all.

c SOCRATES: It doesn't look as though we'll be telling you off for not being ready to offer advice and play your part in the investigation.

LYSIMACHUS: It's up to us now, Socrates—I count you as one of us—so please could you take my place and try, for the good of the boys, to get answers from Laches and Nicias here to the questions we need to ask them, and in the course of your conversation with them offer us your advice. My age makes me forget most of the questions I meant to ask and most of what I hear too, especially if the conversation is interrupted by fresh
d topics, when I can't remember a thing. So why don't the rest of you talk over the matter we raised among yourselves in detail, while I listen? Then afterwards Melesias here and I will do whatever it is you decide we should do.

SOCRATES: Nicias and Laches, we must do as Lysimachus and Melesias request. Now, although it may not be a bad idea for us to ask ourselves questions along the lines of those we tried to consider a short while ago—what teachers there are for the
e kind of education we have in mind, or which people we have improved—I think the following approach will also get us to the same point, and may in fact start from a more basic position. If we know that the gaining of something—it doesn't matter what—improves the thing which gains it, and if moreover we're capable of ensuring that the one thing is gained by the other, it evidently follows that we know about the missing thing and could advise people as to how they might most easily

and effectively acquire it. You may not quite under.
I'm getting at, but you'll grasp my meaning more ea:
look at it this way. If we know that the gaining of sigh
improves the eyes when it is gained by them, and if m
we're capable of ensuring that it is gained by them, it evi
follows that we know what sight is and could advise people is to
how they might most easily and effectively acquire it. I mean, if
we don't even know what sight is or what hearing is, we'd
hardly be in a position to offer useful medical advice about eyes
and ears and about how someone might best acquire hearing or b
sight.

LACHES: You're right, Socrates.

SOCRATES: Now, Laches, these two men here are inviting us to
advise them how their sons' souls might acquire excellence and
so be improved, aren't they?

LACHES: Yes.

SOCRATES: So we have to already know what excellence is, don't
we? I mean, if we don't have any idea at all what excellence
actually is, is there any way we could advise someone how best c
to acquire it?

LACHES: No, I don't think there is, Socrates.

SOCRATES: In other words, Laches, our position is that we know
what it is.

LACHES: That's our position, Socrates.

SOCRATES: And since we know what it is, we can of course say
what it is.

LACHES: Of course.

SOCRATES: Well, let's not rush straight into an investigation of
excellence as a whole, my friend: that would perhaps be too
long a task. Instead, let's first see whether we have sufficient
knowledge of a part of it. That will probably make the investigation easier for us.   d

LACHES: All right, let's do that, Socrates, if that's what you'd like
to do.

SOCRATES: Which part of excellence shall we choose, then?
Doesn't it make sense to take the part to which the skill of
fighting in armour is generally held to be relevant? Most people
link this skill with courage, don't they?

LACHES: Yes, they certainly do.

SOCRATES: So let's start by trying to say what courage is, Laches. Afterwards, we can go on to consider how a young man can
e   gain it, in so far as it can be gained thanks to activities and skills.* Anyway, as I say, do please try to tell us what courage is.

LACHES: By Zeus, Socrates, that's not difficult. You can be certain that anyone who's prepared not to break rank, but to resist the enemy without turning to flight, is a brave man.*

SOCRATES: Well said, Laches! But . . . perhaps it's my fault for being unclear, but you answered a different question and didn't catch the meaning of the one I asked.

LACHES: What do you mean, Socrates?

191a SOCRATES: I'll tell you, if I can find a way to do so. According to you, a man is courageous if he remains at his post in the phalanx and fights the enemy.

LACHES: Yes, I'd call him courageous, anyway.

SOCRATES: So would I. But what about someone who fights the enemy while he's fleeing, not while remaining at his post?

LACHES: What do you mean by 'fleeing'?

SOCRATES: Well, you know how the Scythians are said to fight just as effectively when they're fleeing from their opponents as when they're chasing them.* Then again, at one point Homer praises Aeneas' horses, as you'll remember, for knowing how to
b   'pursue or fly full swift hither and yon', and he also praised Aeneas himself for his knowledge of fear, describing him as an 'instigator of fear'.*

LACHES: Yes, Homer was right to do so, because he was talking about chariots, and the Scythian tactic *you* mentioned involves horsemen. Horsemen fight like that, you see, but what I was talking about applies to hoplites.

SOCRATES: With the possible exception of Spartan hoplites, Laches. There's a story from Plataea that when the Spartan
c   hoplites came up against the Persian troops with their wicker shields, they were *not* prepared to remain at their posts and engage them; they fled, and then, once the Persian lines had broken up, they turned and fought like horsemen, and won the battle there with the help of this tactic.*

LACHES: You're right.

SOCRATES: That's why a short while ago I said that my inadequate question was responsible for your inadequate answer. You see, I meant to ask you not just about courage for d hoplites, but also about courage for horsemen and every other kind of soldier; and I wanted to find out what constitutes courage not just in warfare, but when facing danger at sea, or when up against illness and poverty, or even in political life; and I wanted to know what constitutes courage not just in the face of pain or fear, but also when people fight heroically against desire or pleasure (whether they do so by remaining at their posts or by turning around). After all, Laches, there are people who are e courageous in these situations too.

LACHES: There certainly are, Socrates.

SOCRATES: So all these people are courageous, but some display courage in situations involving pleasure and others in situations involving pain, some in situations involving desire and others in situations involving fear. And presumably cowardice can also be an attribute people display in these situations.*

LACHES: Yes, they do.

SOCRATES: So what actually is each of these attributes, courage and cowardice? *That*'s what I wanted to find out. Let's take courage first, then, and could you please try again to tell me what it is that's the same in all these situations.* Or don't you yet understand what I'm saying?

LACHES: Not quite.

SOCRATES: Well, this is what I mean. Suppose I'd asked you 192a what speed is. Now, speed is something which manifests in a large number of human situations (such as running, playing music, speaking, and learning) and which is an attribute of almost every activity worth mentioning, whether it involves the use of the hands or the legs or the mouth or the voice or the mind. Don't you agree?

LACHES: Yes, I do.

SOCRATES: So if I were asked: 'Socrates, what is this property you call "speed", wherever it occurs?' I'd reply that I use the term 'speed' to refer to the ability to get a lot done in a little b time, whether one is speaking or running or whatever.

LACHES: And you'd be right.

SOCRATES: So, Laches, please can you do the same for courage? Try to tell us what it is that, as the identical ability in all the situations we were just mentioning, such as pleasure and pain, comes to be called courage.*

LACHES: All right. I think it's a sort of mental persistence. That's
c   what I'd say, if I had to identify the nature of courage in all situations.

SOCRATES: Well, that's exactly what we have to do, if we're to answer the question we asked ourselves. Now, I'll tell you what I think: I don't think you take every instance of persistence to be courage. My reason for saying this is that I'm almost sure, Laches, that you count courage as something rather admirable.

LACHES: Yes, it's one of the most admirable things in the world. You need have no doubts on that score.

SOCRATES: Now, intelligent persistence is good and admirable, isn't it?*

LACHES: Yes.

d   SOCRATES: But what about unintelligent persistence? Isn't that, on the contrary, dangerous and harmful?

LACHES: Yes.

SOCRATES: Well, if anything is harmful and dangerous, is it admirable, would you say?

LACHES: No, that wouldn't be a defensible position, Socrates.

SOCRATES: So you wouldn't agree that *this* kind of persistence was courage, since it isn't admirable, but courage is an admirable thing.

LACHES: That's right.

SOCRATES: Only intelligent persistence is courage, then, on your view.

LACHES: I suppose so.

e   SOCRATES: But let's consider the context in which intelligent persistence occurs. Would you describe it as courage in every situation, big or small? For example, if someone persists in spending money and does so with intelligence, in the sense that he knows that by spending now he'll get more later, would you call him a man of courage?*

LACHES: By Zeus, no, I wouldn't.

SOCRATES: What about if a doctor, whose son (or whoever) was suffering from pneumonia and was begging him for something to drink or to eat, were to persist in steadfastly refusing to give 193a him anything?

LACHES: No, that wouldn't be an act of courage either, not in the slightest.

SOCRATES: Well, imagine a man who shows persistence in battle. He's prepared to fight, because he's used his intelligence to calculate the odds: he knows that his comrades will help him, that he'll be fighting opponents who are outnumbered and outclassed by his own side, and also that he has the stronger position. Would you say that this man, whose persistence is supported by this kind of intelligence and these resources, is more courageous, or the man in the opposite camp who's prepared to stand his ground with persistence?*

LACHES: The man in the opposite camp, in my opinion, Socrates. b

SOCRATES: But his persistence is less intelligent than the other man's.

LACHES: True.

SOCRATES: So you'd say that someone who persists in a cavalry engagement on the basis of expert horsemanship is less courageous than someone who lacks such expertise.

LACHES: Yes, *I* think he is.

SOCRATES: And the same goes for anyone who persists on the basis of expertise as a slinger or an archer or something.

LACHES: Yes. c

SOCRATES: What about someone who's willing to climb down into a well and to dive for things there, and persists at this work (or at some similar task), despite not being especially good at it?* You'd say that he was more courageous than people who are good at it.

LACHES: Yes. I mean, there's no alternative, Socrates.

SOCRATES: No, there isn't, at least on this view.

LACHES: Well, that *is* my view.

SOCRATES: And yet people who aren't good at well-diving run risks and display persistence in a less intelligent fashion, I suppose, than those who do it with skill.

LACHES: It seems so.

d SOCRATES: Now, earlier unintelligent daring and persistence struck us as demeaning and harmful, didn't they?*

LACHES: Yes.

SOCRATES: But we agreed that courage was something admirable.

LACHES: Yes, we did.

SOCRATES: As things stand at the moment, however, we're saying, on the contrary, that this demeaning thing, unintelligent persistence, is courage.

LACHES: It does look that way.

SOCRATES: Well, do you think we're right?

LACHES: By Zeus, no, Socrates, I don't.

SOCRATES: It turns out, then, to borrow your words, that you
e   and I haven't been attuned to the Doric mode, Laches, since there is no 'harmonious consistency' between our actions and our words.* I mean, if someone were to judge by our actions, I suppose he might think he was in the presence of courage, but I don't think he'd think so if he'd overheard our present conversation and were to judge us by our words.

LACHES: You're absolutely right.

SOCRATES: Well, do you think this is a good situation for us to be in?

LACHES: Not in the slightest.

SOCRATES: So shall we at least go along to a certain extent with what we've been saying?

LACHES: What do you mean? What are we to go along with?

194a SOCRATES: The suggestion that we are to persist. If you have no objection, let's persevere and persist with the enquiry, otherwise courage itself will laugh at us for not going in search of it courageously, if it turns out after all that persistence actually is courage.*

LACHES: Personally, Socrates, I wouldn't be happy to give up yet, even though I'm not used to this kind of discussion. But our conversation has inspired me with a desire to succeed, and I'm
b   really irritated at this inability of mine to express my thoughts. I mean, I think I understand what courage is, but I'm finding it mysteriously elusive at the moment, and I can't encapsulate it in words and say what it is.

SOCRATES: Well, my friend, a good hunter ought to stay trail and not give up.

LACHES: Absolutely.

SOCRATES: So would you like us to invite Nicias here to join in the hunt? He might find the going easier than we do.

LACHES: Yes, of course I'd like that.   c

SOCRATES: All right, then, Nicias. If you have any resources at your command, please could you help your friends who've been caught in a storm of words and can find no way through. You can see how stuck we've got, but if you tell us what you think courage is, you'll free us from our predicament and secure your point of view by putting it into words.

NICIAS: Well, Socrates, I've been thinking for some time that the problem lies in the way you two have been trying to define courage. You're not making use of a good idea that I've heard from you before.*

SOCRATES: What idea is that, Nicias?

NICIAS: I've often heard you saying that any individual is good at d the things he knows and bad at the things of which he's ignorant.

SOCRATES: By Zeus, Nicias! You're right!

NICIAS: So if a courageous man is a good man, he must be a knowledgeable man.*

SOCRATES: Do you hear this, Laches?

LACHES: Yes, I do, but I don't really understand what he's saying.

SOCRATES: Well, I think *I* do. I think he's saying that courage is a kind of knowledge.

LACHES: What kind of knowledge, Socrates?

SOCRATES: Are you asking him this question?   e

LACHES: Yes.

SOCRATES: All right, then, Nicias. Tell Laches what kind of knowledge courage would be, to your way of thinking. I mean, I imagine that it's not knowing how to play the pipes.

NICIAS: Of course not.

SOCRATES: Nor knowing how to play the lyre.

NICIAS: Not at all.

SOCRATES: Then what knowledge is it? What is it knowledge of?

57

LACHES: This is the right line of questioning, Socrates. Let's hear him tell us what knowledge he thinks it is.

NICIAS: I'll tell you what I think it is, Laches. I think it's the knowledge of what's threatening and what's reassuring in warfare and in all other situations.*

195a

LACHES: What a weird idea, Socrates!

SOCRATES: What makes you think so, Laches?

LACHES: What makes me think so? The fact that courage has nothing to do with knowledge.

SOCRATES: Well, Nicias disagrees.

LACHES: Yes, by Zeus, he does. That's exactly why he's talking nonsense.

SOCRATES: Perhaps we should educate him rather than just abuse him.

NICIAS: Quite, but I think Laches wants to see *my* ideas exposed as empty, Socrates, because the same thing just happened to him.

b

LACHES: That's right, Nicias, and I'll try to prove how vacuous your ideas are. Let's take the first case that comes to mind: in treating illness, aren't doctors the ones with knowledge of what's threatening. Oh, but I suppose you think it's courageous people who have this knowledge, do you? Or perhaps you're describing the doctors as the courageous ones?

NICIAS: No, not at all.

LACHES: Nor, I imagine, would you describe farmers as courageous, and yet, of course, where agriculture is concerned, they're the ones who know what's threatening, and the same goes for every other skilled practitioner of an art or craft: they all know what's threatening and what's reassuring in their own areas of expertise. But that doesn't make them courageous.

c

SOCRATES: Do you understand Laches' point, Nicias? There does seem to be something to what he's saying.

NICIAS: Yes, he's raising a point, but it's not valid.

SOCRATES: Why not?

NICIAS: Because he doesn't realize that a doctor's knowledge of his patients is restricted to health and illness.†* That, surely, is all they know. Laches, do you really think that doctors know whether a particular person finds health or illness threatening?

58

Don't you think that in many cases it's better for people not to recover from illness than it is for them to recover? Go on, tell me: do you believe that it's always better for people to live? d Isn't it often better for people to die?

LACHES: Yes, I agree with you on this, at least.

NICIAS: And do you think those who are better off dead find the same things threatening as those who are better off alive?

LACHES: No, I don't.

NICIAS: Well, do you attribute this knowledge to doctors and other skilled practitioners of their art or craft, or only to the one who knows what is and is not threatening—that is, to the man I'm calling courageous?

SOCRATES: Do you see what he's getting at, Laches?

LACHES: Yes, he's claiming that only diviners are courageous. e After all, who else would know whether it's better for someone to live or die? But what about you, Nicias? Do you think of yourself as a diviner, or, if not, are you not courageous?*

NICIAS: What? Now you're saying that it's a diviner's business to know what's threatening and what's reassuring, are you?

LACHES: Yes, I am. I can't see who else's business it might be.

NICIAS: It's far more likely to be the business of the man I'm talking about, my friend. I mean, all a diviner has to know is how to interpret the signs of the future—whether, for instance, someone is going to die or fall ill or lose money, and whether a battle or some other contest is going to end in victory or defeat. 196a But why should judging whether someone is better off if something does or does not happen to him be the business of the diviner any more than anyone else's business?

LACHES: Well, I don't understand what he's getting at, Socrates. He's not explaining who he thinks is courageous. It's not a diviner, it's not a doctor, but he hasn't told us who else it might be. Perhaps he thinks it's a god. I don't think Nicias has the grace to admit of his own accord that he's wrong; instead, he's b wriggling here and there in an attempt to disguise how stuck he is. And yet you and I could have wriggled just like him, if we'd wanted to hide the fact that we were contradicting ourselves. His behaviour might have been comprehensible if this discussion of ours had been taking place in a lawcourt, but as things

59

are, given the company we're in, I can't understand why anyone would cloak himself in fine but empty words.

c SOCRATES: I can't imagine why anyone would do that either, Laches. But it may be that Nicias thinks he's right and isn't just arguing for argument's sake. So let's ask him to explain his meaning more clearly, and then we'll either concede, if he turns out to be making sense, or show him his mistake, if he turns out not to.

LACHES: If you want to ask him anything, Socrates, go ahead. I've done enough on that front already, I think.

SOCRATES: That's all right with me. After all, I'll be asking questions for both of us, for you as well as for me.

LACHES: Yes.

SOCRATES: So, Nicias, tell me—or rather, tell *us*, because Laches
d and I are both involved in the discussion: your position is that courage is knowledge of what's threatening and what's reassuring, is it?

NICIAS: Yes, it is.

SOCRATES: And you're saying that this isn't something everyone knows, because neither a doctor nor a diviner knows it or is courageous, unless they supplement their expertise with precisely this knowledge. Isn't this what you've been saying?

NICIAS: Yes.

SOCRATES: To paraphrase the proverb,* then, in actual fact it is *not* the case that every pig would know—or, therefore, would be courageous.

NICIAS: No, I don't think it would.

e SOCRATES: Obviously, then, you don't believe that the Crommyonian sow* was courageous either, Nicias. I do have a serious reason for bringing this up. It seems to me that anyone who adopts your view must either deny that any animal is courageous or admit that an animal (a lion or a leopard or a wild boar, perhaps) is clever enough to know things which are too difficult for most human beings.* Anyone whose position on courage is the same as yours must claim that lions and deer, bulls and monkeys, all have the same natural disposition for courage.

197a LACHES: By the gods, Socrates, an excellent point! Come on, Nicias, give us your honest answer: are you claiming that those

60

animals which are universally acknowledged to be courageous are more intelligent than human beings, or would you go so far as to contradict everyone else and say that they aren't even courageous?

NICIAS: No, Laches, I don't call an animal or anything else courageous if it's too mindless to be afraid of threats; I call it 'fearless' and 'irrational'. Or do you imagine that I'm calling children courageous just because they're too stupid to be afraid b of anything?* No, fearlessness and courage aren't the same thing. In my opinion, courage and thoughtfulness are qualities possessed by very few people, whereas boldness, daring, and fearless recklessness are commonly found in men and women and children and animals. The animals and so on that you and most people call 'courageous', I call 'bold', and I reserve the term 'courageous' for the intelligent beings I'm talking about. c

LACHES: Socrates, you can see how successfully he cloaks himself in fine words—or so he thinks. He's trying to strip people who are universally acknowledged to be courageous of the distinction.

NICIAS: Don't worry, Laches, I'm excluding you. I mean, I'd say that you were intelligent, since you're courageous, and the same goes for Lamachus and lots of Athenians.

LACHES: I'm not going to respond to that, though I could if I liked, because I don't want you to think of me as a true man of Aexone!*

SOCRATES: No, don't say anything, Laches. I don't think you've d noticed that Nicias has gained this skill of his from our friend Damon. Now, Damon spends a lot of time in the company of Prodicus, and Prodicus is generally held to be the best of the Sophists at these verbal distinctions.*

LACHES: No, I won't say anything, Socrates, because it's more appropriate for a Sophist to dabble in such subtleties than it is for a man who's been chosen by his fellow citizens as one of their leaders.

SOCRATES: Well, my friend, I dare say that it's appropriate for e someone with the greatest responsibilities to have the greatest intelligence. And I do think we ought to try to see what has led Nicias to use the term 'courage' in this way.

LACHES: You'd better ask him yourself, Socrates.

SOCRATES: That's my plan, my friend, but please don't think I'm cutting you out of the discussion. No, listen carefully and join me in considering the arguments.

LACHES: All right, if you think I should.

SOCRATES: Well, I do. As for you, Nicias, please could you tell us
198a   your position all over again. Do you remember how, when we set out originally to look at courage, we took it to be a part of excellence?*

NICIAS: Yes.

SOCRATES: And when you came to tell us what it is, you did so on the understanding that it was a part of excellence, and that there were also other parts, all of which together are called 'excellence'?

NICIAS: Of course.

SOCRATES: I wonder whether you and I mean the same thing by this. Personally, in addition to courage, what I mean by 'parts of excellence' are self-control, justice, and other similar qualities. Do you agree?

b NICIAS: Yes.

SOCRATES: Now, wait a moment. We're in agreement on this, but let's take a look at what's threatening and what's reassuring, to make sure that you aren't thinking along different lines from us. We'll tell you what we were thinking, and if you disagree, you'll set us straight. We were thinking that threatening things are those which cause fear, and reassuring things are those which don't cause fear—and that it isn't past or current events that cause fear, but events which are anticipated, since fear is the anticipation of future evil.* Do you agree with this, Laches?

c LACHES: Without the slightest hesitation, Socrates.

SOCRATES: That's our position, then, Nicias: what's threatening is future evil, and what's reassuring is a future event which isn't evil or which is good. Do you agree with us on this, or not?

NICIAS: I agree.

SOCRATES: So it's knowledge of these events that you're calling 'courage'?

NICIAS: Absolutely.

62

SOCRATES: Now, we still need to check that you agree with us on a third point.

NICIAS: What's that?

SOCRATES: I'll tell you. My friend here and I deny that there is d any instance of knowing where knowing how things happened in the past is a different branch of knowledge from knowing what's currently happening in the present, which is in turn a different branch of knowledge from knowing how what has yet to happen will turn out or may turn out for the best. No, we think it's all the same branch of knowledge. Let's take health as an example: whatever time is involved, it's just healing, a single branch of knowledge, that surveys current events, past events, and the prospects for the future. The same goes for agriculture where the produce of the soil is concerned, and I imagine that e where warfare is concerned you yourselves would support my assertion that it's generalship which has the most effective and thoughtful approach not just to past and present events, but also and especially to the future. Generalship doesn't expect to be subservient to divination, but to be in command of it, because generalship has superior knowledge of what is happening and what will happen in the military sphere. That's why 199a the law ordains that generals should be in command of diviners, not the other way round.* Is this our view, Laches?

LACHES: It is.

SOCRATES: And what about you, Nicias? Do you too think that, in a single sphere, it's a single branch of knowledge that knows about future, present, and past?

NICIAS: I do. I agree, Socrates.

SOCRATES: Now, according to you, my friend, courage is the knowledge of what's threatening and what's reassuring, isn't it? b

NICIAS: Yes.

SOCRATES: And we've agreed that what's threatening is future evil and what's reassuring is future good.

NICIAS: Yes.

SOCRATES: And, in a single sphere, it's just the one branch of knowledge that knows about the future and about all possible states of its subjects.

NICIAS: True.

63

SOCRATES: It follows, then, that courage isn't restricted to knowing what's threatening and what's reassuring, because it
doesn't know only about what's good and evil in the future, but
c   also about the present and the past,† just as all branches of
knowledge do.

NICIAS: I suppose you're right.

SOCRATES: It follows, then, Nicias, that you specified only about
a third of courage,* despite the fact that we were asking you
about what courage is as a whole. And now it looks as though
courage isn't just knowledge of what's threatening and what's
reassuring, as you claimed. No, your position now turns out to
be that courage must be knowledge of pretty much everything
d   that's good and evil in every possible time. Do you agree that
this is now your position, Nicias, or what?

NICIAS: Yes, I agree, Socrates.

SOCRATES: So, my friend, supposing a person was in this situation—supposing he knew all there was to know about the
present, future, and past of everything that's good and everything that's bad—do you think he would lack any aspect of
excellence? Do you think he would lack self-control or justice
and piety, when he's the only one with the ability to deal
properly with gods and men, in the sense of taking appropriate
e   precautions against threats† and ensuring that good things
come his way?

NICIAS: You're making a fair point, Socrates, I think.

SOCRATES: So what you're currently describing wouldn't be a
part of excellence, Nicias, but excellence in its entirety.

NICIAS: It looks that way.

SOCRATES: But we did say that courage was just one part of
excellence.

NICIAS: Yes, we did.

SOCRATES: And what you're currently describing turns out not
to be just a part of excellence.

NICIAS: Apparently not.

SOCRATES: So we've failed to discover what courage is, Nicias.

NICIAS: It seems so, yes.

LACHES: And I was sure you'd discover it, Nicias, my friend.
200a   After all, you were so contemptuous of the answers I gave

Socrates that I really expected you to discover it with the help of the skill you gained from Damon.

NICIAS: Good for you, Laches! The fact that not long ago you yourself turned out to be utterly ignorant about courage no longer bothers you in the slightest. No, all that concerns you now is to see me in the same boat as you, and it apparently no longer makes any difference to you that you're just as ignorant as me about things which a man really ought to know if he expects to amount to anything. Anyway, although you're behaving, I suppose, in a thoroughly human fashion by looking at b other people and not yourself, I think I've made a reasonable contribution to our discussion, and if there's anything that still needs correction, I'll do that later, not just with the help of Damon—a man whom you seem to think you can mock, even though you've never made his acquaintance—but with others as well. And once I've settled the matter, I'll explain it to you. I won't keep it to myself, because I think you are really badly in c need of education.

LACHES: What a clever fellow you are, Nicias! All the same, my advice to Lysimachus here and to Melesias would be that you and I should not be involved in their boys' education, but that, as I said in the first place, they shouldn't let Socrates here get away. That's what I would do too, if my sons were the right age.

NICIAS: Well, I agree with *that*. If Socrates is prepared to take the boys in hand, they don't need to look for anyone else. After all, I'd be perfectly happy to entrust Niceratus to him, if he was d prepared to take him on. But whenever I broach the topic with Socrates, he introduces me to other people and refuses to help himself.* But maybe you'll find him more compliant, Lysimachus.

LYSIMACHUS: He certainly should be, Nicias, because I'd be prepared to do a great deal for him, more than I would for almost anyone else. So what do you say, Socrates? Will you do as we ask? Will you join us in our efforts to make our boys as good as possible?

SOCRATES: Yes, Lysimachus, it would certainly be shocking e behaviour not to be prepared to contribute towards improving someone. Now, if in the course of our conversation I had turned out to have knowledge, while our two friends here didn't, you'd have been justified in singling me out and getting me involved in the assignment. But as it is we all became equally stuck, so why would anyone prefer one of us over the others? I don't think any of us should be chosen. Under these circumstances, then, see whether you think that the advice I'm about to offer is helpful. Since this is going to be our secret,† I don't mind telling you, my friends, that I personally believe that we all ought to look together for as excellent a teacher as we can find first for ourselves—we need one, after all—and then for the boys. We should do whatever it takes in terms of money or anything else to find such a teacher. But what I advise us *not* to do is leave ourselves in our present state. And if anyone mocks us for thinking that we ought to go to school at our age, I think we should get Homer to defend us with his saying that 'Modesty ill suits a man in need.'* So let's ignore what people say and take care of ourselves and the boys at the same time.

LYSIMACHUS: I like this idea of yours, Socrates, and the fact that I'm the oldest of us will only make me glad to put that much more effort into learning along with the boys. But there is one thing you can do for me. Could you come to my house tomorrow morning without fail, so that we can discuss what to do about this? But for the time being let's go our separate ways.

SOCRATES: Yes, I'll do that, Lysimachus. God willing, I'll be with you tomorrow.

LYSIS

SOCRATES [*addressing an unnamed friend*]: I was walking from 203a
the Academy, taking the direct route outside the city wall towards
the Lyceum, along the road which runs right under the wall.*
When I reached the little gate where the spring of Panops* is, I
came across Hippothales the son of Hieronymus and Ctesippus
of Paeania, along with some other young men, who were all standing in a group. Hippothales spotted me approaching and said,
'Socrates, where are you going? Where have you come from?'   b

'From the Academy,' I replied. 'I'm on my way to the Lyceum.'

'You need go no further than here, then,' he said. 'Why don't
you join us? You won't regret it.'

'Where's "here"?' I asked. 'And who are the "us" I'd be
joining?'

'Look here,' he said, pointing to a kind of enclosure opposite
the wall, with an open door. 'This is where we spend our time,' he
went on, 'and not just those you can see here now, but plenty of
others as well—good-looking ones!'*

'What is this place? What do you do here?'   204a

'It's a wrestling-ground,' he said, 'newly built. We spend most
of the time talking, and we'd be delighted if you'd join in.'

'That's a good way to pass the time,' I said. 'But who's the
teacher here?'

'Your friend and admirer Miccus,' he answered.

'An excellent fellow, by Zeus!' I said. 'Proficient, and a master
of his art!'

'Would you like to come along with us, then,' he said, 'so that
you can actually see who's there?'

'I'd like first to be told what I'm going in for—in other words,   b
who's the main attraction!'

'Each of us has his own favourite, Socrates,' he said.

'Who's yours, Hippothales?' I asked. 'Tell me.'

He blushed at the question, and I said: 'Hippothales, son of
Hieronymus, you certainly no longer need to tell me whether or
not you're in love: I can see that you're not just in love, but well

c and truly smitten. I may be rather hopeless and useless at most things, but one gift I've somehow been granted by the gods is the ability to recognize a lover and his beloved.'*

At these words of mine he blushed even more, and this prompted Ctesippus to say: 'How polite of you to blush, Hippothales! Here you are, coyly refusing to tell Socrates the lad's name, when after just a moment or two in your company, he'll be fed up with hearing you constantly going on and on about him. At any rate, Socrates, he's filled our ears with the name of Lysis until

d we've gone quite deaf. He has to have only a sip or two of wine and it's easy for us to imagine that we can still hear the name of Lysis when we wake up the next morning! His normal conversation is awful, but not totally awful—but then he sets about flooding us with his compositions in prose and verse! As if this weren't awful enough, he also sings about the boy he fancies in an unbelievable voice and we have to put up with listening to these songs! And now he blushes at your question!'

e 'Lysis is a still young, I suppose,' I said. 'The reason I think so is that I didn't recognize his name when you mentioned it.'

'That's because people don't often use his name,' he said. 'They still use his father's name in referring to him, because his father is extremely well known. Anyway, I'm sure you can hardly fail to know what the boy looks like, because his looks alone are enough to get him recognized.'

'Why don't you tell me who his father is?' I asked.

'He's the eldest son of Democrates of Aexone,' he replied.

'Well, Hippothales!' I said. 'What an aristocratic and vigorous love you've come upon! Why don't you make me your audience, as you do your friends here? I'd like to be sure that you know what

205a a lover should say about his beloved when he's talking to him, or when he's talking to other people, for that matter.'

'Do you take anything Ctesippus says seriously, Socrates?' he asked.

'Do you deny being in love with the boy he mentioned?' I said.

'No, I don't,' he answered. 'But I do deny composing prose and verse pieces about my beloved.'

'He's not well,' Ctesippus said. 'He's out of his mind, talking nonsense.'

'Hippothales,' I said, 'I don't need to hear any of your verses or any song you might have composed about the lad. Just give me the gist, so that I can understand how you treat the boy you fancy.' b

'I'm sure Ctesippus will tell you,' he said. 'He must know it off by heart, if what he says is true and I've done nothing but din his ears with it all.'

'By the gods,' said Ctesippus, 'all right, I will! Actually, it's totally absurd, Socrates. I mean, how could it not be absurd for a lover, someone who thinks about the boy far more than anyone else does, to have nothing personal to say? Even a child could c come up with the same material. All the qualities for which everyone in Athens celebrates Democrates and his father Lysis and all their ancestors—their wealth, their horse-breeding, their victories at the Pythian, Isthmian, and Nemean games in the four-horse-chariot events and the horse-races*—this is what forms the content of his verse and prose compositions. There's even more antiquated stuff as well: just the other day, he told us in verse the story of the entertainment of Heracles—how their ancestor, as a relative of Heracles (their ancestor was the son of Zeus and the daughter of the founder of the deme),* made d Heracles welcome. But this is what our old women sing about already, Socrates! The verse and prose which Hippothales composes and forces us to listen to consist of all these sorts of stories.'

'That *is* absurd, Hippothales,' I said, when Ctesippus had finished. 'Are you making up poems and singing your own praises before you've won the victory?'*

'It's not about me, Socrates,' he protested. 'That's not the point of my poems and songs.'

'That's what you *think*, anyway,' I said.

'Then what's the truth of the matter?' he asked.

'These songs of yours have more to do with you than with e anyone else,' I said. 'If you win your beloved, everything you've said and sung about him will redound to your credit, given what he's like: the winning of such a boyfriend will make your songs the equivalent of victory odes. If you fail to catch him, however, the more extravagant your praises of him were, the more beautiful and good he'll seem, and the more you'll become a laughing-stock for having lost him. That's why anyone who's skilful at love, my 206a

71

friend, waits until he's won his beloved before praising him, in case the future doesn't turn out as he hopes. And another point is that praise and flattery of beautiful people fills them with pride and arrogance, don't you think?'

'Yes, I do,' he said.

'And the more arrogant they are, the harder they are to win, aren't they?'

'I suppose so.'

'How would you describe a hunter whose hunting frightens off his quarry and makes it harder to catch?'

b   'Useless, obviously.'

'And it's hardly a sign of a good musicianship to make someone fierce rather than tame with one's words and songs, is it?'

'I don't think so.'

'You'd better be careful, then, Hippothales, in case your compositions make you liable to all these charges. And yet I personally doubt you'd be prepared to agree that a man whose poetry harmed his own interests was a good poet, given that he harms himself.'

'No, by Zeus, I wouldn't,' he said. 'That would be deeply stupid. But that's why I'm consulting you, Socrates. If you've any

c   further advice to give, do please tell me what a man should say or do to endear himself to the boy he fancies.'

'It's hard to know what to say,' I said, 'but if you'd be prepared to get him to talk to me, I might be able to provide you with a sample of the kind of conversation you should be having with him, instead of the prose and verse your friends tell me you come up with at the moment.'

'That shouldn't be difficult,' he said. 'If you go inside with Ctesippus here and sit down and start talking, I'm sure he'll come over and join you. You see, Socrates, he really hates to miss out on

d   conversations, and also, since it's the time of the Hermaea, the young men and the boys have been lumped together—so he'll come and join you.* If he doesn't, Ctesippus and he have got to know each other well through Ctesippus' cousin Menexenus, who's Lysis' best friend, and so Ctesippus can call him over, if he doesn't come of his own accord.'

'That sounds like a good plan,' I said, and with these words I entered the wrestling-ground along with Ctesippus. All the e others followed us. Inside, we found that, since the boys had finished their sacrifice and by now the rites were almost over, they were playing knucklebones and were all dressed in their finery.* Most of them were playing outside in the courtyard, but there were a few in a corner of the changing-room, playing odd-or-even with a large quantity of knucklebones, which they picked out of little baskets. Others were standing around these players and watching them, and one of the spectators was Lysis, who was standing among the boys and young men with a wreath on his 207a head. He was by far the best-looking of them, and looked as though he deserved to be called not just beautiful, but a model of the noble combination of beauty and excellence. We went over to the opposite side of the room, where it was quiet, and sat down and struck up a conversation among ourselves. Lysis kept turning around and frequently looked in our direction; it was obvious that he wanted to come over. For a while, he didn't know what to do— he was too shy to come over on his own—but then Menexenus took a break from the game and came in from the courtyard. b When Menexenus saw Ctesippus and me, he came and sat down next to us, and the sight of him doing so spurred Lysis to do likewise. After Lysis had joined Menexenus next to us, others came over as well. As for Hippothales, once he saw that there were quite a few people standing near by, he used them as a screen and stood where he thought he'd be out of Lysis' sight, because he didn't want to irritate him. He listened to our conversation from this position.

I looked at Menexenus and said: 'Tell me, son of Demophon: which of you two is the oldest?' c

'That's a bone of contention between us,' he said.

'And do you also argue about which of you has more noble blood?' I asked.

'Yes, we do,' he said.

'And likewise about which of you is better looking?'

They both laughed, and I went on: 'But I won't ask which of you has more money, because you're friends, aren't you?'

'We certainly are,' they said.

'And, as the proverb says, friends share, which means that, as long as you're being honest about your friendship, neither of you will be better off in this respect.'

d   They agreed with me on this, and I was getting ready to ask them next whether one of them was more just than the other, and more clever, when someone came over and interrupted us. He made Menexenus get up, saying that the trainer wanted to see him, and I got the impression that Menexenus was responsible for the performance of the rites. Once Menexenus had left, I began to question Lysis instead.

'Tell me, Lysis,' I said, 'do your parents love you a lot?'

'Definitely,' he said.

'So they want you to be as happy as possible?'

'Of course.'

e   'Do you think a man can be happy if he's a slave, without the freedom to do whatever he wants?'

'By Zeus, no, I don't think so,' he said.

'If your parents love you, then, and want you to be happy, it must follow that they do their best to ensure your happiness.'

'Of course,' he said.

'Do they allow you to do what you want, then? Do they never tell you off and stop you doing what you want?'

'By Zeus, Socrates, no: there are a great many things they stop me doing.'

'What do you mean?' I said. 'Even though they want you to be 208a happy, they stop you doing what you want? Tell me this: suppose you wanted to ride on one of your father's chariots and take the reins in a chariot-race, would they stop you? Wouldn't they let you do that?'*

'By Zeus, no,' he said, 'they certainly wouldn't.'

'Who would they allow to do so, then?'

'There's a charioteer, who's paid by my father.'

'What do you mean? They let a common labourer rather than you do what he wants with the horses, and then they pay him as well?'

b   'Of course,' he said.

'But I'm sure they let you take control of their mule team. If you wanted to take whip in hand and beat the mules, they'd let you.'

'What makes you think they'd let me do that?' he asked.

'What?' I exclaimed. 'Is no one allowed to beat them?'

'Yes,' he said, 'the mule-man is.'

'And is he a slave or a free man?'

'A slave,' he said.

'Apparently, then, they think more highly even of a slave than they do of you: they entrust their affairs more to him than they do to you, and they allow him to do what he wants, but stop you doing what you want. Is that right? And here's another question c for you: do they let you keep yourself under control, or don't they even let you do this?'

'Of course they don't,' he said.

'But who keeps you under control?'

'My attendant here,' he said.*

'He's not a slave, is he?'

'Of course he is,' he said. 'He's one of ours.'

'It's extraordinary to find someone who's free being controlled by a slave,' I said. 'What does this attendant do to keep you under control?'

'He attends me, of course,' he said, 'when I go to school.'

'Surely they don't keep you under control as well, your teachers, do they?'

'They most certainly do.' d

'So your father has set a lot of masters and controllers over you, then. But when you go home to your mother, does her desire for your happiness mean that she lets you do what you want? Does she let you do what you want with the wool and the loom when she's weaving? I'm sure she doesn't stop you touching the blade or the shuttle* or any of her other spinning tools.'

'By Zeus, Socrates,' he said with a laugh, 'she doesn't just stop e me: she'd thrash me if I touched anything.'

'By Heracles,' I said, 'you haven't offended your parents in some way, have you?'

'By Zeus, no, I haven't,' he said.

'Then what have you done to make them restrict your happiness in such a frightful manner and stop you doing what you want? Why do they bring you up in a constant state of subjection to others, day in and day out? Why, in short, do they let you do almost nothing you want? On the face of it, it turns out that your 209a great wealth does you no good at all, because you've less authority over your possessions than anyone else, and the same goes for your body too, for all its noble blood, because someone else has the job of tending to it and looking after it. But you're the master of no one and nothing, Lysis, and you never get to do what you want.'

'That's because I haven't yet come of age, Socrates,' he said.

'That may not be what's stopping you, Lysis. After all, I'm sure your parents give you a certain amount of responsibility, without waiting until you've come of age. For example, when they want someone to read to them or to write something for them, I'm sure it's you they give the job to, rather than any other member of the b household. Am I right?'

'Yes,' he said.

'So in this area you can choose which letter to write first, and which second, and you have the same freedom in your reading too. Moreover, I imagine that when you take up your lyre, neither of your parents stops you tightening or slackening whichever of the strings you want, and that you can also choose which string to pluck or strike with your plectrum. Or do they stop you doing this?'

'No, of course not.'

'What's the explanation for this, Lysis? Why don't they stop you doing what you want in these cases, but do in all the cases we c mentioned a short while ago?'

'I suppose it's because I know about these things, but not the others,' he said.

'All right, then, my friend,' I said. 'So your father isn't waiting for you to come of age before he lets you take responsibility for everything. No, once he reckons that you understand things better than him, he won't wait another day before entrusting both himself and his possessions to you.'

'Yes, I suppose so,' he said.

'All right, then,' I said. 'Now, does your neighbour apply the same criterion in your case as your father does? Do you think that, d once he reckons that you understand how to manage households better than he does, he'll let you manage his own household, or will he continue to preside over it himself?'

'I should think he'll leave it to me.'

'And what about the Athenians? Do you think they'll entrust the city's affairs to you, once they see that you know enough to do so competently?'

'Yes, I think so.'

'In the name of Zeus,' I said, 'what about the Great King, then?* When his meat is being boiled, would he let his eldest son, the future ruler of Asia, add whatever ingredients he wanted to the sauce, or would he entrust the job to us, if we arrived in his court e and proved to him that our knowledge of the preparation of food was superior to his son's?'

'He'd give the job to us, obviously,' he said.

'Yes, and he wouldn't let his son add even a pinch of anything, but he'd let us add whole handfuls of salt, if that's what we wanted to do.'

'Of course.'

'And suppose his son had an eye infection? If the king didn't think his son knew medicine, would he let him treat his own eyes, 210a or would he stop him?'

'He'd stop him.'

'Whereas, if he took us to be expert doctors, I doubt he'd stop us even if we wanted to open his eyes and dust them with ash, as long as he thought we knew exactly what we were doing.'*

'You're right.'

'And the same goes for every other area where he felt us to be more knowledgeable than himself and his son: he'd leave all such things to us, wouldn't he?'

'He'd have to, Socrates,' he said.

'So this is how things stand, my dear Lysis,' I said. 'Every-one—Greeks and non-Greeks, men and women—will entrust to b us those fields where we have knowledge. In these cases we'll do whatever we want, and no one will intentionally stop us getting our way; we'll have freedom in these areas and authority over others,* and these matters will constitute our line of business, because we'll profit from them. On the other hand, when it comes to fields where we remain ignorant, no one will let us do as we c please. Everyone—not just outsiders, but also our parents and any even closer relatives we may have—will do all they can to stop us getting our way; we'll be subordinate to others in these cases, and these matters won't be our line of business, because we won't profit from them. Do you agree?'

'Yes, I do.'

'Now, will we be anyone's friends—will anyone love us—in those areas where we're useless?'

'Of course not,' he said.

'So if your father doesn't love you at the moment, that's because no one loves anyone else in so far as he's useless.'

'So it seems,' he said.

d 'It follows, my boy, that everyone will love you and be on familiar terms with you if you become knowledgeable, because you'll be helpful and beneficial, but if you don't, no one will love you—not your father, nor your mother, nor your relatives, nor anyone else for that matter. Can anyone feel proud of himself, then, Lysis, for something he doesn't yet understand?'

'Of course not,' he said.

'And as for you, if you still need a teacher, you're not yet knowledgeable.'

'True.'

'So you're not proud of yourself, since you lack understanding.'

'By Zeus, Socrates,' he said, 'I don't feel proud.'

e When I heard him saying this, I looked at Hippothales—and almost made a mistake. I was on the point of saying: 'That's how one should talk to the boy one fancies, Hippothales. One should make him humble and unpretentious, not boastful and conceited, as you do.' But the sight of how the conversation had distressed and upset him reminded me that, although he was standing close by, he didn't want to be seen by Lysis.

211a Just then, Menexenus returned and sat down next to Lysis, where he'd got up from before, and Lysis whispered in my ear in a very playful and friendly fashion, without Menexenus noticing. 'Socrates,' he said, 'please have the same conversation with Menexenus that you've been having with me.'

'You'll be able to do it yourself, Lysis,' I replied. 'At any rate, you were paying close attention to what was being said.'

'Yes, I was,' he said.

'So try to remember as much of it as you can,' I said, 'and then you can reproduce the whole thing for him exactly. If you forget b anything, you can ask me again when we next meet.'

'All right,' he said, 'I'll most definitely do that, Socrates. You can be sure of that. But have a different conversation with him, then, so that I can listen too, until it's time for me to go home.'

'Well, I'd better do as you say,' I said, 'since that's what you want to see happen. But it's up to you to support me if Menexenus tries to challenge me. You know how he always tries to win arguments, don't you?'

'By Zeus, yes, I most certainly do,' he said. 'That's why I want *you* to be the one to talk to him.'   c

'So that I can make a fool of myself?' I asked.

'By Zeus, no,' he said. 'So that you can teach him a lesson.'

'How?' I said. 'That won't be easy. He's a formidable person, with Ctesippus as his teacher. Ctesippus is here, you know. Look: there he is.'

'Put Ctesippus and everyone else out of your mind, Socrates,' he said, 'and do please talk to Menexenus.'

'All right,' I said.

At this point of our private discussion, Ctesippus said: 'Why are you two feasting alone? Why don't you share your d conversation?'

'Yes, we'd better let others join in,' I said. 'You see, our friend here doesn't understand something I've been saying, but he says he thinks Menexenus does, and he's suggesting that I ask him.'

'Why don't you ask him, then?' he said.

'I will,' I said. 'Menexenus, please respond to any question I ask. Ever since I was a boy, there's something I've wanted to have. Different people want different things—horses, maybe, or dogs, or gold, or political offices—but whereas I'm not bothered about e any of these things, I'm deeply passionate about acquiring friends. I'd prefer to have a good friend than the best quail or cock in the world; I'd prefer a good friend, by Zeus, to both a horse *and* a dog. By the Dog,* I think I'd much rather gain a friend than

79

Darius' wealth—in fact, I'd rather gain Darius as a friend.†*
That's how dedicated I am to the cause of friendship. So the sight
212a of you two—you and Lysis—impresses me. I count you very
fortunate to have gained what I want while you're still young, and
to have done so rapidly and effortlessly: it took neither of you
much time to gain the other as a firm friend. I'm so far from
getting what I want,* however, that I don't even know how one
person becomes another's friend. And so that's exactly the question I want to put to you, as someone who'll know what he's
talking about. Please tell me, then: when a person is fond of
b another person, who is whose friend? Is the one who loves the
friend of the one who is loved, or is it the other way around? Or is
there no difference between them?'

'Personally,' he said, 'I don't think there's any difference.'

'What do you mean?' I said. 'All it takes is for just one of them
to love the other, and then they're both each other's friends?'

'That's what I think,' he said.

'But isn't it possible for the one who loves not to be loved back
by the one he loves?'

'Yes, that can happen.'

'In fact, isn't it possible for the one who loves even to be hated
by the other person? For instance, as you know, this is supposed to
be the response even lovers sometimes meet from the boys they
fancy: even though they love them passionately, some feel that
c their love isn't returned and others even that they meet with
loathing. Or do you think that this doesn't really happen?'

'No, it most certainly does,' he said.

'In this situation, then,' I went on, 'one of them loves and the
other is loved.'

'Yes.'

'Then which of them is whose friend? Is the one who loves the
friend of the one who's loved, whether his love is not returned†
or he even meets with hatred? Or is the one who's loved the friend
of the one who loves? Or, on the other hand, in this situation is
neither of them the friend of the other, unless they *both* love each
other?'

'Yes, I suppose that's right.'

d   'So we've changed our minds. Previously, we thought that if just one of them loved the other, they were both friends, but now we're saying that, unless both of them love each other, neither of them is a friend to the other.'

'It looks that way,' he said.

'It follows that A isn't a friend to B, who loves him or it, unless B returns A's affection.'

'It seems not.'

'So people aren't fond of horses unless their horses return their affection, and the same goes for people who love quails* or dogs or wine or sports. And no one can love learning unless learning returns his love. Or do these people love what they love even though what they love isn't fond of them? If so, the poet got it e wrong when he said:

Blessed is he whose children are fond of him, his whole-hooved horses, His hunting hounds, and his guest-friend from abroad.'*

'I don't think he was wrong,' he said.

'You think he got it right?'

'Yes.'

'In that case, Menexenus, if A is loved, it is, apparently, dear to B, who loves it, whether A doesn't love† B or even hates B. Very young children, for instance, don't feel love and may even hate their parents when they're being punished by them, but that 213a doesn't make any difference: even at the precise moment when they're hating their parents, they're still unconditionally dear to their parents.'

'Yes, that's what I think,' he said.

'It follows from this argument, then, that it's not the one who loves who is the friend, but the one who's loved.'

'Apparently so.'

'And it's the one who's hated, then, who's an enemy, not the one who hates.'

'That seems to follow.'

'In that case, it's common to be loved by one's enemies and hated by one's friends. If a friend is not the one who loves but b the one who's loved, a lot of people are friends to their enemies and enemies to their friends. But it seems absurd, my dear friend—impossible, actually, not just absurd—for someone or something to be a friend of an enemy and an enemy of a friend.'

'I think you're right, Socrates,' he said.

'Well, if that's out of the question, it must be the one who loves who's the friend of the one who's loved.'

'Apparently.'

'And by the same token it must be the one who hates who's the enemy of the one who's hated.'

'That necessarily follows.'

'We've been forced to the same conclusion as before, then: that c a man may often be the friend of a non-friend or even of an enemy. This happens when he either loves something that doesn't love him, or loves something that even hates him. And a man may often be the enemy of a non-enemy or even of a friend, when he hates something that doesn't hate him or hates something that even loves him.'

'I suppose so,' he said.

'What are we going to do, then,' I asked, 'if friends aren't those who love, nor those who are loved, nor those who both love and are loved? Are we to say that there are others, from outside these categories, who are friends of one another?'

'By Zeus, Socrates, I'm really stuck,'* he said.

d 'Are we going about the enquiry in completely the wrong way, perhaps, Menexenus?' I asked.

'Yes, I think so, Socrates,' said Lysis. He blushed as he spoke, because—or so I thought—the words had slipped out by accident, as a result of the intensity with which he'd been following the discussion. It was obvious that he'd been listening very carefully, and so, since I wanted to give Menexenus a rest and was delighted with Lysis' love of learning, I turned to continue the discussion with Lysis instead.

e 'Lysis,' I said, 'I think you're right. If we'd been going about our investigation in the right way, we'd never have gone astray like this. But let's take a different route on the difficult journey, as I see it, of our enquiry. I think we should take the road we turned down before and look at what the poets have to say on the matter, 214a given that where knowledge is concerned they are, so to speak, our fathers and guides. Now, they do, of course, come up with some significant statements about which people constitute friends. At any rate, they say that it's the god himself who makes people friends, by attracting them to one another. They put it somewhat as follows, I think: "Ever the god draws like to like"* and makes them get to know each other. Have you come across the b verses I mean?'

'I have,' he said.

'And have you also come across the writings of our cleverest men, making the same claim that like must always be friend to like? I'm thinking of those who talk and write about natural science and about the universe as a whole.'*

'You're right,' he said.

'Well, is this idea of theirs a good one?' I asked.

'Maybe,' he said.

'Maybe it's half right,' I said, 'or maybe it's wholly right, but we don't fully understand it. I mean, we tend to think that the closer a bad man gets to another bad man and the more time he c spends in his company, the more he becomes hated as a result of the wrong he does the other person.* It is of course impossible for criminals and their victims to be friends, don't you think?'

'Yes,' he said.

'In which case half of the idea would be untrue, since bad men are like one another.'

'You're right.'

'But I think what they mean is that good men resemble one another and are friends, whereas what the proverb says about bad men is correct: they're never similar even to themselves, but are impulsive and unstable. And anything which is constantly† dis- d similar to and unlike itself can hardly be similar or friendly to something else. Don't you think so?'

'Yes, I do,' he said.

'So, my friend, I think the statement that like is friend to like is an obscure way of saying that only good men can be friends with one another, whereas true friendship can never exist between a bad man and either a good man or another bad man. Do you agree?'

He nodded his assent, and I went on: 'So we're now in a position to say which people are friends: the argument suggests that it's good men.'

e 'I quite agree,' he said.

'I think so too,' I said. 'But there's an aspect of the idea which is still bothering me. In the name of Zeus, then, come and help me expose my suspicion to scrutiny. If A is a friend of B in so far as he's like B, is A useful to B? Perhaps it would be better to look at it this way: can anything that is similar to anything else affect that other object, for good or ill, in a way that the object couldn't affect itself? Or could it be affected by that other object in a way that it 215a couldn't be affected by itself? But then how could these similars value one another when they're no help to one another? Is there any way they could?'*

'No, there isn't.'

'But how can something that isn't valued be a friend?'

'It couldn't be.'

'Then like is *not* friend to like. But maybe a good man is a friend to another good man in so far as he's good, not in so far as he's similar to him. What do you think?'

'Perhaps.'

'But wouldn't a good man be self-sufficient, precisely in so far as he's good?'*

'Yes.'

'And self-sufficiency is what makes a self-sufficient person have no need of anything.'

'Of course.'

'But a person who has no need of anything wouldn't value anything either.'

b 'No.'

'And where there's no valuing, there's no love either.'

'Definitely not.'

'And where there's no love, there's no friendship.'

'I suppose not.'

'Then how are we to maintain that good men are to any extent friends with one another, when they won't miss one another when they're apart—because they're self-sufficient even when they're apart from one another—and they won't need one another when they're together? Is there any way that such people could prize one another?'

'No,' he said.

'But they won't be friends unless they prize one another.'   c

'True.'

'Can you see where we're going wrong, Lysis? Are we in fact completely mistaken?'

'In what sense?' he asked.

'I've just remembered something I once heard someone say, to the effect that like is utterly hostile to like, and that therefore good men are the bitterest enemies. This person brought up Hesiod to support his case, because Hesiod says that, as it turns out, "Potter is piqued with potter, singer with singer, beggar with beggar."* d And my source added that in all other cases too this was bound to be the case—that it was chiefly things which resemble one another most that are filled with envy and rivalry and hostility, while friendship is the property of things which are utterly different from one another. He pointed out that poor people have no choice but to be friends with rich men, that weak people are forced to be friends with strong people, whose support they rely on, that sick people are bound to be close to doctors, and that laymen must inevitably value and love experts. In fact, he went on in an even more grandiose vein, saying that it was completely out e of the question for like to be friend to like and that the truth was the exact opposite: the more A is contrary to B, the more they're bound to be friends. Everything, he argued, desires its opposite, not something similar: that which is dry desires that which is wet, the cold desires the hot, the bitter the sweet, the sharp the blunt, the empty the full, the full the empty, and so on and so forth. The reason for this, he said, was that opposites nourish each other, whereas similars don't derive any advantage from similars.* And his argument did strike me as elegant, my friend; he made his 216a point well. But what do you two think of what he said?'

'It sounds good,' Menexenus said, 'at least, in your version of it.'

'So shall we say that opposites are best friends?'

'Yes.'

'All right,' I said, 'but it's a weird position, isn't it, Menexenus?

Those all-round geniuses, the ones who are good at contradicting what one says,* will gleefully leap on us straight away, asking b whether hostility and friendship aren't contradictory. How shall we respond to this question? We have to accept that they're right, don't we?'

'Yes, we have to.'

'Then they'll go on to ask whether, in that case, an enemy loves a friend or a friend an enemy.'

'Neither is true,' he said.

'Well, what about something that is honest and something that is dishonest? What about something that has self-control and something that lacks self-control? What about the good and the bad? Are they friends?'

'No, I don't think so.'

'But if it's opposition that makes something the friend of something else, these things must be friends.'

'Yes.'

'So not only is like not friend to like, but opposite isn't friend to opposite either.'

'Apparently not.'

c 'Here's another point for us to consider. It's possible that the truth is still evading us more than we realize, and that none of the approaches we've been trying so far can capture what it is to be a friend. At any rate, friendship puts one in mind of something soft and smooth and sleek, which is presumably why it finds it easy to give us the slip; if that's what it's like, it's hardly surprising that it eludes us.† But there may be a way for that which is neither good nor bad sometimes to become a friend of the good.'

'What way?' he asked. 'What do you mean?'

'By Zeus,' I said, 'I'm not sure. Personally, the argument has got me so puzzled that I'm actually feeling dizzy, and it seems possible that the old saying is right—that "what is fair is a d friend". What I'm getting at, you see, is that anything good is fair or beautiful. What do you think?'

'I agree.'

'And I think—though this is no more than a guess—that what is neither good nor bad is a friend of what is fair and good. I'll tell you what prompted this guess of mine. I think that there are three

86

families, so to speak: the good, the bad, and that which is neither good nor bad. Do you agree?'

'Yes,' he said.

'And I also think that what is good is not the friend of what is good, that what is bad is not the friend of what is bad, and that what is good is not the friend of what is bad. The discussion we've been having also excluded these possibilities. There remains the possibility—assuming that anything can be the friend of anything, and given that nothing can be the friend of the bad— that what is neither good nor bad is the friend either of the good or of something which has the same nature as itself.'

'True.'

'But we also ruled out the possibility that like is friend to like, didn't we?'

'Yes.'

'Then something with the same nature as that which is neither good nor bad will not be the friend of that which is neither good nor bad.'

'I suppose not.'

'The only remaining possibility, then, is that what is neither good nor bad may be the friend of what is good.'* 217a

'That necessarily follows, apparently.'

'Well, boys,' I said, 'let's see whether this present idea of ours is a good guide. It's true, at any rate, that a healthy body (if we may use this as an example) has no need of the kind of help provided by the art of healing, because it's in a good enough state on its own. In other words, no healthy person is the friend of a doctor on account of his health, is he?'

'No.'

'Whereas a sick person is, on account of his illness.'

'Of course.'

'And illness is a bad thing, while healing is beneficial and good.' b

'Yes.'

'And a body, in itself, is neither good nor bad.'

'Quite so.'

'It's illness that compels a body to welcome and love the healing art.'

'I'd say so.'

'It's the presence of something bad, then, that makes what is neither bad nor good become a friend of the good.'

'So it seems.'

c 'And obviously this happens before it has been made bad by the presence of the bad. I mean, once it has become bad, it can no longer desire the good and be the friend of the good, because we said that bad can never be friend to good.'

'Yes, that's impossible.'

'See what you make of my idea, then. I'm thinking that there are some things which take on the attributes of whatever is present to them, and some things which don't. Suppose, for example, that we were to apply colouring to something: the colouring is, in a sense, present to the thing to which it has been applied.'

'Yes.'

'And in this instance is the thing which has had colouring applied to it really the same colour as that which was applied to it?'

d 'I don't understand,' he said.

'Look at it this way, then,' I said. 'You've got fair hair. Suppose someone were to daub your hair with ceruse.* Would it then be white, or would it only look white?'

'It would look white,' he said.

'But there would be whiteness present.'

'Yes.'

'Nevertheless, your hair still wouldn't actually be white. Although whiteness is present to it, it's no more white than it is black.'

'True.'

'However, my friend, once your hair has had this same colour bestowed upon it by old age, it has really taken on the property: the presence of whiteness has really made your hair white.'

e 'Of course.'

'So the question I'm asking at the moment is whether something which has a quality present to it will take on the attributes of the quality which is present to it. Or is it the case that it will under certain circumstances, but not under others?'

'I prefer this latter alternative,' he said.

'There may be occasions, then, when something that's neither bad nor good is not yet really bad, despite the presence of badness, but there may also be occasions when it already has really become bad.'

'Yes.'

'So when, despite the presence of badness, it's not yet really bad, the presence of badness makes it desire goodness; but when the presence of badness makes it really bad, it loses both the desire for and the friendship of the good. This is because it's no longer neither bad nor good, but actually bad, and it's impossible 218a for bad to be friend to good.'

'Yes, that's impossible.'

'That's why we'd say that those who are already learned—be they gods or men*—no longer love learning, and also that those who've been corrupted by their ignorance don't love learning either (since no one who is bad and empty-headed loves learning).* That leaves those who are bad, in the sense that they're ignorant, but who haven't yet succumbed to their ignorance to the extent of becoming empty-headed dolts, and remain aware of the extent of their ignorance.* It follows that those who aren't yet b good or bad love learning, while neither those who are bad nor those who are good do. After all, earlier we concluded that neither opposites nor similars can love and be friends. Do you remember?'

'Of course,' they both said.

'At last!' I said. 'Lysis and Menexenus, we've discovered, beyond the shadow of a doubt, what it is to be a friend and what it is that a friend is a friend of.† Our position is that, in every sphere—in the body and the soul and so on—it's what's neither bad nor good that is a friend of the good because of the presence c of badness.'

They both expressed their total agreement with what I'd said, and personally I felt as delighted as a hunter at the satisfactory capture of my quarry. But then a ridiculous suspicion entered my mind—I can't explain why—that this conclusion of ours was wrong, and I immediately said: 'Damn! Lysis and Menexenus, this may be no more than fool's gold.'*

'Why on earth do you say that?' asked Menexenus.   d

'I'm afraid that the arguments we've met about friendship are the logical equivalent of impostors,' I said.

'What do you mean?' he asked.

'Let's look at it this way,' I said. 'In any case of friendship, is there or isn't there something to which the friend is a friend?'

'There must be,' he said.

'So does his friendship have no end in view and is he a friend for no reason, or does he have an end and some reason for being a friend?'

'He has an end and some reason.'

'Is that thing—the end of the friendship between the friend and his friend—itself a friend, or is it neither a friend nor an enemy?'

e   'I don't quite understand what you're asking,' he said.

'That's hardly surprising,' I said. 'But perhaps you'll follow if I put it like this—and I should think I'll gain a better understanding of what I'm saying too! Not long ago we said that a sick man was a friend of a doctor, didn't we?'

'Yes.'

'And is he a friend of the doctor because of his illness and with health as the end he has in view?'

'Yes.'

'And illness is a bad thing?'

'Of course.'

'What about health?' I asked. 'Is it good, bad, or neither?'

'It's good,' he said.

219a   'So we were saying, apparently, that the body (which is neither good nor bad), befriends the healing art (which is good), because of its illness (which is to say, because of something bad). And health—the end for the sake of which the healing art has won this friendship—is a good thing, isn't it?'

'Yes.'

'And is health lovable, like a friend, or not?'

'It is.'

'Whereas illness is hateful, like an enemy.'

'Yes.'

b   'So that which is neither bad nor good is a friend of the good because of something bad and hateful, and with an end that is good and lovable.'

'So it seems.'

'It follows, then, that a friend's friendship† has something lovable as its end and is caused by something hateful.'

'Apparently.'

'Now, boys,' I said, 'having come this far, let's make sure that we don't make any mistakes. I'm going to overlook the fact that we said that a friend befriends a friend—which is to say that a similar is a friend of a similar, which we said was impossible*—but there's something else we need to consider, to ensure that our present position doesn't lead us astray. The healing art, we're saying, is lovable because health is the end the person has in view.' c

'Yes.'

'And is health lovable too?'

'Yes, it is.'

'And if it's lovable, it's a means to some end.'

'Yes.'

'In fact, if it's to be consistent with our earlier conclusion, its end is something lovable.'

'Yes.'

'And will that lovable object too be befriended as a means to a lovable end?'

'Yes.'

'Well, won't we inevitably either go on and on like this until we're too exhausted to carry on, or else reach some source which won't pass us on to a further friend, but will stop doing so† when we reach that which is a primary lovable object, the final end d which makes everything else that is lovable lovable?'*

'Inevitably.'

'That's what I was getting at. I'm worried that all the other friends, which we said are lovable because of this final end, might lead us astray, since they are, so to speak, mere reflections of it, while it is the primary and truly lovable object. Let's look at it this way. When someone counts something as important (as, for instance, a father may prize a son more than all his other posses- sions), does the fact that he regards his son as of supreme import- e ance make other things important to him too? For example, if he saw that his son had swallowed some hemlock, would he count wine as important, if he thought that wine would save his son's life?'

'Of course he would,' he said.

'And also the bowl which contained the wine?'

'Yes.'

'At that moment, then, what is their relative importance? Is the earthenware cup as important to him as his son? Are three *kotylai* of wine?* Or is this how things are? In situations such as this, the focus of concern is never those things which are brought in as 220a means to some end, but only the end for the sake of which they're all brought in. Not that we don't often say that we count gold and silver as important, but all the same the truth may well be different: what we really take to be important is that thing—whatever it may turn out to be—for the sake of which we have gold and all our instruments at our disposal. Is this right, do you think?'

'Yes.'

'And does the same argument apply to a friend too? We're obviously using the term "friend" or "lovable" in a derivative b sense when we apply it to all the things we said were dear to us as means to a further lovable end. But it looks as though the only truly lovable object is the one which is the goal of *all* these so-called friendships.'

'Yes, it looks that way,' he said.

'That which is truly lovable, then, is not loved as a means to a lovable end. Right?'

'Yes.'

'So we've freed ourselves from the notion that any and every friend is lovable as a means to a lovable end. But let's ask instead whether something good is a friend.'

'I'd say so.'

'Is something good loved, then, because of something bad? If c so, suppose we were to keep two of the three things we were talking about just now—good, bad, and neither good nor bad— and get rid of badness. If there were no badness to affect any of the things, such as bodies and souls, that we said were in themselves neither bad nor good, would it be the case under these circumstances that something good would be no help to us at all?

Would goodness have been rendered useless? You see, if there's no longer anything to harm us, we wouldn't need anything to help us, and this would make it perfectly clear that we value and love d the good because of the bad. It's as if the good were a remedy for the sickness that is the bad: if there's no sickness, there's no need for a remedy. Is that what something good is like? Is it because of something bad that anything good is loved by us, who are between badness and goodness? Is it no use in its own right?'

'It looks that way,' he said.

'If so, that lovable object, the goal of all other lovable objects— the one we were talking about when we said that all other lovable e objects are lovable as means to a lovable end—is different from other lovable objects. They're called "lovable" or "friends" as means to a lovable end, but that which is truly lovable obviously has quite the opposite nature. I mean, we've come to the conclusion that it's lovable because of something hateful, and that if this hateful thing were to depart, it apparently stops being loved by us.'

'I agree,' he said, 'at least, on the basis of what we're saying at the moment.'

'In the name of Zeus,' I went on, 'what if badness really were eradicated? Will it stop being possible to feel things like hunger 221a and thirst? Or will there still be hunger—provided that human beings and other living creatures exist, that is—but it will stop being harmful? And will there still be thirst and the other appetites and desires, but they'll stop being bad, given that badness has been eradicated? It may be that asking what will or will not be the case under these circumstances is ludicrous; after all, how could one know? What we do know, however, is that at the moment it's possible for hunger to harm a person, though it can also help him.* Yes?'

'Yes.'

'And does the same go for thirst and all the other appetites and b desires? Sometimes it's possible for the desire to benefit the person experiencing it, sometimes it harms him, and sometimes it does neither.'

'Definitely.'

'So imagine a situation in which bad things are being

eradicated: does that mean that things which aren't bad should be eradicated along with them?'

'Not at all.'

'So even if bad things are eradicated, desires which are neither good nor bad will still exist.'

'Presumably.'

'Now, is it possible for someone who desires and loves something not to feel that what he desires and lusts after is dear to him, like a friend?'

'No, I doubt it.'

'So apparently, even if bad things are eliminated, there'll still c be things that are friends.'

'Yes.'

'But if badness were the reason for something's being a friend, there could be no friendship between one thing and another once badness was eradicated. I mean, the eradication of a cause necessarily entails the non-existence of things whose existence depends on the cause.'

'You're right.'

'Now, we've agreed that a friend loves something as a friend and does so for some reason, and at the time we thought that something bad was the reason that what is neither good nor bad loves what is good.'

'True.'

d 'But now we seem to have found that badness is *not* the cause of loving and being loved.'

'So it seems.'

'In actual fact, then, desire is the cause of friendship, as we were saying a moment ago;* a person feeling desire is a friend to what he desires for as long as he desires it. What we were saying before about what it is to be a friend was as pointless as a long-winded verse composition.'

'It does look that way.'

'But in any case of desire,' I pointed out, 'the desirer desires what it lacks, doesn't it?'

e 'Yes.'

'And it follows that anything in need is a friend of what it lacks. Yes?'

'I agree.'

'And it lacks what it has lost.'

'Of course.'

'Apparently, then, the object of lust and friendship and desire is something that is close to one. That's what we've discovered, Menexenus and Lysis.'

They both agreed. 'So if you're each other's friends,' I went on, 'you're naturally close to each other* in some respect.'

'Absolutely,' they said.

'So whenever one person desires or lusts after another person, boys,' I said, 'he wouldn't feel desire or lust or affection 222a unless he were in some respect close to his beloved, thanks to his soul or to some cast of his mind or to his personality or to his appearance.'

'Quite so,' Menexenus said, but Lysis kept quiet.

'All right, then,' I said. 'What we've found is that we're bound to love that to which we are naturally close.'

'So it seems,' he said.

'It follows, then, that a genuine lover, one who is not pretending, is bound to be loved by the boy he fancies.'

Lysis and Menexenus could hardly bring themselves to nod b their assent to this, but Hippothales' pleasure showed in the variety of colours he turned.* But I still wanted to look into the position we'd reached, and so I said: 'Lysis and Menexenus, I think our position on friendship would be correct if there were any difference between closeness and likeness, but if they're actually identical, we can hardly reject our earlier position* that because of their likeness like is no use to like, and that it would be misguided to admit that anything useless is a friend. So, since the c argument is putting us into something like a drunken stupor, shall we concede the point and assert that closeness and likeness are different?'

'Yes, let's.'

'Shall we assume, then, that what is good is close to everything, while what is bad is alien to everything? Or shall we say that the bad is close to the bad, the good to the good, and what's neither good nor bad to what's neither good nor bad?'

They agreed with this and said that, in their opinion, each type d of thing was close to things of its own type. 'Boys,' I said, 'we've stumbled back into the positions on friendship we rejected at the beginning of our discussion, since dishonest people and bad people will be friends just as much as good people.'

'So it seems,' he said.

'And if we say instead that goodness and closeness are identical,* it surely turns out that only good people can be friends,* doesn't it?'

'Yes.'

'But we thought we'd successfully challenged ourselves on this point too, if you remember.'

'We remember.'

e 'So can we take the argument any further, or have we clearly come to a standstill? If so, I shall imitate one of those clever speakers in the lawcourts and ask your permission to recapitulate the entire course of the argument. If neither those who are loved, nor those who love, nor those who are alike, nor those who are unlike, nor those who are good, nor those who are close, nor all the other possibilities we covered (there were so many that I can't now remember them all) . . . anyway, if none of these is a friend, I've no longer got anything to say.'

223a These words of mine were supposed to stimulate the interest of one of the others, one of the older men who were present, but just then, like supernatural beings,* Menexenus' and Lysis' attendants came over with the boys' brothers and, since it was now late, began to tell them, in no uncertain terms, that it was time to go home. At first, we and the people standing around us tried to shoo them away, but they took no notice of us; displaying traces of their foreign accents,* they just repeated their summons, now with some

b irritation. It occurred to us that they'd had a bit to drink during the Hermaea and that this was what was making made them intractable. So we conceded defeat and called the meeting to a close. But as they were leaving I said: 'Lysis and Menexenus, we've made fools of ourselves today, you and I—and I'm an old man. Our friends here will say as they leave that although we imagine that we're one another's friends—I count myself as one of you, you see—we've not yet been able to discover what it is to be a friend.'

MENO

MENO: I wonder whether you can tell me, Socrates, whether 70a
excellence is teachable or, if not teachable, at least a product of
habituation. Or perhaps it isn't the kind of thing one can practise or learn, but is a natural human endowment. If not, how *do*
people become good?*

SOCRATES: Meno, in the past the Thessalians were famous and
admired throughout the Greek world for their skill with horses
and for their wealth,* but I get the impression that now they're
admired for their knowledge too—and the foremost Thessal- b
ians in this respect are the people of Larisa, the fellow citizens
of your friend Aristippus. You have Gorgias to thank for this
new attainment of yours. When he came to Larisa, he ignited a
passion for his wisdom in the leading Aleuadae, including your
lover Aristippus, as well as in the general population. One of
the main things he did was get you into this habit of fearlessly
giving grand answers to any question that is put to you. But
this is no more than one would expect from men of knowledge,
given that he himself invites questions on any topic from any- c
one in Greece and never fails to provide them with answers.*

We're in the opposite situation here in Athens, though, my
dear Meno: we're parched of knowledge, so to speak, and it
looks as though it has emigrated from hereabouts to you. At 71a
any rate, if you were to put your question to anyone here, you
would undoubtedly meet with a laugh and the reply: 'Stranger,
you must take me to be high in the gods' favour, if you really
think I know whether or not excellence is teachable or how
people come to get it. So far from knowing whether or not it's
teachable, I don't even have the faintest idea what excellence
is.' So that's how I'm placed as well, Meno: I'm no better off b
than my fellow citizens in this matter, and I tell myself off for
my utter ignorance about excellence. And if I don't know what
a thing is, how can I know what sort of a thing it is? Or do you
think that someone who is utterly ignorant of who Meno is
could know whether he's good-looking or rich or well born, or

whether he has the opposite attributes? Do you think that's possible?*

MENO: No, I don't. But do you really not know what excellence
c   is, Socrates? Is this part of what we're to tell people at home about you?

SOCRATES: Yes, my friend, and you can add that I don't think I've yet met anyone else who knew what it was.

MENO: What? Didn't you meet Gorgias when he was here?

SOCRATES: Yes, I did.*

MENO: And did you still not think he knew?

SOCRATES: I'm rather forgetful, Meno, so I can't say now what I thought of him then. Maybe he does know—and maybe you know what he used to say. If so, remind me what it was, or, if
d   you prefer, tell me in your own words, since I suppose you share his opinion.

MENO: Yes, I do.

SOCRATES: Then let's leave him out of it: he's not here, after all. But in the name of the gods, Meno, please do tell me in your own words what you think excellence is. Don't hold back because, if it turns out that you and Gorgias know, you'll be converting my mistaken claim that I had never met anyone with this knowledge into a piece of extraordinary good fortune.

e   MENO: Well, it's not hard to put it into words, Socrates. If you'd like me to start with masculine excellence, that's easy, because the excellence proper to a man is to be capable of managing the affairs of his community, and of doing so in a way that enables him to help his friends, harm his enemies, and avoid suffering any harm himself.* Or if you'd rather hear about a woman's excellence, that's easy to explain: she should be a good house-keeper, which is to say that she should keep the indoor prop-erty safe and obey her husband. And then what it is to be a good child (male or female) is different again, and so is excel-lence in an old man, never mind whether he's free or a slave.
72a   There are a great many other excellences too,* and this makes it easy to say what excellence is. For every task we undertake, there is, for each of us, the excellence that depends on our walk of life and our age, and I should imagine, Socrates, that by the same token there is for each of us the appropriate defect too.

SOCRATES: I am indeed extraordinarily lucky, apparently, Meno. In the course of looking for a single excellence, I've found that a veritable swarm of them have settled in your house. Well, Meno, let's stick with this image of a swarm. Suppose I asked b what it is to be a bee and you said that there were many bees, of many varieties. What answer would you give me if I then asked: 'Are you saying that these bees are many, and of many different varieties, in that they are bees? Or do they not differ from one another at all in that they are bees, but differ from one another in some other respect—in beauty, for example, or size or something like that?' Tell me: what answer would you give to this question?

MENO: I'd say that they don't differ one from another at all, in so far as they are bees.

SOCRATES: So what if I went on to say: 'Here's the crucial ques- c tion, then, Meno: what, in your opinion, is it that makes them all no different from one another, but the same?' I imagine you'd be able to tell me, wouldn't you?

MENO: Yes, I would.*

SOCRATES: So do the same for excellence as well, please. Even if there are many aspects of excellence, of different kinds, they all share a single characteristic, thanks to which they are aspects of excellence, and it's this single characteristic which a person should look to when he's replying to someone who has asked him to explain what excellence actually is. But perhaps you're d not following what I'm saying.

MENO: No, I think I understand, but I'm not quite as clear as I'd like to be about the point of the present enquiry.

SOCRATES: Well, Meno, is it only excellence that seems to you to be like that—to be different for a man and for a woman and so on—or does the same go, in your opinion, for health and height and strength? Do you think that health is different in a man and in a woman? Or is it the same characteristic wherever there's health, whether it's in a man or a woman or anything e else?

MENO: As far as health is concerned, I think it's the same for a man and for a woman.*

SOCRATES: And height and strength too? If a woman is strong, will she be strong thanks to the same characteristic, the same strength? By 'the same' I mean that, in so far as it's strength, strength is no different whether it's in a man or in a woman. Or do you think there's a difference?

MENO: No, I don't.

73a SOCRATES: What about excellence? In so far as it's excellence, does it make any difference whether it's found in a child or an old man, in a woman or a man?

MENO: I don't think this case is quite the same as the others, Socrates.

SOCRATES: But weren't you saying that male excellence consisted in managing a community well and that female excellence consisted in managing a household well?

MENO: Yes.

SOCRATES: Now, a good manager of anything, not just of a community or a household, must go about it in a self-controlled and just way, mustn't he?

MENO: Of course.

b SOCRATES: And if they manage things in a self-controlled and just way, they'll do so thanks to justice and self-control, won't they?

MENO: They're bound to.

SOCRATES: If they're to be good,* then, they'll both need the same qualities. It doesn't matter whether they're male or female: they'll both need justice and self-control.

MENO: So it seems.

SOCRATES: What about a child and an old man? Could they possibly be good people if they were undisciplined and unjust?

MENO: Of course not.

SOCRATES: Only if they're self-controlled and just?

c MENO: Yes.

SOCRATES: It follows that anyone who's good is good in the same way, since their goodness depends on their possession of the same qualities.

MENO: Apparently.

SOCRATES: But they wouldn't be good in the same way, I imagine, unless they had the same excellence.*

MENO: Of course not.

SOCRATES: All right, then. Since everyone's excellence is the same, try to tell me what that excellence is. Try to remember what Gorgias—and you along with him—say it is.

MENO: What else could it be other than the ability to rule men? Yes, that's it, if you're looking for some one thing to cover all d cases.

SOCRATES: Yes, that's exactly what I'm looking for. But is that also what it is to be a good child, Meno, or a good slave—to have the ability to rule over one's master? Do you think that a ruler can still be a slave?

MENO: No, I can't really say I do, Socrates.

SOCRATES: No, it would hardly be tenable, my friend. And here's another point for you to consider: you're saying that excellence is 'the ability to rule'—but shouldn't we add to it 'justly, rather than unjustly'?

MENO: I'd say so. After all, Socrates, justice is excellence.*

SOCRATES: Is it excellence, Meno, or *an* excellence? e

MENO: What are you getting at?

SOCRATES: A point of universal application. Let's take round-ness, if you like: I'd say that it is *a* shape, not simply that it is shape, and the reason I'd put it this way is that there are other shapes as well.

MENO: Yes, you're right: I too would say that there are other aspects of excellence in addition to justice.

SOCRATES: What are they? Tell me. I mean, I'd name other 74a shapes for you, if you wanted me to, so why don't you tell me some other aspects of excellence?

MENO: All right. I think courage is an excellence, as are self-control, wisdom, and nobility—but there are a great many others too.

SOCRATES: The same thing has happened to us again, Meno. In the course of our search for just one excellence, we've once more—though not in the same way that we did just now—found many of them. But we can't discover the one excellence that runs through them all.

MENO: That's because I can't yet do what you're asking, Socrates. I can't grasp a single excellence which covers all b cases, as in the other examples.

SOCRATES: That's hardly surprising. Well, I'll do my best to get us close,† if I can. I mean, I'm sure you can see that there's a universal principle involved here. Suppose someone were to ask you, as I did just now, 'What is shape, Meno?', and you said 'Roundness'. Then suppose he asked you the same question I put to you: 'Is roundness shape or a shape?' You'd say, I suppose, that it was a shape.

MENO: Yes.

c SOCRATES: The reason being that there are other shapes as well. Yes?

MENO: Yes.

SOCRATES: And if he went on to ask you what other kinds of shapes there were, you'd tell him.

MENO: I would.

SOCRATES: And if he next asked you, along the same lines, what colour is, and you answered 'White', and he came back at you with the further question 'Is white colour or a colour', you'd say that it was a colour, because there are others as well. Yes?

MENO: Yes, I would.

SOCRATES: And if he asked you to name other colours, you'd do
d   so, wouldn't you, and they'd be colours just as much as white was?

MENO: Yes.

SOCRATES: So suppose he pursued the issue as I did, and said: 'We keep reaching a plurality. Please don't give me this kind of answer. Instead, since you use a single word to refer to all the members of this plurality—you say that the word "shape" applies to them all, even when they are opposites—tell me what this thing is which covers "round" just as much as "straight", which you call "shape", a term you apply equally to "round"
e   and to "straight".' That *is* how you use the term, isn't it?

MENO: Yes, I do.

SOCRATES: And on the occasions when you talk like this, are you saying that something round is no more round than straight, or that something straight is no more straight than round?

MENO: Of course not, Socrates.

SOCRATES: No, you're saying that 'round' is a shape no less than 'straight', and vice versa.

MENO: Right.

SOCRATES: What exactly is it, then, which is the bearer of this name 'shape'? Try to tell me. [*Meno hesitates*] Suppose you told 75a the person who was asking you those questions about shape or colour: 'I'm sorry. Personally, I don't understand what you're after, sir. I don't know what you mean.' He might well be astonished, and he'd say, 'Don't you understand that I'm looking for that which is the same in all these cases?' Would you still not be able to reply, Meno, if under these circumstances you were asked: 'What is it that is always the same, in roundness and in straightness and in all those things you call "shapes"?' Try to answer, as practice for your answer about excellence.

MENO: No, Socrates, *you* answer instead. b

SOCRATES: You're asking me for a favour?

MENO: Yes.

SOCRATES: Will *you* be prepared to give me an answer about excellence, then?

MENO: Yes, I will.

SOCRATES: In that case, I'll do my best. It'll be worth the effort.

MENO: I'm sure it will.

SOCRATES: All right, then, let's try to tell you what shape is. See whether you can accept that this is what it is: let's take shape to be the only thing that always accompanies colour. Will that do, or would you prefer an alternative answer? Speaking for myself, I'd be quite happy if you were to describe excellence for me c along these lines.

MENO: But this is simplistic, Socrates.

SOCRATES: What do you mean?

MENO: If I understand you, you're saying that shape is what always accompanies colour. All well and good, but if someone were to say that he didn't know what colour was and was just as puzzled about colour as he was about shape,* what reply would you have given him, do you think?

SOCRATES: I'd tell him the truth. And if the person asking me the question was one of those clever, disputatious men who always try to win arguments, I'd say: 'You've heard what I have d to say. If I've made a mistake, it's up to you to challenge me and get me to explain myself.' On the other hand, if people are willing to join in the kind of friendly conversation you and I are having now, a less aggressive reply, one better suited for conversation, is appropriate. And I suppose what's more suitable for conversation is not just to tell the truth, but to make use of points to which the questioner† too has given his assent. So that's how I too will try to talk to you. Tell me, then: do you acknowledge the existence of something called an 'end'? By

e 'end' I mean the same kind of thing as a 'limit' or an 'extremity'; I'm using the terms interchangeably. Prodicus might well take issue with us for this, but I'm sure that you, at any rate, recognize that there's such a thing as 'having been limited' and 'having come to an end'. This is the kind of thing I mean, nothing complicated.

MENO: Yes, I do acknowledge its existence, and I think I see what you're getting at.

76a SOCRATES: Well, then, do you acknowledge the existence of something called 'plane', and then again something called 'solid'—as they occur, for instance, in one's geometrical studies?

MENO: Yes, I do.

SOCRATES: Well, you may already be able to use them as a basis for understanding what I say shape is. In every instance of shape, what I mean by 'shape' is that at which something solid terminates. In short, I'd say that 'shape' is 'the limit of a solid'.

MENO: And what would you say colour is, Socrates?

SOCRATES: You bully, Meno! You're making work for an old man, getting him to tell you what he thinks, while remaining unwill-

b ing yourself to recall and tell me what Gorgias said excellence is.

MENO: No, I'll tell you, Socrates—once you've answered this question of mine.

SOCRATES: Even someone with his eyes covered up, Meno, could tell from talking to you that you're good-looking and are still pursued by admirers.

MENO: How?

SOCRATES: Because you issue orders every time you open your mouth, which is a sure sign of being spoiled, since young men rule the roost as long as they're in bloom.* At the same time,

you've probably recognized my weakness, that I'm susceptible c
to good looks. So I'll indulge you; I'll answer your question.

MENO: Yes, please indulge me.

SOCRATES: Shall I answer in the manner of Gorgias, to make it
easy for you to follow?

MENO: Yes, please. Of course I'd appreciate that.

SOCRATES: All right, then. Do you and Gorgias agree with
Empedocles that there are certain emanations from things?*

MENO: Definitely.

SOCRATES: And that there are channels into which and through
which the emanations travel?

MENO: Yes.

SOCRATES: And that some of the emanations fit some of the
channels, while others are too small or too big? d

MENO: That's right.

SOCRATES: Now, you acknowledge the existence of something
called 'sight', don't you?

MENO: Yes, I do.

SOCRATES: So now you're in a position to 'mark well what I
say',* as Pindar puts it: colour is an emanation emitted by
shapes which is commensurate with sight and so is perceptible.

MENO: I think this is a truly excellent answer, Socrates.

SOCRATES: That's probably because it's in the manner to which
you are accustomed. At the same time, I think you're bearing in
mind that you'd be able to use my answer as a basis for saying
what sound is as well, and smell, and so on and so forth.* e

MENO: Quite so.

SOCRATES: Yes, because it's a grandiose answer, Meno, and so
you prefer it to the one about shape.

MENO: Yes, I do.

SOCRATES: But it isn't a better answer, son of Alexidemus, I'm
convinced: the previous one was.†* And I don't suppose you'd
think it was better either, if (as you told me yesterday) you
didn't have to leave before the Mysteries, but could stay and be
initiated.*

MENO: I would stay, Socrates, if you'd do me the favour of 77a
including plenty of those sorts of ideas in our discussion.

SOCRATES: Well, I'll try my hardest to do so, for both our sakes,

but I doubt I'll be able to include *plenty* of them. But come on, now: try to keep your promise and tell me what excellence is as a whole. Stop 'turning one into many' (as wags say when someone breaks something); leave excellence whole and intact, and tell me what it is. I've already supplied you with some models
b to follow.

MENO: All right, Socrates. I think that excellence is—to borrow the words of the poet—'to enjoy fine things and to have power'.* So that's what I say excellence is: desiring fine things and having the ability to procure them for oneself.

SOCRATES: When you say that a person desires fine things, do you mean that he desires good things?

MENO: Yes, certainly.

SOCRATES: Is your assumption that there are some people who desire bad things and others who desire good things? Don't
c you think that everyone desires good things, my friend?

MENO: No, I don't.

SOCRATES: Some people desire bad things, then?

MENO: Yes.

SOCRATES: Do you mean that they do so because they mistake the bad things for good things, or that they desire them even though they recognize them as bad?

MENO: Both, I think.

SOCRATES: So do you really think, Meno, that someone can recognize something bad as bad and still desire it?

MENO: Certainly.

SOCRATES: What do you mean when you say he desires it? He desires it as a possession?

MENO: Yes, of course.

d SOCRATES: And does he do so because he thinks that bad things help those who get them, or because he recognizes that bad things harm their possessors?

MENO: There are people who think that bad things do them good, and then there are others who recognize that they do them harm.

SOCRATES: Do you also think that people who think that bad things do them good are recognizing the bad things as bad?

MENO: No, I don't think *that*.

SOCRATES: Obviously, then, in these cases, when people don't recognize something bad as bad, it's not that they're desiring something bad; they desire what they take to be good, even e though in actual fact it's bad. And this means that people who fail to recognize something bad as bad, and take it to be good, are obviously desiring something good, aren't they?*

MENO: It looks as though they are, in these cases at least.

SOCRATES: Well, then, take those people who, in your opinion, desire something bad, but think that bad things are harmful to their possessors: I suppose they realize they're going to be harmed by it?

MENO: They must do.

SOCRATES: Well, don't they think that people who suffer harm 78a are in a bad way, precisely because they are suffering harm?

MENO: Again, they must do.

SOCRATES: Aren't people who are in a bad way unhappy?

MENO: I'd say so.

SOCRATES: Well, is there anyone who wants to be in a bad way and unhappy?

MENO: I don't think so, Socrates.

SOCRATES: No one wants bad things, then, Meno, if he doesn't want to be unhappy. After all, being in a bad way is just that—desiring bad things and getting them*—isn't it?

MENO: I suppose you're right, Socrates: it looks as though no one b wants bad things.

SOCRATES: Now, weren't you saying just now that excellence is wanting good things and having the ability to get them?

MENO: Yes, I did say that.

SOCRATES: Now, the 'wanting' aspect of what you said† is common to everyone. In this respect, no one is better than anyone else.

MENO: I suppose so.

SOCRATES: Plainly, then, if one person is better than another, it would be in respect of ability.

MENO: Yes.

SOCRATES: It seems to follow that what excellence is, to your way of thinking, is the ability to procure good things for c oneself.

MENO: Socrates, I think you've understood me perfectly correctly now.

SOCRATES: So let's see if you're right too; you might be. You're saying that excellence is the ability to procure good things for oneself?

MENO: Yes.

SOCRATES: And you use the term 'good' for things like health and wealth, don't you?

MENO: Yes, I mean not just getting gold and silver, but acquiring positions of prestige and political authority as well.

SOCRATES: And that's it, isn't it? There aren't any other good things, in your opinion, are there?

MENO: No, but I'm including everything else of this kind.

d SOCRATES: All right, then. According to Meno, the hereditary guest-friend of the Great King,* excellence is procuring gold and silver. Would you add 'by fair and moral means' to this 'procurement' of yours, Meno, or does it make no difference to you? I mean, would you still call it excellence even if one gained these things unjustly?

MENO: No, of course I wouldn't, Socrates.

SOCRATES: You'd count it a defect, then.

MENO: Absolutely.

SOCRATES: Apparently, then, even though it procures good things, this procurement must be attended by justice or self-
e   control or morality, or some other aspect of excellence, if it is to be excellence.

MENO: Yes. I mean, it would hardly count as excellence otherwise.

SOCRATES: But what about avoiding the procurement of gold and silver (whether oneself or someone else is the beneficiary) when it would be unjust to get them? Isn't this non-procurement excellence too?

MENO: I suppose so.

SOCRATES: So excellence is no more the procurement of good things of this sort than it is the failure to procure them. It turns out that any behaviour that is attended by justice is excellence
79a and any behaviour that is not attended by any such thing is a defect.

MENO: I don't see any alternative to what you're saying.

SOCRATES: Now, didn't we say a short while ago that each of these things—justice, self-control, and so on—was a *part* of excellence?

MENO: Yes.

SOCRATES: Are you playing games with me, then, Meno?

MENO: How so, Socrates?

SOCRATES: Because not long ago I asked you not to break excellence up into bits or pieces, and I came up with models of the kind of answer you should give. But you took no notice and now you're telling me that excellence is the ability to procure b good things with justice—which is a part of excellence, in your view, isn't it?

MENO: Yes.

SOCRATES: So it follows, from your own premises (since you admit that justice and so on are parts of excellence), that excellence is doing whatever one does with a part of excellence.

MENO: What of it?†

SOCRATES: What I'm getting at is this. I asked you for your opinion about excellence as a whole, but so far from saying what it is in itself, you're saying that excellence is any action that is accompanied by a part of excellence. But this would make sense c only if you'd already said what excellence as a whole is, so that I'd then be in a position to understand what you were saying even if you chopped it up into pieces. So I think you have to face up to the original question all over again, my dear Meno: if excellence is any action that is accompanied by justice, which is to say that excellence is any action that is accompanied by a part of excellence, what is excellence? Or don't you think we need to go back to the original question? Do you think that it's possible for anyone to understand what is meant by a part of excellence if he doesn't know what excellence is?

MENO: No, I don't.

SOCRATES: No, and if you cast your mind back a few moments to d when I gave you my answer about shape, I'm sure you'll remember that we rejected the kind of answer which tries to make use of terms that are still under investigation and have not yet been agreed upon.*

MENO: Yes, and we were right to do so, Socrates.

SOCRATES: But then *you* shouldn't think, my friend, that while we're still looking into the question of what virtue as a whole is, an answer in terms of its parts will elucidate it for anyone. That kind of answer won't work with anything. You'd better

e   appreciate that we still need an answer to the same question: you talk about excellence, but what *is* it? But perhaps you don't think I'm right.

MENO: No, I think you're right.

SOCRATES: Then make a fresh start and answer the question: what is it that you and your friend* say excellence is?

MENO: Before I'd even met you, Socrates, I'd heard that all you

80a   do is infect other people with the bewilderment you suffer from yourself. And that seems to me to be what you're doing now too: you're using magic and witchcraft on me. It's hardly an exaggeration to say that you're casting a spell on me, to make me utterly stuck. If you'll allow me a little joke, I think I know the perfect image for you: in appearance* and all other respects you're just like one of those flat sea-fish, torpedoes. I mean, the torpedo numbs anyone who comes near enough to touch it, and I think you've done the same kind of thing to me.

b   My mind and my mouth are literally torpid, and I have no answer for you, despite the fact that I've spoken at length about excellence on countless occasions, to a great many people, and, though I say so myself, have done so rather fluently and well. But at the moment I can't even begin to say what it is. I think it was a sensible decision of yours to stay here and not to travel abroad, because if you were to behave like this elsewhere, as a foreigner, you'd probably be arrested as a magician.*

SOCRATES: You're full of mischief, Meno: I nearly fell into your trap.

MENO: What do you mean, Socrates?

c SOCRATES: I know why you came up with an image for me.

MENO: Why, do you think?

SOCRATES: To make me come up with one for you in return. I'm well aware that all good-looking people enjoy being compared to something: it works in their favour, because, I suppose, attractive people are bound to be compared to something attractive. But I'm not going to come up with an image for you in return. As for me, if the torpedo numbs other people by virtue of the fact that it's numb itself, I am indeed like it, but otherwise I'm not. It's not that I make other people stuck while being clear myself; no, I make other people stuck by virtue of the fact that I'm stuck myself. In the present instance, I don't know what excellence is, and although you probably did know d before you came into contact with me, you seem not to know now. But I'd be happy if the two of us together could investigate the issue and try to find out what it is.

MENO: And how will you search for something, Socrates, when you don't know what it is at all? I mean, which of the things you don't know will you take in advance and search for, when you don't know what it is? Or even if you come right up against it, how will you know that it's the unknown thing you're looking for?*

SOCRATES: I see what you're getting at, Meno. Do you realize e what a controversy you're conjuring up? The claim is that it's impossible for a man to search either for what he knows or for what he doesn't know: he wouldn't be searching for what he knows, since he knows it and that makes the search unnecessary, and he can't search for what he doesn't know either, since he doesn't even know what it is he's going to search for.*

MENO: Well, doesn't† the argument strike you as sound, 81a Socrates?

SOCRATES: No, it doesn't.

MENO: Can you say why not?

SOCRATES: Yes, I can, because I've heard both men and women who are wise in sacred lore . . .

MENO: Saying what?

SOCRATES: Something which I think is true, as well as being attractive.

MENO: What did they say? Who are they?*

SOCRATES: They are those priests and priestesses who've taken an interest in being able to give an account of their practices, though the idea also occurs in Pindar and many other inspired b poets. Here's what they say; see if you think they're right. They say that the human soul is immortal—that it periodically comes to an end (which is what is generally called 'death') and is born again, but that it never perishes.* And that, they say, is why one should live as moral a life as possible, because

In the ninth year Persephone restores once more to the upper light
The souls of those from whom she has accepted requital for ancient woe.

c   From them grow glorious kings, full mighty men, and great sages,
And henceforth they are known on earth as holy heroes.*

Given, then, that the soul is immortal and has been incarnated many times, and has therefore seen things here on earth and things in the underworld too—everything, in fact—there's nothing that it hasn't learnt. Hence it isn't at all surprising that it should be possible for the soul to recall what, after all, it also knew before about excellence and about everything else.* For

d   since all nature is akin* and the soul has learnt everything, there's nothing to stop a man recovering everything else by himself, once he has remembered—or 'learnt', in common parlance—just one thing; all he needs is the fortitude not to give up the search. The point is that the search, the process of learning, is in fact nothing but recollection.* So we shouldn't trust that controversial argument of yours: it would make us lazy and appeals to faint-hearted people, but the doctrine I've

e   just expressed makes us industrious and inquisitive. For my part, I will put my trust in this doctrine and take it to be true, and on that basis I'm prepared to try to find out, with your help, what excellence is.

MENO: Yes, Socrates, but what do you mean when you say that we don't learn—that what we call 'learning' is actually 'recollection'? Can you teach me how this is so?

SOCRATES: Didn't I describe you a moment ago as mischievous, Meno? And now, just when I'm insisting that there's no such

82a   thing as teaching, only recollection, you're asking me whether I can teach you something. You're trying to catch me out in an immediate contradiction.

MENO: By Zeus, no, Socrates, that's not what I had in mind when I spoke; it was just a natural question. But if you can find some way to demonstrate the truth of what you've been saying, please do so.

SOCRATES: Well, it isn't easy, but I'm prepared to do my best, for your sake. Call over one of your many attendants there for me—it doesn't matter who: you choose—and I'll use him to b prove the point to you.

MENO: By all means. [*To a slave*] Come over here!

SOCRATES: He is Greek, isn't he, and speaks Greek?

MENO: Yes, certainly. At any rate, he was born and bred at home.*

SOCRATES: Pay careful attention, then, and see whether you get the impression that he's remembering or learning from me.

MENO: I will.

SOCRATES [*drawing in the sand of the gymnasium*]: Tell me, boy,* do you know that this is what a square looks like?

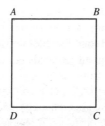

SLAVE: Yes.

SOCRATES: So is it a rectangular figure with all these sides—all c four of them—equal in length?

SLAVE: Yes.

SOCRATES: And is it a figure with these lines here through the middle equal in length as well?*

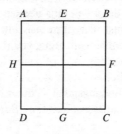

SLAVE: Yes.

SOCRATES [*pointing to the two sizes of square*]: So a figure of this kind can be larger or smaller, can't it?

SLAVE: Yes.

SOCRATES: Now, let this side [*AB*] be 2 feet long,* and this one as well [*BC*]. How big would the whole figure be, in square feet? [*The slave hesitates*] Look at it this way: if it's 2 feet long here [*AB*], but only 1 foot long here [*BF*], then the area must be 2 feet taken once, mustn't it?

SLAVE: Yes.

d SOCRATES: But since it's 2 feet long here too [*BC*], then it must be 2 feet taken twice, mustn't it?

SLAVE: Yes.

SOCRATES: So it's 2 times 2 square feet?

SLAVE: Yes.

SOCRATES: And how many square feet does that make? Work it out and tell me.

SLAVE: Four, Socrates.

SOCRATES: Now, could there be another figure, twice the size of this one [*ABCD*], but the same shape, with all its sides equal, just like this one?

SLAVE: Yes.

SOCRATES: How many square feet will it be?

SLAVE: Eight.

SOCRATES: All right, then. Next try to tell me how long each line

e of this new figure will be. Each line of this figure here [*ABCD*] is 2 feet long. What about the line of our new figure, which is double in size?

SLAVE: Obviously, Socrates, each line must be double in length.

SOCRATES: Do you see, Meno, that I'm not teaching him anything, but just asking him questions?* At the moment he thinks he knows what length of line will produce a figure of 8 square feet. Don't you think that's the position he's reached?

MENO: Yes, I do.

SOCRATES: Well, does he *know*?

MENO: Plainly not.

SOCRATES: But he *believes* it will be produced by a line that's twice as long?

MENO: Yes.

SOCRATES: Now watch how he remembers what comes next, which is the right way to go about remembering.* [*To the slave*] Tell me: are you saying that it's a line double in length that will produce a figure with double the area? I don't mean that this line of the figure should be long [*he extends AB to J*], while this one is short [*AD or JM*],* but that it should be equal on all sides, just like this one [*ABCD*], but double in size, making 8 square feet. Do you still think that it will be produced from a line which is double the length of the original? 83a

SLAVE: Yes, I do.

SOCRATES: Well, isn't this line [*AJ*] twice as long as this one [*AB*], once we've added to the original another line of the same length [*BJ*]?

SLAVE: Yes. b

SOCRATES: And it's from this line [*AJ*], according to you, that we can produce an area of 8 square feet, if we make four lines of this length?

SLAVE: Yes.

SOCRATES: All right, let's draw four equal lines, using this line [*AJ*] as our starting-point. [*He draws JK, KL, and LA, in addition to AJ*] This must now be the figure which you say has an area of 8 square feet, mustn't it?

SLAVE: Yes.

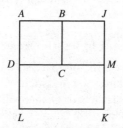

SOCRATES: Now, doesn't this figure contain these four figures [*ABCD, BJMC, CMKN, DCNL*], each of which is equal in size to this one [*ABCD*], which is 4 square feet?

MENO

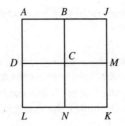

SLAVE: Yes.

SOCRATES: How big is it, then? Isn't it four times as big?

SLAVE: Of course.

SOCRATES: Is something which is four times as big double the size?

SLAVE: By Zeus, no!

SOCRATES: How many times as big is it?

SLAVE: Four times.

c SOCRATES: It follows, boy, that a line double in length gives us a figure with not double the area, but four times the area.

SLAVE: You're right.

SOCRATES: Because a figure of 4 times 4 square feet has an area of 16 square feet, doesn't it?

SLAVE: Yes.

SOCRATES: So what length of line is needed to produce a figure with an area of 8 square feet? We've got a figure four times the size from this one [*AJ*], haven't we?

SLAVE: I'd say so.

SOCRATES: And this quarter-sized one† [*ABCD*] is produced by this half line here [*AB*], isn't it?

SLAVE: Yes.

SOCRATES: Well, then, a figure with an area of 8 square feet is double the size of this one [*ABCD*], and half the size of this one [*AJKL*], isn't it?

SLAVE: Yes.

SOCRATES: So in order to produce a figure with an area of 8 square feet, we need as a starting-point a line which is longer than this one [*AB*], but shorter than this one [*AJ*], don't we?

d SLAVE: I think so.

SOCRATES: Good. Your answers should always express your

118

beliefs. Now, tell me: wasn't this line [*AB*] 2 feet long, and this one [*AJ*] 4 feet long?

SLAVE: Yes.

SOCRATES: So the side of a square whose area is 8 feet must be longer than this 2-foot line and shorter than this 4-foot line.

SLAVE: Yes, it must be.

SOCRATES: Then try to tell me how long you think it is.　　　　e

SLAVE: Three feet.*

SOCRATES: Now, if 3 feet is correct, shall we add half of this one [*BJ*], to make one 3 feet long [*AP*]? I mean, we've got 2 feet here [*AB*] and 1 foot here [*BP*], and then, in the same way, we've got 2 feet here [*AD*] and 1 foot here [*DR*]. And we can now produce the figure you wanted [*APQR*].

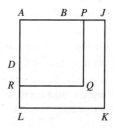

SLAVE: Yes.

SOCRATES: Now, if it's 3 feet this way and 3 feet this way, the whole area is going to be 3 times 3 square feet, isn't it?

SLAVE: I suppose so.

SOCRATES: And how many square feet is 3 times 3 feet?

SLAVE: Nine.

SOCRATES: But what we wanted was a double-size square of how many square feet?

SLAVE: Eight.

SOCRATES: So we haven't yet produced our figure of 8 square feet. It isn't produced by a line 3 feet long either.

SLAVE: No, it certainly isn't.

SOCRATES: How long would the line have to be to produce it, then? Try to give us an accurate answer. If you don't want to use numbers, at least point to the line that would produce it.　84a

SLAVE: By Zeus, Socrates, I just don't know.

SOCRATES: Meno, can you see where our friend here has got to on his journey towards recollection? At first, he didn't *know* which line would produce the figure with an area of 8 square feet—just as he doesn't yet know the answer now either; but he still *thought* he knew the answer then, and he was answering confidently, as if he had knowledge. He didn't think he was stuck before, but now he appreciates that he *is* stuck and he also

b   doesn't think he knows what in fact he doesn't know.

MENO: You're right.

SOCRATES: So is he now better off with regard to what he didn't know?

MENO: Again, yes, I think so.

SOCRATES: So have we done him any harm by making him stuck and by our torpedo-like numbing of him?

MENO: No, I don't think we have.

SOCRATES: At any rate, it would seem that we've increased his chances of finding out the truth of the matter, because now, given his lack of knowledge, he'll be glad to undertake the investigation, whereas before he was only too ready to suppose

c   that he could talk fluently and well to numerous people on numerous occasions about how a double-sized figure must have double-length sides.*

MENO: I suppose so.

SOCRATES: Do you think he'd have tried to enquire or learn about this matter when he thought he knew it (even though he didn't), until he'd become bogged down and stuck, and had come to appreciate his ignorance and to long for knowledge?

MENO: No, I don't think he would, Socrates.

SOCRATES: The numbing did him good, then?

MENO: I'd say so.

SOCRATES: Have a look, then, and see what he'll discover even under these circumstances as he undertakes the enquiry with me, with his puzzlement as our starting-point. All I'll be doing is asking him questions, not teaching him anything, but you

d   should make sure that you don't catch me teaching and explaining things to him, rather than just asking him for his thoughts. [*To the slave*] Tell me, then. This is our figure with an area of 4 square feet [*ABCD*], isn't it? Do you understand?

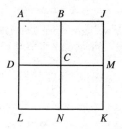

SLAVE: Yes.

SOCRATES: And we could add another one, equal in size [*BJMC*], couldn't we?

SLAVE: Yes.

SOCRATES: And here's a third square, which is again the same size as either of the other two [*DCNL*]. Right?

SLAVE: Yes.

SOCRATES: And we could also fill up the corner with this one [*CMKN*], couldn't we?

SLAVE: Yes.

SOCRATES: And then, of course, we'd have these four equal figures here, wouldn't we?

SLAVE: Yes.   e

SOCRATES: Well, now, how many times as big as this figure [*e.g. ABCD*] is this whole figure here?

SLAVE: It's four times as big.

SOCRATES: Whereas what we wanted was one twice as big, didn't we? Do you remember?

SLAVE: That's right.

SOCRATES: Now, here's a line that runs from one corner to another and cuts each of these figures in two [*DBMN*].* 85a Right?

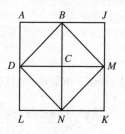

SLAVE: Yes.

SOCRATES: And what we've got are four equal lines which form the perimeter of this figure here [*DBMN*]. Yes?

SLAVE: Yes.

SOCRATES: Here's a question for you, then. How big is this figure [*DBMN*]?

SLAVE: I don't understand.

SOCRATES: Hasn't each line [*e.g. DB*] cut off the inner half of each of these four squares [*e.g. ABCD*]? Well, has it?

SLAVE: Yes.

SOCRATES: Well, how many half-squares are there in this figure [*DBMN*]?

SLAVE: Four.

SOCRATES: And how many are there in this figure here [*ABCD*]?

SLAVE: Two.

SOCRATES: And 4 is what in relation to 2?

SLAVE: Double.

SOCRATES: So how many square feet is this one [*DBMN*]?

b SLAVE: Eight.

SOCRATES: Which line produces it?

SLAVE: This one [*DB*].

SOCRATES: The one that runs from one corner to another of the square whose area is four square feet?

SLAVE: Yes.

SOCRATES: The technical term for this line is a 'diagonal', so— making use of this term 'diagonal'—what you're saying, boy, is that it is the diagonal that will produce the double-sized figure we were after.

SLAVE: Absolutely, Socrates.

SOCRATES: What do you think, Meno? Did he come up with any reply that was not his own opinion?

c MENO: No, they were all his own.

SOCRATES: But, as we said a short while ago, he didn't *know* the answer.

MENO: That's right.

SOCRATES: But these views of his were inside him, weren't they?

MENO: Yes.

SOCRATES: So someone who doesn't know about whatever it is

that he doesn't know has true beliefs inside him about these things that he doesn't know.

MENO: So it seems.

SOCRATES: At the moment, these beliefs have only just been stirred up in him and it all feels like a dream, but if he were to be repeatedly asked the same questions in a number of different ways,* he'd certainly end up with knowledge of these matters that is as good and as accurate as anyone's.　　　d

MENO: I suppose so.

SOCRATES: And it won't be as a result of any teaching that he'll have become knowledgeable: he'll just have been asked questions, and he'll recover the knowledge by himself, from within himself.

MENO: Yes.

SOCRATES: And recovering knowledge from within oneself is the same as recollection, isn't it?

MENO: Yes.

SOCRATES: And isn't the case either that at some point he acquired the knowledge he now has,* or that he always had it?

MENO: Yes.

SOCRATES: If he always had it, there's never been a time when he wasn't knowledgeable, and if he acquired it at some point, he couldn't have done so in *this* lifetime—unless you tell me that someone has taught him geometry. After all, he'll do the same　e for any aspect of geometry, and for all other subjects too.* So has anyone taught him every subject there is? You should know, I suppose, especially since he was born and bred in your household.

MENO: Yes, I do know—and what I know is that he's never had a teacher.

SOCRATES: But he does have these opinions, doesn't he?

MENO: It looks as though we have to say so, Socrates.

SOCRATES: But if he didn't acquire them in this lifetime, then it immediately follows that he had already learnt them and gained　86a them at some other time.

MENO: Apparently so.

SOCRATES: And this other time must be when he wasn't a human being, mustn't it?

MENO: Yes.

SOCRATES: So if during both periods of time—both when he is and when he isn't a human being—there are true beliefs inside him which are awoken by questioning and become pieces of knowledge, doesn't it follow that his soul will have been in a state of knowledge for all time?* After all, throughout the whole of time he clearly either is or is not a human being.

MENO: I suppose you're right.

b SOCRATES: So if the truth of things is always in our souls, the soul must be immortal, and this means that if there's something you happen not to know at the moment—which is to say, something you happen not to remember at the moment—you can confidently try to search for it and recall it. Yes?

MENO: I can't quite explain it, Socrates, but I think you're right.

SOCRATES: Yes, I think so too, Meno. I wouldn't support every aspect of the argument with particular vigour,* but there's one proposition that I'd defend to the death, if I could, by argument and by action: that as long as we think we should search for what we don't know we'll be better people—less faint-hearted and less lazy—than if we were to think that we had no

c chance of discovering what we don't know and that there's no point in even searching for it.*

MENO: I think you're right about this too, Socrates.

SOCRATES: Well, since we're in agreement on the importance of undertaking a search in cases of ignorance, shall we combine forces and try to find out what excellence is?

MENO: By all means. However, Socrates, above all I'd like to consider and hear what you have to say on the issue I raised right at the beginning. That is, as we attempt to find out what excellence is, are we taking it to be something teachable or a

d natural endowment?* And if not, how do people come to have excellence?

SOCRATES: Well, Meno, if I could regulate not just myself, but you too, we wouldn't investigate whether or not excellence is teachable until we'd first looked into the question of what it is in itself. But since you're not even trying to regulate yourself—because you want to preserve your status as a free man, I suppose—and since you're trying, successfully, to tell me what to

do, I'll give in to you. What else can I do? And so it seems that
we've got to consider what sort of thing excellence is before we e
know what it is. But please relax your control of me just a little,
at least, and let us get away with making use of an assumption,
as we consider whether it's teachable or whatever.

What do I mean by 'making use of an assumption'? Think of
how geometricians often go about their investigations. When
someone asks them a question about an area, perhaps—
whether a given area can be inscribed as a triangle inside a
given circle—a typical geometrician's reply might be: 'I don't 87a
yet know whether this is the sort of area that can do that, but I
think I can come up with an assumption, so to speak, which
will prove useful in this context. If this figure is such that,
when placed alongside its given line, the shortfall is a figure
similar to the original figure that was placed alongside the line,
then I think we will get one result, whereas if it is such that this
cannot happen, we'll get a different result. So if I can make an
assumption, I'm prepared to tell you what follows, in terms of b
whether or not it's possible, for inscribing the area inside a
circle.'*

We should do the same where excellence is concerned. Since
we don't know what it is or what sort of thing it is, let's look
into the question of whether or not it's teachable by making the
following assumption: what *sort* of mental quality would it have
to be for it to be or not to be teachable? Above all, we should ask
whether or not it's teachable (or recollectable, as we were saying
just now, but let's not argue over which term to use*)—so let's
ask whether it's teachable if it's *different* from knowledge or if c
it's *similar* to knowledge. But perhaps it's perfectly clear that no
one is taught anything except knowledge.

MENO: I think that's right.

SOCRATES: So if excellence is a kind of knowledge, it evidently
follows that it will be teachable.

MENO: Of course.

SOCRATES: It didn't take us long, then, to dispose of the question
of what kind of thing excellence must be if it is to be or not to
be teachable.

MENO: Yes.

SOCRATES: Next, I suppose, we should consider whether excellence is knowledge or is different from knowledge.

d MENO: Yes, I agree: that's the next point to look into.

SOCRATES: All right, then. Well, we say that it—excellence, I mean—is good, surely, don't we? That's a stable assumption for us, that it's good, isn't it?

MENO: Certainly.

SOCRATES: Now, if there's something else that is also good,† while having nothing to do with knowledge, the possibility remains that excellence might not be a kind of knowledge. But if there's nothing good that is not encompassed by knowledge, we'd be right to suspect that it is knowledge of some kind.*

MENO: True.

SOCRATES: Now, it's excellence that makes us good, isn't it?

e MENO: Yes.

SOCRATES: And if we're good, we do good, because that's what everything good does. Do you agree?

MENO: Yes.

SOCRATES: Excellence does good as well, then?

MENO: That necessarily follows from the premises we've agreed.

SOCRATES: So let's consider what kinds of things do us good, taking them one by one. We say that health does us good, and strength and good looks—and wealth, of course. We say that these things and others like them are good for us, don't we?

88a MENO: Yes.

SOCRATES: But we also say that these same things sometimes actually harm us. Or don't you agree with this?

MENO: No,† I agree.

SOCRATES: Let's ask ourselves, then, what it is that has to guide us in the case of each of these things for them to do us good, and what it is that guides us when they do us harm. Won't they do us good when guided by correct use and harm otherwise?

MENO: Yes.

SOCRATES: Well, let's go on to consider mental qualities. You acknowledge the existence of the qualities called 'self-control', 'justice', 'courage', 'cleverness', 'memory', 'nobility', and so on and so forth, don't you?

b MENO: Yes, I do.

SOCRATES: Now, among these qualities, take those that you think aren't knowledge—those that are different from knowledge—and let me ask you whether they're sometimes harmful and sometimes beneficial. Take courage, for instance, when it isn't wisdom but is something like recklessness. Isn't it the case that unintelligent recklessness harms people, while intelligent boldness does them good?

MENO: Yes.

SOCRATES: And does the same go for self-control and cleverness? Are intelligent learning and training beneficial, while unintelligent learning and training are harmful?

MENO: Most definitely.

SOCRATES: In short, then, mental endeavour and persistence c always end in happiness when they are guided by knowledge, but in the opposite if they are guided by ignorance.

MENO: So it seems.

SOCRATES: It follows that, if excellence is a mental quality and is necessarily beneficial, it must be knowledge, since no mental quality is in itself either beneficial or harmful, but it takes the presence of knowledge or ignorance to make it beneficial or d harmful. If this is right, then, excellence must be a kind of knowledge, just because it does us good.

MENO: Yes, I agree.

SOCRATES: Doesn't the same go for all the other things—wealth and so on—that we said just now may be good or harmful? Basically, we found that, when knowledge guides the soul, mental qualities become beneficial, and when ignorance guides them, they become harmful. Isn't it the same for wealth and so on too? When the soul makes correct use of e them and guides them correctly, they become harmful, and vice versa?

MENO: Yes.

SOCRATES: And isn't it a knowledgeable soul that offers correct guidance and an ignorant soul that leads us astray?

MENO: That's right.

SOCRATES: So we can state as universal principles that for a human being everything else depends on the soul and that the faculties of the soul itself depend on knowledge for their

89a goodness. And it follows from this that what does us good is knowledge. But didn't we say that excellence does us good?

MENO: Yes, we did.

SOCRATES: So we're saying that excellence is knowledge—either the whole of knowledge or some part of it—aren't we?

MENO: I'm sure these ideas are right, Socrates.

SOCRATES: And if this is so, excellence cannot be a natural endowment.

MENO: No, I think not.

b SOCRATES: There's another point to take into consideration too: if excellence were a natural endowment, I imagine that we'd have people who could tell which of our young men were naturally good, and that once they'd pointed them out to us, we'd seize these young men and keep them in secure quarters on the Acropolis. We'd seal them up much more carefully than our gold,* to stop them being corrupted and to make sure that when they reached adulthood they could serve the city well.

MENO: Yes, that certainly makes sense, Socrates.

SOCRATES: But since the excellence of good people isn't a natural

c endowment, it must be a result of education, mustn't it?

MENO: I think that conclusion is now inevitable. It also clearly follows from our assumption, Socrates, that if excellence is knowledge it must be teachable.

SOCRATES: Perhaps so, by Zeus. But perhaps we weren't right to agree to this.†

MENO: But we *thought* it was right a moment ago.

SOCRATES: But if the idea has any validity, we should presumably think it right not just a moment ago, but also now and in the future.

d MENO: What's going on? What consideration has made you unhappy with the idea? Why are you doubting whether excellence is knowledge?

SOCRATES: I'll tell you, Meno. I'm not taking back my commitment to the correctness of the view that if excellence is knowledge it's teachable, but see if you think I have good grounds for doubting that in fact it *is* knowledge. Tell me this: if anything (not just excellence) is teachable, mustn't there be both teachers and students of the subject?

MENO: I'd say so, yes.

SOCRATES: And conversely, wouldn't we be right to suppose that e something which has neither teachers nor students isn't teachable?*

MENO: True—but don't you think there are teachers of excellence?

[*Anytus enters the gymnasium and sits down next to Meno and Socrates*

SOCRATES: Well, I've often tried to see if there are any teachers of excellence, but despite my best efforts I've failed to find any, even though I enlist the support of a lot of other people for my enquiries, and especially those whom I take to be the greatest experts in the matter. In fact, Meno, Anytus has sat down here next to us at just the right time: let's get him to help us in our enquiry. It makes sense for us to do so, not least because Anytus 90a here is the son of a clever and wealthy father, Anthemion. Now, Anthemion became rich not by accident—not as a result of a gift, that is, which is how Ismenias of Thebes recently gained Polycrates' money*—but thanks to his own skill and care; moreover, he was generally held to be essentially a decorous and well-behaved member of his community, not overbearing or offensively authoritarian, and in addition he did a good job of raising and educating his son—or so the Athenian people b think, to judge by the fact that they elect Anytus to the most important posts. So Anytus is typical of the kind of person with whom one ought to try to see whether or not there are any teachers of excellence, and if so who they are.

So, Anytus, do please join us—your guest-friend Meno here and me—as we try to find out who the teachers of this subject might be. And here's a question for you. If we wanted your friend here to become a good healer, where would we send him for his education? We'd send him to the healers, wouldn't we? c

ANYTUS: Yes.

SOCRATES: And if we wanted to turn him into a good cobbler, we'd send him to the cobblers, wouldn't we?

ANYTUS: Yes.

SOCRATES: And the same goes for all other cases?

ANYTUS: That's right.

SOCRATES: Let's just go back over the same instances. What we're saying is that sending him to the healers would be the right thing to do if we wanted him to become a healer. Now, when we say this, are we saying that, if we're sensible, we'd send him to those who lay claim to this skill, rather than to those who don't, and to those who are paid for doing exactly this and declare themselves willing to teach anyone who wants to go and study with them? Are these the factors we should take into consideration to help us send him to the right people?

ANYTUS: Yes.

SOCRATES: And does the same go for learning to play the pipes and so on? If we want to get someone to learn the pipes, it's extremely stupid to refuse to send him to those who undertake to teach the technique and who charge for it, and instead to trouble others, so that the prospective student sets out to learn from people who don't claim to be teachers of this subject and who also haven't got a single student in the subject which we expect whoever we send to learn from them. Doesn't that strike you as the height of stupidity?

ANYTUS: Yes, by Zeus, it does. It's a sign of great ignorance too.

SOCRATES: You're right. Well, here's your chance to join me in deliberating about your guest-friend Meno here. You see, Anytus, he's been telling me for a while now that he'd like to gain this skill, the excellence which enables people to manage their households and their communities well, to care for their parents, and to know how to deal as a good man should with fellow citizens and with foreigners on their arrival and departure. What do you think? Where should we send him to learn this excellence? But perhaps it's obvious, if we keep to what we were saying a moment ago, that we should send him to those who undertake to teach excellence and who declare their availability for any Greek who wants to learn from them, as long as he pays the ordained fee they charge. Yes?

ANYTUS: And who are these people, Socrates?

SOCRATES: I'm sure you know as well as I do that they are those who are generally called 'Sophists'.*

ANYTUS: By Heracles, Socrates, watch what you say! I pray that

all my relatives and friends, from here or elsewhere, may avoid
the kind of insane fit that would make them go and be damaged
by these Sophists. I mean, it's plain to see that Sophists do
nothing but corrupt and harm those who associate with them.

SOCRATES: What do you mean, Anytus? Is it really the case that
the Sophists are so uniquely different from all those who claim
to know how to do people some good or other, that not only do
they not benefit whatever is entrusted to them, as all the rest
do, but they even do the opposite and corrupt them? And they d
make no secret of the fact that they expect to get paid for this?*
I can't believe what you're saying. I mean, I know of one man,
Protagoras, who earned more money from this branch of wisdom than not just Pheidias (the creator of such conspicuously
beautiful works of art), but ten other sculptors too. What
you're saying is extraordinary. If people who mend old shoes
and repair clothes tried to conceal the fact that they were
returning those items in a worse condition than they received
them, they wouldn't last thirty days before being found out; if e
they behaved like that, they'd soon starve to death. And yet
you're saying that Protagoras took in the whole of Greece: he
was corrupting those who associate with him and sending them
back home in a worse condition than when he took them on,
and no one noticed for . . . well, it must have been more than
forty years, because I think he was getting on for 70 when he
died, and so he'd been engaged in his profession for forty years.
And you're saying that Protagoras took everyone in for that
long—right up to the present day, in fact, because his good
reputation has not yet been dented.* Actually, it's not just
Protagoras, because there are a great many others too, some 92a
born earlier than him and some still alive today. Are we really to
go along with your suggestion and say that they are knowingly
deceiving and damaging their young associates, or that they
haven't realized themselves what they're doing? Some people
regard them as the wisest men on earth, but if you're right we
shall have to count them as insane.

ANYTUS: They're not insane in the slightest, Socrates. The
young men who pay their fees are far more insane—but even
they are not as crazy as their relatives who let them do so, and b

then the most insane of all are the citizens of the communities the Sophists visit, who let them in when they arrive and fail to banish anyone, whether he's a foreigner or a fellow citizen, who tries to do what they do.

SOCRATES: Has one of the Sophists done you wrong, Anytus? Why are you so hostile towards them?*

ANYTUS: By Zeus, no, I've never had anything to do with any of them, and I wouldn't let anyone close to me study with them either.

SOCRATES: So you have absolutely no experience of these men?

ANYTUS: A situation that I hope will continue.

c SOCRATES: Then how on earth, Anytus, could you know what's good and what's worthless about the enterprise, when you have no experience of it at all?*

ANYTUS: Easily! At any rate, it doesn't make any difference whether or not I have personal experience of them: I know what they're like.

SOCRATES: Perhaps you're a diviner, Anytus, for your own words make it extremely difficult for me to see how else you could know about these people. But the point of our enquiry was not

d to find to whom we could send Meno to make him bad—let it be the Sophists, if you like. No, do please tell us—and you'll be doing your family friend here a favour—to whom in this great city of ours he could go to become distinguished for the kind of excellence I outlined a short while ago.*

ANYTUS: Tell him yourself, why don't you?

SOCRATES: Actually, I did name those who I *thought* were teachers in this field, but I was wrong, according to you. And

e you may be right, but now it's your turn: give us the name of any Athenian you think he could go to.

ANYTUS: Why should I tell him the name of any particular individual? Any decent Athenian gentleman he comes across will do a better job of improving him than the Sophists, as long as he's prepared to do as they say.

SOCRATES: Did these decent gentlemen become decent and gentlemanly by accident? If so, are they still capable, without having had teachers, of teaching other people things which

93a they themselves never learnt?

ANYTUS: Personally, I expect that they too learnt from the previous generation of decent gentlemen. Don't you think there have been plenty of good men in this city of ours?

SOCRATES: Well, to tell you the truth, Anytus, I do think we've got men here who are good at politics,* and I imagine there have been as many of them in the past as there are now. But the question before us at the moment is whether they've also proved to be good teachers of their own excellence. We're not asking whether or not there are good men here now, nor whether there have been any in the past, but we've been trying for a while now to find out whether excellence is teachable. As b part of this enquiry we're also asking whether the good men of present or past generations knew how to transmit their own excellence to anyone else, or whether excellence is not the kind of thing that can be transmitted to someone else or received by anyone from anyone else. This is what Meno and I have been looking into for quite a while. Anyway, look at it this way, taking your own ideas as a starting-point: would you say that Themistocles was a good man? c

ANYTUS: Yes, he was exceptionally good.

SOCRATES: So do you also think that he, if anyone, was a good teacher of his excellence?

ANYTUS: Yes, I'd say he was, if he wanted to be.

SOCRATES: Well, don't you think he'd have wanted others to become decent gentlemen, and especially his own son? Or do you think he was too mean, and deliberately kept his own particular brand of excellence to himself? Haven't you heard that d Themistocles had his son taught to be a good horseman, at least, in the sense that he could keep an upright seat on horses, could throw a javelin from horseback while remaining upright,* and could perform a lot of other amazing feats? In other words, Themistocles provided him with the kind of training that made him good at everything that depended on good teachers. Haven't you heard elderly men telling this story?

ANYTUS: Yes, I have.

SOCRATES: So in respect of natural ability, no one could charge his son with being bad.

ANYTUS: Presumably not. e

SOCRATES: But have you ever in the past heard from anyone, elderly or not, that Themistocles' son Cleophantus turned out to be good at the same things his father was good at, and had the same skills?

ANYTUS: No, certainly not.*

SOCRATES: Are we to suppose, then, that Themistocles was happy to have his son educated in certain respects, but wasn't prepared to make him better than any of his neighbours at his own particular skill—that is, *if* excellence is teachable?

ANYTUS: By Zeus, perhaps he wasn't!

SOCRATES: So that's the kind of teacher of excellence Themistocles was—and according to you he was one of the best men of times past! But let's look at someone else, then: Aristeides the son of Lysimachus—unless you don't agree that he was a good man.

ANYTUS: No, of course I think he was, without any doubt.

SOCRATES: Now, although he too had his son Lysimachus educated better than anyone else in Athens in all the subjects that depend on teachers, do you think he's made him a *better* man than anyone else? I imagine that you've met him and can see what he's like. Or, if you like, let's take Pericles, a man of stupendous wisdom. You know that he raised two sons, Paralus and Xanthippus, don't you?

ANYTUS: Yes.

SOCRATES: And, as you know, he taught them to be among the best horsemen in Athens and trained them to be as good as anyone at everything that depends on skill, such as music and sports. Does it look as though he didn't want them to be good men? I think he wanted them to be good, but it's just that it may not be teachable. I don't want you to suppose that it's just a few Athenians who've found this business beyond them, who you might then judge simply to be particularly incompetent, so take Thucydides too. He raised two sons, Melesias and Stephanus, and trained them well in everything, but especially in wrestling, for which he entrusted one of them to Xanthias and the other to Eudorus, the acknowledged best wrestlers of their generation. Do you remember?

ANYTUS: Yes, I've been told about that.

SOCRATES: Well, can't we safely assume that, if it were teachable, he'd never have failed to teach his sons how to be good men, which wouldn't have cost him anything, while having d them taught those subjects where the teaching was bound to cost him money? Unless, perhaps, Thucydides was incompetent, and didn't have very large numbers of loyal friends both here in Athens and among the allies abroad?* He also came from an important family and wielded a great deal of power both here in Athens and among the allies, and this means that if excellence were teachable, he'd have found someone—a local resident or someone from abroad—to make his sons good people, if he himself was too busy looking after the city's e affairs.* So you see, Anytus, it may be that it just isn't teachable.

ANYTUS: You don't seem to have any qualms about running people down, Socrates. If you want my advice, I'd recommend caution. You should appreciate that, as easy† as it may be to do people harm or good elsewhere, here in Athens it's particularly easy. But I think you're already aware of this. 95a

[Anytus departs in a huff, but stays within sight in the gymnasium

SOCRATES: It looks as though Anytus is angry,* Meno, but that's hardly surprising: in the first place, he thinks that I'm speaking ill of these men and, second, he counts himself as one of them. If he ever comes to realize what it is to speak badly of someone, he'll stop being angry, but he lacks that insight at the moment. But tell me, Meno, don't you have good and decent men in Thessaly?

MENO: Certainly.

SOCRATES: Well, then, are they prepared to take on the education b of the younger generation? Do they agree that they are teachers and that excellence is teachable?

MENO: No, by Zeus, Socrates, they don't. Sometimes you'd find them assuming that it's teachable and sometimes that it isn't.

SOCRATES: So can we call them teachers of this business, when they don't agree even about this?

MENO: No, I don't think so, Socrates.

SOCRATES: What about these Sophists, then, who are the only ones who claim to teach excellence? Do you think they really can?

c MENO: Actually, Socrates, one of the things I particularly admire about Gorgias is that you'd never hear him making any such promise. In fact, he used to laugh at his peers when he heard them offering to teach excellence. His intention, by contrast, was to make people good speakers.

SOCRATES: According to you too, then, the Sophists aren't teachers of excellence?

MENO: I can't really say, Socrates. My position is the same as most people's: sometimes I think they are, and sometimes that they aren't.

SOCRATES: You know, don't you, that it's not only you and politicians in general who vacillate about whether or not it's teach-
d able? Are you aware that the poet Theognis also says exactly the same?

MENO: Where?

SOCRATES: In his elegies, where he says:*

> Drink and eat with the high and mighty,
> Sit with them, make them like you.
> For from good company you will learn good things,
e > While the bad will rob you even of the wits you had.

You realize that in these lines he's assuming that excellence is teachable, don't you?

MENO: It looks that way.

SOCRATES: Elsewhere, however, he changed his mind a bit.

> If wits could be made and implanted in a man,

he says, and then goes on, I think, to say of those who could do this:

> Full many a time would they reap handsome rewards,

and:

> Never would a bad son be born to a good father,
96a > As long as he hearkened to words of wisdom.
> But never by teaching will you make a bad man good.

136

Do you see that he's saying something quite different here, even though the issue is the same?*

MENO: It looks as though he is.

SOCRATES: Can you think of any other matter, then, where those who claim to be teachers not only are not acknowledged as teachers of others, but aren't even accepted as experts in their field—where, in fact, they're agreed to be no good at the very matter they claim to teach—and where b those who are acknowledged as good and decent people vacillate on whether or not it is teachable† . . . can you say that people who are so confused on any subject are, strictly speaking, teachers at all?

MENO: By Zeus, no, I can't.

SOCRATES: Now, if neither the Sophists nor the good and decent gentlemen themselves are teachers of this matter, there can't be any others, can there?

MENO: I don't think so.

SOCRATES: And if there aren't any teachers, there aren't any c students either?

MENO: I think you're right.

SOCRATES: But didn't we agree* that any matter for which there are no teachers and no students is not in fact teachable?

MENO: We did.

SOCRATES: And we haven't found any teachers of excellence anywhere?

MENO: True.

SOCRATES: And no teachers means no students?

MENO: I suppose so.

SOCRATES: It follows, then, that excellence cannot be teachable.

MENO: Apparently not, if we've gone about the enquiry cor- d rectly. And all this makes me really wonder, Socrates, whether there might not be any good men at all, or at least, if there are any good men, how they come to be good.

SOCRATES: It rather looks, Meno, as though you and I are incompetent and were inadequately educated by Gorgias, in your case, and Prodicus in mine.* So we'd better focus on ourselves and try to find someone to somehow make us better people. The reason I say this is because, looking back over our e recent enquiry, it's clear that we made fools of ourselves in not realizing that success and effectiveness in human affairs do *not* depend only on the guidance of knowledge. This is presumably also why we've found recognizing how good men become good so elusive.

MENO: What do you mean, Socrates?

SOCRATES: This is what I'm getting at. We were surely right to agree* that good men are absolutely bound to do good, weren't we?

MENO: Yes.

SOCRATES: And I suppose we were also right to agree that they'll do us good if they guide our affairs well. Yes?

MENO: Yes.

SOCRATES: But it looks as though we were wrong to agree that good guidance is impossible without knowledge.

MENO: What do you mean?

SOCRATES: I'll tell you. If someone who knows† the road to Larisa (or anywhere else you like) walks there and shows others the way, he'd be giving good and beneficial guidance, wouldn't he?

MENO: Yes.

SOCRATES: Well, what about someone who *thinks* he knows the way, and is right, but has never travelled the road and so doesn't *know* it?* Wouldn't he too be a good guide?

MENO: Yes.

SOCRATES: And as long as he correctly believes what the other person knows, he'll be just as good a guide as the one with knowledge, because his thinking is correct, even though he doesn't have knowledge.

MENO: Yes, he'll be just as good.

SOCRATES: True belief, then, is just as good a guide as knowledge, when it comes to guaranteeing correctness of action. This is what we were overlooking before, during our enquiry into the nature of excellence, when we were saying that knowledge is the *only* good guide of our actions. In fact, though, there's true belief as well.

MENO: Yes, apparently so.

SOCRATES: So true belief is just as useful as knowledge.

MENO: Yes, except with this qualification, Socrates, that a person with knowledge will always be successful, whereas one with true belief will sometimes be right and sometimes wrong.

SOCRATES: What do you mean? Won't someone with true belief always be right, as long as his beliefs are true?

MENO: I suppose he's bound to be. All this is making me wonder, Socrates, why, if this is so, knowledge is so much more highly d valued than true belief* and on what grounds one can distinguish between them.

SOCRATES: Well, do you know why this is puzzling you, or shall I tell you?

MENO: Tell me, please.

SOCRATES: Because you haven't paid attention to Daedalus' statues. Perhaps there aren't any in Thessaly.*

MENO: What are you getting at?

SOCRATES: The fact that his statues too must be anchored, or else they run away and escape. They stay put only if they're anchored.

MENO: What of it? e

SOCRATES: There's as little point in paying a lot of money for an unrestrained statue of his as there is for a runaway slave: it doesn't stay put. But Daedalus' pieces are so beautiful that they're worth a great deal if they're anchored. What am I getting at? I mean this to be an analogy for true beliefs. As long as they stay put, true beliefs too constitute a thing of beauty and do nothing but good. The problem is that they tend not to stay 98a for long; they escape from the human soul and this reduces their value, unless they're anchored by working out the reason.* And this anchoring is recollection, Meno, my friend, as we agreed earlier.* When true beliefs are anchored, they become pieces of knowledge and they become stable. That's why knowledge is more valuable than true belief, and the difference between the two is that knowledge has been anchored.

MENO: By Zeus, Socrates, that sounds very plausible.

SOCRATES: I'm not speaking from a position of knowledge, b though; it's just what seems plausible. But I certainly don't think the distinction between knowledge and true belief is just a plausible inference. There's not a lot I'd say I know, but I'd certainly say it about this; I'd count this as one of the things I know.

MENO: Yes, and you're right, Socrates.

SOCRATES: So isn't it right to say that the guidance of true belief produces results, whatever the activity, which are no worse than those of knowledge?

MENO: Yes, I think you're right on this too.

c SOCRATES: For all practical purposes, then, true belief will do us just as much good as knowledge and be no less beneficial than knowledge, and armed with true belief a man will do just as much good as anyone with knowledge.

MENO: True.

SOCRATES: And we've agreed that a good man does good.

MENO: Yes.

SOCRATES: So knowledge isn't the only thing that makes men good and enables them (if there are any such men) to do their communities good: true belief does this too. However, neither

d of them—neither knowledge nor true belief, nor in fact anything that is an acquisition—is a natural human endowment. You don't think that either of them is a natural endowment, do you?

MENO: No, I don't.

SOCRATES: Now, since they aren't natural endowments, the goodness of good people can't be a natural endowment either.

MENO: No indeed.

SOCRATES: And since goodness isn't a natural endowment, the next thing we considered was whether it's teachable.

MENO: Yes.

SOCRATES: And didn't we decide that excellence is teachable if it's knowledge?

MENO: Yes.

SOCRATES: And also that if it were teachable, it would be knowledge?

MENO: Yes.

e SOCRATES: And also that if there were teachers of it, it would be teachable, but not if there weren't?

MENO: That's right.

SOCRATES: Well, haven't we agreed that there are no teachers of it?

MENO: True.

SOCRATES: Haven't we therefore agreed that excellence isn't teachable and that it isn't knowledge either?

MENO: Yes.

SOCRATES: But we agree that it's good, don't we?

MENO: Yes.

SOCRATES: And that good guidance is something beneficial and good?

MENO: Yes.

SOCRATES: And that only these two things, true belief and know- 99a ledge, offer good guidance? It's only when a man has one or the other of these that he can guide others well. Things may sometimes just happen to turn out right by chance, but that doesn't involve any human guidance; when a human being is the one offering guidance towards some appropriate goal, it's always these two things, true belief and knowledge, that are doing the guiding.

MENO: I think this is right.

SOCRATES: Now, since excellence isn't teachable, we can no longer say that it's due to knowledge,† can we?

MENO: I suppose not.

SOCRATES: Of the two things that are good and beneficial, then, b one has been eliminated: it cannot be knowledge that guides us in political action.

MENO: I agree.

SOCRATES: So when politicians such as Themistocles and the ones Anytus here mentioned not long ago guide their communities, they don't do so thanks to any special intellectual capacity and because they are wise. This also explains why they're incapable of getting others to take after themselves: it's because they don't owe their political abilities to knowledge.

MENO: It does look as though you're right, Socrates.

SOCRATES: If knowledge isn't responsible, the only remaining possibility is that it's sound belief. This is what politicians use c to steer their communities aright, since as far as knowledge is concerned they're in the same state as soothsayers and inspired diviners. I mean, these men too often speak the truth when they're possessed by some god, but they don't understand anything they say.*

MENO: It rather looks as though you're right.

SOCRATES: Therefore, Meno, shouldn't we really call these men 'inspired', because all the important work they accomplish by their actions and their words gets done despite the fact that they have no knowledge?*

MENO: Yes.

SOCRATES: So we'd be right not just to use the term 'inspired' for the soothsayers and diviners we mentioned a moment ago, and for all poets, but also to say that politicians are at least as inspired and possessed as them. When they raise important issues in their speeches and see them through to a successful conclusion, despite not understanding anything they say, they're inspired: they've been taken over by the gods.

MENO: Yes.

SOCRATES: Yes, and as you know, Meno, women do use the term 'divine' to describe good men, and when the Spartans praise someone for his goodness they too say, 'He's a divine man.'†

e MENO: Yes, and it looks as though they're right, Socrates— though Anytus here may not like what you're saying.*

SOCRATES: That doesn't bother me; we'll talk things over with him later, Meno. For the time being, however, if our enquiry has gone well and we've been right in what we've been saying throughout our discussion, excellence cannot be a natural endowment and cannot be teachable either. No, the excellence of good people comes to them as a dispensation awarded by the gods, without any knowledge—short of there being a politician with the ability to make someone else an expert politician too. If there were such a person, pretty much the same description could be given of him here among the living as Homer gives of Teiresias among the dead, when he says that of those in the underworld 'he alone still has wisdom, while the rest dart around like shadows'.* In the same way, here in the upper world, such a man would be, where excellence was concerned, a piece of concrete reality, so to speak, compared to shadows.

b MENO: I think you're absolutely right, Socrates.

SOCRATES: So, Meno, our argument has led us to suppose that the excellence of good people comes to them as a dispensation awarded by the gods. We'll confirm this, however, only by undertaking an enquiry into what excellence is in itself before asking how men come to get it.* But now I've got to be elsewhere, and it's up to you to try to win your guest-friend Anytus here over to the point of view of which you've become convinced, so that he'll be more even-tempered. After all, if you do manage to convince him, you'll be doing the people of c Athens a favour too.

EXPLANATORY NOTES

See also the Index of Names (pp. 186–90) for information on characters appearing or mentioned in the dialogues.

CHARMIDES

153a *addressing an unnamed friend*: the few 'stage directions' that occur in the translations are my own editorial insertions.

153a *Potidaea*: this allows us to pinpoint the dramatic date of the dialogue with more precision than usual. The Athenian campaign against the town of Potidaea (in northern Greece, on the Chalcidice peninsula) lasted from 432 to 430. Socrates' presence there is also attested by Plato at *Symposium* 219e–220e. Comparison of the accounts and time indications in *Charmides* and *Symposium* suggests that Socrates spent quite a long time up north, and returned to Athens in the early summer of 429 (C. Planeaux, 'Socrates, Alcibiades, and Plato's τὰ Ποτειδεατικά. Does the *Charmides* Have an Historical Setting?', *Mnemosyne*, 52 (1999), 72–7).

153a *the shrine of the Queen*: the shrine lay to the south of the Acropolis, but we do not know exactly where. The 'Queen' worshipped there was apparently the personification of ancient Athenian royalty, but the cult is obscure.

153c *I was*: Socrates was of hoplite status, rather than being wealthy enough to serve in the cavalry, as most of his aristocratic friends would have.

153d *in the field of education*: Socrates' calmness contrasts with the understandable frenzy of interest in the war, which was new at the time and whose major front was in the north, where Socrates had been serving. The contrast perhaps hints at Socrates' self-control, and shows how different his values were from those of his contemporaries. For similar speculations, based largely on the artistry of the dialogue, see especially Schmid, *Plato's Charmides*; on the prologue in particular, see M. McAvoy, 'Carnal Knowledge in the *Charmides*', in E. Benitez (ed.), *Dialogues with Plato* (Edmonton: Academic Printing & Publishing, 1996 = *Apeiron*, 29/4), 63–103, and especially M. McPherran, 'Socrates and Zalmoxis on Drugs, Charms and Purification', *Apeiron*, 37 (2004), 11–33.

154a *on his way here*: homoeroticism was an accepted feature of ancient Athenian life, and was not held to be perverted, against a standard of heteroeroticism as normal. It was acknowledged that at a certain phase of his development, between the onset of puberty and the time of beard-growth, a teenage boy was beautiful, or had a certain 'bloom', as the Greeks also put it. Such a boy would be pursued by admirers (usually older men, in their twenties, before the age of marriage), and would probably end by picking one of them as his lover. The sexual favours he was expected to give were largely limited to masturbation or intercourse between the thighs, rather than anal penetration. Lifelong partnerships were rare, and the sexual side of the relationship died down after a few years, in favour of friendship and, in particular, a form of mentorship for the boy: the older man helped to acculturate him into the ways of Athenian life, and to introduce him into the right political and social circles. It was, for this reason, largely an upper-class phenomenon in Athens. The essential book is K. J. Dover, *Greek Homosexuality* (London: Duckworth, 1978).

154b *a white line*: proverbial for someone incapable of discrimination or otherwise useless. Ancient Greek builders coloured a piece of string with red ochre, stretched it tight, and then twanged it down on to the marble to make a good, straight line to follow as they cut. White chalk, however, would not show up on the marble, and so a 'white line' was no help at all.

154c *his height as well as his beauty*: the ancient Greeks found height attractive in both men and women. The average height for men was about 168 centimetres (5 feet, 6 inches), for women about 155 centimetres (a little over 5 feet).

154c *as if he were a statue*: apparently a Greek idiom for being thunderstruck by love: see also Plato, *Phaedrus* 251a.

154d *if he can be induced to strip*: that is, to join in the wrestling taking place at the school. All sports were practised naked, and the gymnasia and wrestling-grounds were notoriously places where men came to watch the boys exercise naked and to eye up the talent. The sixth-century poet Theognis of Megara was probably not being too outrageous when he claimed: 'Happy is the lover who exercises in the gymnasium and then goes home to spend the rest of the day in bed with a beautiful boy' (1335–6).

154d *By Heracles*: the mighty Heracles was, naturally, one of the guardian deities of Greek sports. The others were Eros, the god of love or, more literally, sexual passion, and Hermes for communication: the gymnasia were always places where those with the time to do so would meet, make conversation, and admire the young men at their training—just as Socrates and his friends are doing here. But though Socrates was undoubtedly attracted towards boys like Charmides, and although they found him attractive too (for his mind, at any rate—he was not good-looking), he turned the dynamics of such a situation towards educational purposes: see especially Plato, *Symposium* 215a–219e.

154e *an attractive soul*: the Greek word for 'soul'—*psykhē*—is notoriously difficult to capture in modern English. Sometimes it certainly does mean 'soul', with enough of the metaphysical implications of the English word for that to be an accurate translation. But *psykhē* is also what receives and interprets sense-impressions, and has feelings, fancies, memories, thoughts, and so on, and is the agent of choice and action—all of which makes 'mind' a better translation in these contexts. Here 'character' would capture some of Socrates' point, but would overlook the fact that for Plato and Socrates your *psykhē* was your true self; on this, see especially L. P. Gerson, *Knowing Persons: A Study in Plato* (Oxford: Oxford University Press, 2003). In this volume, I have generally translated the word as 'soul', but I have used 'mental' as the corresponding adjective, since 'psychic' has some misleading connotations.

154e *strip this part of him too*: notice the assumption that to engage in conversation with Socrates is to bare one's soul (see also Plato, *Protagoras* 352a–b, *Theaetetus* 169b). This says something about the personally challenging, even caustic, nature of Socratic enquiry.

155a *his guardian as well as his cousin*: Charmides' father was already dead, and so Critias had become the boy's guardian. The frequency of early death, and the inability of women to inherit property under Athenian law, meant that it was common for fatherless children to be put in the care of a male guardian, who was usually a close relative. Although homoeroticism was accepted in Athens, it was improper for a teenager to behave in any way that might seem flirtatious (at bottom because this was considered to be slavish or feminine behaviour), and so a boy would be chaperoned by an adult, usually a slave, in such public situtations.

155b *pretending . . . you know a medicine for the head*: Socrates also uses false pretences to lure an interlocutor into discussion at *Lysis* 211d.

156c *cure the part along with the whole*: the 'good healers' just mentioned include Hippocrates, the founder of a more scientific approach to medicine, to whom Plato attributed the same notion at *Phaedrus* 270c.

157c *an unexpected piece of good fortune*: in Greek, literally 'a gift from Hermes': Hermes was the god of, among other things, prosperity and mystery. So coming across something unexpectedly was a gift from the god.

158d *I don't know what reply to give you*: Charmides' modesty is probably a front, since elsewhere he seems to be portrayed as immodest: he considers himself a good poet (154e), and we may assume that he likes all the flattering attention of his admirers (154c). We may also note that he has been suffering from morning headaches (155b); such headaches are generally caused either by excessive drinking the night before, or by oversleeping, neither of which are signs of a self-controlled character. These indications of conceit are important, because they bear on the question whether Plato intended the dialogue to convey any message about Socrates' influence on Charmides, who grew up to be a notorious oligarch. Charmides' deference to Critias (161b, 176c) is perhaps a hint that the moral influence Socrates may have exerted on the young man was interrupted or in some way stymied by Critias. For Socrates' alleged hostility towards Critias, see especially Xenophon, *Memoirs of Socrates* 1.2.

159c *isn't it?*: all the activities mentioned in the last few sentences are those encountered by an Athenian schoolboy at the various schools he attended (see the note on *Laches* 187c). They would still be fresh in Charmides' memory. They are, however, bizarre as counter-examples to Charmides' definition: for instance, it is not always better to play the lyre quickly; it depends on the pace of the music. Socrates is assuming that 'slowly' or 'unhurriedly' means 'hesitatingly' or 'laboriously'.

159c *the pankration*: pankration was similar to wrestling, except that, whereas in wrestling the loser was the one who lost his footing and ended up on the ground, in pankration the winner had to compel defeat rather than throwing his opponent, because in this event the contestants were allowed on the ground—and in fact were allowed to do almost anything. See M. B. Poliakoff, *Combat Sports in the Ancient World: Competition, Violence, and Culture* (New Haven: Yale University Press, 1987).

160b *a self-controlled life has to be admirable*: for reflections upon Socrates' rejection of this first definition of self-control, see L. A. Kosman, 'Charmides' First Definition: Sophrosyne as Quietness', in J. P. Anton and A. Preus (eds.), *Essays in Ancient Greek Philosophy*, vol. 2 (Albany: State University of New York Press, 1983), 203–16. The essential error of the argument is that if self-control is admirable, and if quick actions are admirable (though in fact the argument licenses the conclusion only that they *may* be more admirable than unhurried actions), it hardly follows that quick actions are more self-controlled: the fallacy is treating accidental properties (the admirableness of the properties in question) as essential properties.

161a *"Modesty ill suits a man in need"*: *Odyssey* 17.347, also quoted at *Laches* 201b. Socrates (and Charmides) take Homer's authority to be enough to undo his second definition, but Charmides could have replied by refusing to accept an old poet's authority.

162a *in these and similar situations*: clearly, Plato has Socrates miss the point, or he fails to allow Charmides properly to defend the definition. (Perhaps this is why Charmides admits that it is not his own definition: he has not thought it through enough to defend it.) After all, self-control applies to one's own behaviour, or to the internal state of mind that motivates or inhibits certain kinds of behaviour. Whether or not that behaviour has an effect on other people is a secondary issue. Moreover, it is very unfair to have Socrates describe the definition as obscure and 'enigmatic', when it is Socrates himself who has made it so, by interpreting it in a peculiar fashion. The tactic is designed to provoke Critias into joining the discussion in order to defend his view.

162e *all artisans make something*: the reference is to 161e, even though there Socrates used *making* things only as a example of the general rule that they *do* something. Socrates' shift from *doing* to *making* becomes pronounced in the next few sentences, and Critias is forced to distinguish the two verbs. In *Republic*, Plato shows himself to be perfectly happy with people *making* what pertains to others (e.g. a cobbler making shoes for others), but not with people *doing* what pertains to others (e.g. a cobbler making cheese for others).

163b *production was no disgrace*: *Works and Days* 311. However, Critias is already well on the way to distorting Hesiod's meaning, since Hesiod said: 'Work is no disgrace, but idleness is.' The rest of Critias' argument is riddled with false reasoning and snobbery. The snobbery is obvious (and typical of upper-class Greeks); the false reasoning lies essentially in the identification of 'doing' with 'producing'.

164b *both for himself and for the person he's curing*: the addition of 'for himself' is nonsense, of course: the benefit is the patient's, not the healer's.

164d *"Be well and happy"*: under the circumstances, I have to give a literal translation of the standard Greek greeting, *khaire*, though really, of course, it was as simple and straightforward as 'hello' (which is itself related etymologically to 'hail', meaning originally 'health'). The famous inscription, now lost, on the entrance to the temple at Delphi was 'Know yourself'. The god referred to is Apollo, to whom the sanctuary, oracular shrine, and monumental temple at Delphi were sacred.

165b *I don't have any knowledge myself*: the sincerity of this common claim by Plato's Socrates is hotly debated by scholars.

165d *its product was houses*: there is of course a slight disanalogy between healing and house-building in that the product of healing (health) is also what it is knowledge of, whereas the product of house-building (houses) is not what it is knowledge of, which is how to build houses.

But for the present argument Socrates needs only to argue that all branches of knowledge have products.

166b *what I was getting at, Socrates*: it is unclear why Critias does not just give a direct reply to Socrates' question. He could just say, 'Yes, self-control is knowledge of oneself, and this self is different from self-control itself.' Perhaps Plato fails to give him this straightforward response as a way of initiating the shift from self-control as knowledge of *oneself* to self-control as knowledge of *itself* (166c). The substitution is abrupt. The usual meaning of knowing oneself, as in the Delphic maxim (164d–165a), was knowing one's limitations, or knowing one's proper place in society or in relation to some wider force or forces; it was not usually taken as the kind of introspection which is just knowing what one knows. However, it is worth noting that at 167a knowledge of oneself is said to be equivalent to knowing what one does and what one does not know (which is an odd, but not entirely implausible substitution, provided that what consitutes one's self is taken to be the sum total of one's knowledge, and Critias says at the beginning of 170a that they are one and the same thing). The formulation 'knowledge of itself', then, is best taken as an awkward first stab at the definition of 167a: see also 169d–e. For more on the Socratic conception of the self, see J. Annas, 'Self-Knowledge in Early Plato', in D. J. O'Meara (ed.), *Platonic Investigations* (Washington, DC: Catholic University of America Press, 1985), 111–38. Additional bibliography on the relation between 'knowledge of oneself' and 'knowledge of itself' in *Charmides*: R. Wellman, 'The Question Posed at *Charmides* 165a–166c', *Phronesis*, 9 (1964), 107–13; R. McKim, 'Socratic Self-Knowledge and "Knowledge of Knowledge" in Plato's *Charmides*', *Transactions of the American Philological Association*, 115 (1985), 59–77; T. Tuozzo, 'Greetings from Apollo: *Charmides* 164c–165b, *Epistle III*, and the Structure of the *Charmides*', in the collection edited by Robinson and Brisson.

166c *you recently promised not to do*: this may refer to 165b–c; 161c is another possibility, but is perhaps too remote. The core of Critias' criticism is doubt about the Socratic analogy between the knowledge that is excellence and craft-knowledge; Plato, however, has Socrates continue to ignore Critias' point and make use of the analogy (at 170a–171c, for instance).

166e *knowledge of lack of knowledge*: it is a common Platonic assumption that one and the same branch of knowledge knows the opposites relevant to that branch of knowledge: see e.g. *Euthyphro* 5c–6e, *Phaedo* 97d, *Republic* 329d–e, 333e–334a. In any case, awareness of one's lack of knowledge is intuitively central to the *sōphrosynē*, which involves knowing one's limitations, and so it is natural for Socrates to introduce it in a discussion of *sōphrosynē*.

167a *and no one else will be capable of doing this*: the examination of others' claims to knowledge is exactly what Socrates undertook as his mission in life (according to Plato at *Apology* 21a–23c). If Plato now argues that knowledge of either one's own or others' knowledge and ignorance is impossible, is he casting doubt on Socrates' mission and/or on Socrates' self-control? Probably not: the conclusion of this stretch of argument is not refutation, but puzzlement (see 169b–c). Besides, even if Plato claims that it takes an expert to distinguish experts from frauds, this 'does not conflict with the claim that, even without moral expertise, Socrates can *identify* some of those who lack moral knowledge' (J. Gentzler, 'How to Distinguish between Experts and Frauds: Some Problems for Socratic Peirastic', *History of Philosophy Quarterly*, 12 (1995), 227–46, at 240). Others also dissolve the problem: G. R. Carone, 'Socrates' Human Wisdom and Sophrosyne in *Charmides* 164c ff.', *Ancient Philosophy*, 18 (1998), 267–86); T. F. Morris, 'Knowledge of Knowledge and of Lack of Knowledge in the *Charmides*', *International Studies in Philosophy*, 21 (1989), 49–61. Other views: Plato intends to refute the position which he recognizes to be that of Socrates in *Apology* (Kahn, *Plato and the Socratic Dialogue*, 197–203); Plato intends to refute only the possibility of recognizing knowledge in someone else while being ignorant oneself (H. H. Benson, 'A Note on Socratic Self-knowledge in the *Charmides*', *Ancient Philosophy*, 23 (2003), 31–47); Critias' views differ subtly from those of Socrates (V. Tsouna, 'Socrates' Attack on Intellectualism in the *Charmides*', in McPherran (ed.), 63–78).

167b *a third libation to Zeus the Saviour*: Zeus the Saviour was the deity traditionally offered the third libation during religious ceremonies such as symposia. The phrase means more or less 'Third time lucky'. Plato seems to be dividing Socrates' discussion with Critias as follows: the first part ended at 164c, the second at 165e, and the third is about to begin. However, as I understand the argument with Critias, these points do not mark major breaks in the discussion, such that each time Critias offers a new definition. Each idea he comes up with is a refinement of or attempt to explicate the definition of self-control as doing what pertains to oneself. Each refinement, however, takes us further away from the commonsensical approach to self-control exemplified by Charmides' first two attempts at a definition, and by Aristotle's discussion in *Nicomachean Ethics* 1117b–1119b.

167e *all other cases of wanting*: the distinction between 'desiring' and 'wanting' is important for Plato: we 'desire' pleasure and short-term satisfaction, but we 'want' only what is good for us; we desire means, but we want only ends (even if they turn out to be intermediate ends). See Plato, *Gorgias* 466a–468e. The distinction perhaps originated with Prodicus: see Plato, *Protagoras* 340a–b. But Plato pushes the distinction only when he feels the need; at other times (as, probably, at *Meno* 77b–78b), he uses the terms interchangeably.

167e *love of anything beautiful*: in *Symposium* Plato deepens this analysis of love: the object of love may be beauty, but the ultimate goal of love is the permanent possession of goodness.

168a *doesn't fear anything threatening at all*: actually, it does make some sense to think that a soldier might be afraid of being afraid. Perhaps this is why Plato is not so dogmatic at 169a; perhaps he is doing no more than arguing *ad hominem* against Critias, while expecting readers to pick up on the obvious disanalogies between the various cases of relativity he puts forward. The issue is this: some of Plato's counter-examples are truly reflexive, in the sense that it is impossible for a double to be double all other doubles and itself (168c), but others are not. If a soldier fears fear, the fear that he fears is not the same fear as the fear he is experiencing. Likewise, in the formula 'knowledge of knowledge', if the two knowledges are not identical, there is no true reflexivity and no impossibility. Hence, perhaps, Plato's less-than-definite conclusion (see the note on 167a).

168b *greater than something, isn't it?*: in Greek, the italicized phrases in 'knowledge *of something*' and 'greater *than something*' are identical: Greek effectively says 'greater *of something*'. There is no equivocation here: it is enough for Plato's arguments that the concepts are relative in some way.

170e *we attributed that to self-control alone*: one of the basic flaws of the argument is here particularly apparent, in the sense that we want to protest: 'But a healer can be self-controlled as well as being a healer.' Plato is assuming that all branches of knowledge have just a single domain, with a single product, but self-control could be something of a different, more general order, which people from all or many walks of life and areas of professional expertise could possess.

171a *a branch of knowledge*: this is an odd thing for Plato to say, since a healer must be taken to know about healing and is so taken by Plato at 170a–b, for instance. There has been a suggestion that the lines should be excised (M. Schofield, 'Socrates on Conversing with Doctors', *Classical Review*, 23 (1973), 121–3), but we can retain them if we understand Plato to be saying that a healer does not know about the art of healing in so far as the art of healing is just a branch of knowledge.

171c *as well as being self-controlled*: there must be something wrong with this, since it is not only those with expert knowledge of healing who can distinguish true healers from frauds. One does not need full knowledge of all aspects of health and healing, but just enough to recognize that someone, perhaps oneself, is being made worse, not better (and the same goes, *mutatis mutandis*, for distinguishing experts from frauds in other areas of expertise).

171e *things they knew about*: this is remarkably similar to the ideal (and unrealizable) state of Plato's *Republic*, whose stability and perfection is supposed to be guaranteed by the fact that everyone 'does only what pertains to himself' (the same formula as at *Charmides* 161b ff.). For the suggestion that *Charmides* (and other early dialogues) are 'proleptic' (they prepare the reader for doctrines introduced more formally in later dialogues), see C. H. Kahn, 'Plato's *Charmides* and the Proleptic Reading of Socratic Dialogues', *Journal of Philosophy*, 85 (1988), 541–9, and Kahn, *Plato and the Socratic Dialogue*.

172e *By the Dog*: the full oath is preserved at Plato, *Gorgias* 482b: 'By the divine dog of the Egyptians!'—i.e. Anubis, the dog-headed god. The euphemistic oath 'By the Dog' was a favourite of Socrates (though not unique to him) and occurs quite a few times in Plato's dialogues.

173a *the Gate of Horn or the Gate of Ivory*: true dreams were said to come through the Gate of Horn, deceptive ones through the Gate of Ivory (Homer, *Odyssey* 19.562–7).

174d *and will do us good*: see Plato, *Meno* 87d–89a, *Euthydemus* 278e–282a.

175b *the legislator named "self-control"*: it is a conceit of Plato's that in the distant past an all-wise legislator named all the items and concepts of the world: see *Cratylus* 388c–390e.

175b *the argument disallowed and denied it*: 167c–169a.

175c *and branches of knowledge*: this was agreed to at 173a–d, despite having been denied at 171c.

175c *a more irrational idea*: the idea that one can know what one does not know is not at all irrational if it is understood (as it was originally meant by Critias) as knowing the limitations of one's knowledge: I know that I do not know how to build a house and awareness of this limitation is what makes me behave appropriately, by giving the work to the appropriate expert. Plato is now teasing us with something similar to Meno's paradox (*Meno* 80d–e): if I do not know a person, how can I know whether or not he is in the same room as me on a given occasion?

176d *you'd better not resist me either*: the erotic byplay of the beginning of the dialogue here comes to a conclusion—with Charmides flirting with Socrates, rather than the other way around, as at the start of the dialogue. See A. Reece, 'Drama, Narrative, and Socratic Eros in Plato's *Charmides*', *Interpretation*, 26 (1998/9), 65–76.

LACHES

178a *fighting in hoplite armour*: in the course of the fifth century, the demand for professionalism in a number of fields increased. The teachers who supplied this demand were commonly known as 'Sophists'; they were professional teachers who, in democratic Athens, offered above all to teach 'excellence' in the sense of those skills which would literally enable one to excel—to be better than others at debate, argument, rhetoric, and other useful political skills. Here Plato imagines that a teacher of armed combat, who we learn at 183c is called Stesilaus, has just finished a display (in one of the city's gymnasia, or perhaps in a stoa) designed to attract fee-paying students. Other dialogues too start at the end of a Sophistic display: *Hippias Minor, Gorgias, Protagoras*. Hoplites were the heavy infantry of the Greek world. They were armed, typically, with a bronze helmet (the designs of which found various ways to balance protection, visibility, and a fearsome appearance), a bronze breastplate, greaves for the shins, and above all a large, round, two-handled shield, about 90 centimetres in diameter, made of bronze-covered wood, and weighing about 7 kilograms. They carried a long, iron-tipped spear and a short, iron sword. On their fighting techniques, see V. D. Hanson, *Infantry Battle in Classical Greece* (New York: Knopf, 1989).

179a *his grandfather's name*: in classical Athens eldest sons were normally named after their paternal grandfathers.

179c *our own fathers*: see the Index of Names under 'Lysimachus' and 'Melesias'.

179c *the allies*: for much of the fifth century Athens had hundreds of allies among Greek cities all over the Aegean, eastern Mediterranean, north African coast, and the Black Sea region, who made up what gradually became not so much an alliance as an Athenian empire. See my *Athens: A History* (London: Macmillan, 2004).

180b *managing it*: the failure of great Athenian leaders to pass their virtues on to their sons is a recurrent theme in Plato: *Meno* 93b–94e, *Protagoras* 319e–320b, *Alcibiades I* 118d–e.

180c *same deme as you*: for administrative purposes, all Athenian citizens had been divided since the end of the sixth century among 139 demes ('parishes' or 'wards'), which underpinned the administration and structure of the Athenian democracy in many ways. Socrates' deme was Alopece.

181b *on that occasion*: in 424, the eighth year of the Peloponnesian War, the Athenians, in a mood of overconfidence, devised a plan to remove their Boeotian enemies from the war by fomenting democratic rebellions in the cities there and simultaneously launching a large invasion. The secret leaked out and the Boeotians massed an army to meet the Athenian invasion. The battle of Delium was the first major land battle of the war, and the Athenians were soundly beaten. Apart from light-armed troops, they lost about 1,000 hoplites. Socrates' bravery during the retreat is again mentioned by Plato at *Symposium* 220e–221b, where it is said that he kept Laches safe.

182a *appropriate for a free man*: the casual snobbery is typical of a slave-owning society such as ancient Athens, where the ideal was not to work for another person, but to work or manage one's own land, and where it was the duty of every citizen ('free man') to be ready to serve in the army as a foot soldier or, if he was well off, as a horseman.

182a *the contest in which we are engaged*: the Peloponnesian War. Since the battle of Delium is in the past (181a–b) and Laches is still alive, we have upper and lower limits of 424 and 418 BCE for the dramatic date of the dialogue. The fact that there were some years of relative peace—brokered above all by Nicias—from 421, suggests that a dramatic date closer to 424 than 418 is plausible. Socrates is described as a young man (181d—or at least as younger than Nicias and Laches), but he was 45 years old in 424. Plato rarely fixes the dramatic dates of his dialogues with precision, and even allows himself the occasional glaring anachronism, so we have to be content with these clues.

182a *alongside large numbers of other people*: hoplites fought in a phalanx—a tightly packed formation in lines. While advancing, the shield on a hoplite's left arm protected the left half of his body and the right half of the body of his neighbour; even in combat, when the necessity of standing sideways-on in order to wield his spear meant that his shield offered less protection to his neighbour, it was vital for the line of battle to remain solid. Hoplite battles tended to be brief: one phalanx would give way and the men scattered in flight, while being pursued by the victors. Nicias thinks the kind of training offered by Stesilaus will be more useful after the massed confrontation, because it is designed to improve a man's personal battle skills, whereas while the phalanx was unbroken its members received plenty of support from their neighbours.

183a *here in Athens*: the contrast between the cultural values of Athens and the military values of Sparta was a common topic in the last quarter of the fifth century, and was firmly grounded in truth. But Laches' grasp of the law of supply and demand is weak: the Spartans did not need to import such training, because they had their own home-grown variety, and of course those places which felt themselves to be weak in such training would hire coaches such as Stesilaus.

183b *Attica*: the district around and governed by Athens.

183e *got stuck there*: he was presumably trying to cut the merchant vessel's rigging—a sensible thing to do, given that merchant ships relied solely on wind power, not on oarsmen.

185a *ignore everyone else*: a familiar Socratic point: see especially *Crito* 47a–c. It may seem somewhat gratuitous here, since Socrates was recommended to Lysimachus at 180b–d as an expert, but Socrates habitually disclaimed such knowledge.

185e *the souls of the young men*: notice how Socrates has shifted the terms of the argument from the young men's bodies (e.g. 181e) to their souls: the ground is being shifted away from the Homeric assumptions of Nicias and Laches.

186a *product of their own skill*: Since Plato's Socrates believes that craft expertise and excellence are in important respects analogous or even identical, the issue of the criteria by which one recognizes expertise is far from trivial. In this passage, Socrates has mentioned two of the most central: that an expert should be able to show good products and that he should be able to point to his teachers. Others guide the argument with Critias in *Charmides*, for instance that most crafts have a product, that this product is something valuable within human life (165c–d), and that a craftsman is expert in the *whole* of his field (166e). For further criteria thrown out here and there in the Socratic dialogues, and for discussion, see e.g. J. Annas, 'Virtue as a Skill', *International Journal of Philosophical Studies*, 3 (1995), 227–43; G. Klosko, 'The Technical Conception of Virtue', *Journal of the History of Philosophy*, 19 (1981), 95–102; D. Roochnik, *Of Art and Wisdom: Plato's Understanding of Techne* (University Park: Pennsylvania State University Press, 1996); P. Woodruff, 'Plato's Early Theory of Knowledge', in S. Everson (ed.), *Companions to Ancient Thought*, vol. 1: *Epistemology* (Cambridge: Cambridge University Press, 1990), 60–84 (repr. in Benson (ed.), 86–106).

186a *good men in their own right*: the analogy between excellence and skill (see the previous note) is partially sustained by an ambiguity which is as possible in English as in Greek. So here the translation 'good men in their own right' smacks of moral goodness, but the Greek could also mean that they were *good at* what they did. But the analogy must not be pushed too far: Plato did not mean that excellence was exactly like craft-knowledge, with its product being happiness. On this view, excellence is merely instrumental in producing the goal of human life. It is more likely that Plato believed that excellence was the chief and overriding component of a life of happiness, though there were other good things too (see e.g. *Meno* 78c).

187b *Carian . . . starting your pottery with a wine-jar*: two proverbs are alluded to in this sentence. Carians, from the south-west of the Asia Minor coast, were commonly used as mercenary soldiers. Since they were more expendable than citizen soldiers, the proverb 'Try it out on a Carian' meant, as we would say, 'Use Carians as your guinea-pigs.' The second proverb is more obvious: a novice potter should start work on something smaller and less ambitious than a *pithos*, a large storage jar.

187c *old enough to be educated*: a telling remark. Their sons were all teen-agers, who had already been through what passed for education for the sons of well-to-do households (that is, they had studied sports, music, Homer and the lyric poets, reading, writing, and basic arith-metic), but by the end of the fifth century even conservatives were beginning to realize that this did not count as a proper education. This is the gap the Sophists filled. On ancient Athenian education, see J. Bowen, *A History of Western Education*, vol. 1: *The Ancient World: Orient and Mediterranean 2000 B.C.–A.D. 1054* (London: Methuen, 1972).

187d *of critical importance to us*: see 185a.

188b *what Solon said*: the relevant saying of Solon is Fragment 22 (Diehl) of his poems, which contains the rather banal sentiment: 'As I grow old, I'm constantly learning more and more.'

188d *the only mode that is truly Greek*: the musical 'modes' or attunements (originally ways of tuning a lyre) were held, especially by Damon, to have different emotional effects, with the Dorian being masculine and martial, and the others (there were six others in all, named after regions of Asia Minor, rather than mainland Greece) more effemin-ate. For technical details, see S. Michaelides, *The Music of Ancient Greece: An Encyclopaedia* (London: Faber and Faber, 1978), and for discussion of the debate Plato is reflecting, see E. Csapo, 'The Polit-ics of the New Music', in P. Murray and P. Wilson (eds.), *Music and the Muses: The Culture of Mousike in the Classical Athenian City* (Oxford: Oxford University Press, 2004), 207–48.

188e *experienced him in action*: see 181a–b. Laches' only concerns are practical, and that is why he will shortly become irritated with Nicias' intellectual pretensions (194d–196c, 197a–e).

190e *thanks to activities and skills*: this second stage of the investigation is not undertaken in the dialogue, since the first stage is never com-pleted to the interlocutors' satisfaction. Socrates' hestitation here ('in so far as . . .') is due to his awareness of the debate (which forms the background of this dialogue, but more particularly of *Meno* and *Protagoras*) about whether goodness is learnable or is innate.

190e *is a brave man*: Laches' first stab at a definition is rooted in tradition. For instance, Tyrtaeus, the Spartan war poet of the later seventh century, once described a man as courageous if he 'keeps his place in the front line without flinching and with no thought of foul flight' (12.16–17); and he went on to say that such a man should have an enduring heart and mind, which is effectively Laches' second definition of 192b.

191a *when they're chasing them*: the Scythians (a nomadic people from the steppes of southern Russia) are here attributed with the light-cavalry tactic of pretending to retreat in order to entice their opponents to break ranks and give chase, and then firing their arrows behind them at their disorganized opponents—an extremely difficult operation in the days before saddles and stirrups. In Roman times, the tactic was made famous by the Parthians, from further east, and in Plato's own time Xenophon came across it from elements of the Persian cavalry, while fighting in what is now Iraq (*The Expedition of Cyrus* 3.3.10).

191b *'instigator of fear'*: the Homeric quotations and paraphrase are from *Iliad* 8.105–8 (the first three lines of which are repeated at 5.221–3). Obviously the description of Aeneas as the 'instigator of fear' has nothing to do with any ability to fight while retreating, but Plato is fond of adapting Homeric lines to his own purposes, and may even be gently mocking some of the more extreme interpretations of Homeric passages which were current in his day.

191c *with the help of this tactic*: in the account of Herodotus (9.30–84), our main source for the battle of Plataea (479 BCE), one of the critical Greek victories of the second Persian invasion of Greece, the Spartans do not behave in this way. Plato seems to be confusing Plataea with Thermopylae, fought in the previous year, when the Spartans did employ a series of feigned retreats (Herodotus 7.211), although they famously lost the battle in the end. Plato has Socrates pick on a Spartan manoeuvre as a counter-example to Laches' 'definition' of courage, because in Laches' eyes the Spartans were the supreme hoplite warriors of Greece (182e–183a).

191e *in these situations*: Socrates has somewhat extended the normal range of 'courage', since resisting pleasure and desire was normally called self-control (*sōphrosynē*, the aspect of excellence investigated in *Charmides*). But this extension merely foreshadows the tendency of the dialogue to take us in the direction of thinking that all aspects of excellence are identical or mutually entailing.

191e *what it is that's the same in all these situations*: the assumption that there is just the one unchanging quality or characteristic which constitutes courage (or whatever) in absolutely every situation is a constant in the Socratic dialogues, and one of the most striking features of Socratic and Platonic thought. See especially *Meno* 72a–d and *Euthyphro* 6d.

192b *comes to be called courage*: Plato has Socrates ask for a definition of courage in terms of the 'ability' to do something, but this will not work. No behavioural account of a virtue can act as a proper definition, because it will either be too narrow (the problem with Laches' definitions) or too vague (see further Irwin, *Plato's Moral Theory*, 42–6). Perhaps Socrates makes this request as a step in the right direction, a kind of temporary working definition.

192c *intelligent persistence is good and admirable, isn't it?*: Socrates is aware that the definition is inadequate: mental persistence may be common to all cases of courage, but it does not uniquely identify courage— mental persistence may be a feature of other things too—and so Socrates wants an addition. In a typical example of a leading question, he suggests the addition of intelligence, which will lead to Nicias' intellectualist definition, which is the direction in which Socrates wants the discussion to go. The difference, however, between Laches' and Nicias' definitions is that for Laches the cognitive aspect is a necessary condition of courage, whereas for Nicias it is identical with courage.

192e *a man of courage*: the argument contains multiple, related equivocations. (1) Laches wants courage to be intelligent persistence (as opposed to unintelligent persistence), but Socrates here shifts the terms of the argument from 'intelligent persistence' to 'persisting in doing something intelligently' (as opposed not to 'unintelligent persistence', but to 'persisting in doing something unintelligently'). (2) Socrates equivocates on the notion of intelligence: the type of prudential intelligence required in courage (weighing up the good to be gained from an action that could endanger one's life) is not the same as the type of skilled knowledge required in the examples Socrates uses. (3) There is an ambiguity in 'harmful' (192d, 193d). By contrast, courage should be beneficial. But beneficial to whom? It is obvious that courageous action is often harmful to the agent, while being beneficial to some wider community. Nevertheless, Socrates appears to slide between the notion that courage should be beneficial to the community and the notion that it should somehow be beneficial to the agent himself. (4) The ill-equipped soldier of 193a is described as unintelligent, but he is unintelligent only if intelligence is applied to his own welfare; he may very well be intelligently thinking of wider aims (such as the benefit to his community). The best discussion of the passage is in Hobbs, pp. 86–99.

193a *with persistence*: Aristotle reflects on the difference between informed and uninformed 'courage' at *Eudemian Ethics* 1230a; see also his wide-ranging discussion of courage at *Nicomachean Ethics* 1115a–1117b. Socrates' counter-example is somewhat puzzling. If we assume that the second soldier, the one with the weaker position, does not know that he has a weaker position, his case is parallel to the ignorant or unskilled well-diver of 193c, but then it is hard to see why he could be called courageous. Someone is courageous, surely, if he *knows* that there is danger and still acts (as in the Charge of the Light

Brigade). If, then, we assume that the second soldier *knows* the weakness of his position, it is hard to see why Socrates describes him as 'foolish': he has, after all, weighed things up and decided to fight. Moreover, at 197a–b it is precisely the possession of knowledge that distinguishes courage from mindless daring.

193c *good at it*: people dived into wells for the purposes of cleaning them, and to retrieve lost objects. Oddly, Plato uses both these examples (trained cavalry fighting and experienced well-diving) in *Protagoras* to prove more or less the opposite point, in an argument designed to identify courage and knowledge (*Protagoras* 350a–c). For an argument that there is no real contradiction between the two dialogues, and that Plato is not here in *Laches* intending to dent the constant Socratic equation of excellence and knowledge, see the essay 'The *Protagoras* and the *Laches*', in Vlastos's *Socratic Studies*.

193d *didn't they?*: this appears to be a combination of 192d, where Laches and Socrates agreed that unintelligent persistence is harmful, and 184b, where Laches himself suggests that 'boldness' (presumably synonymous with 'unintelligent daring') exposes one to ridicule.

193e *'harmonious consistency' between our actions and our words*: see 188d.

194a *persistence actually is courage*: it is the opinion of quite a few commentators that the definition of courage as intelligent persistence is the one Plato means us to regard as the most promising. The main attraction of this view is that it accounts for the detailed characterization of the two generals: Nicias' focus is always intellectualist, while Laches focuses on a man's character and actions; perhaps Plato is suggesting that a courageous person must combine both temperament and intelligence (understood by the end of the dialogue as knowledge of what is good and bad for him). However, Plato here not only has Socrates reject the view, but the entire discussion is in fact a red herring, in the sense that Socrates raises the issue of intelligence only to drive a wedge between the possession of knowledge and courage: courage is not in an unqualified sense persistence, but nor is it in an unqualified sense intelligent persistence.

194c *I've heard from you before*: the idea that courage is knowledge of what is and is not to be feared is put into Socrates' mouth at *Protagoras* 360c–d and *Republic* 429b–430c. Plato has Laches take Nicias to task over the next few pages presumably in part because he did not want to have Socrates appear to criticize an idea of his own; Socrates' part is more to seek clarification than to refute the definition.

194d *he must be a knowledgeable man*: the equivocation between being 'good' and being 'good at' (see the second note on 186a) is here particularly acute.

195a *and in all other situations*: Hobbs rightly paraphrases Nicias' meaning as follows: 'If it is always better for someone to pursue the morally noble course, and physical wellbeing and even life itself are always less important, then it makes sense to conclude that the only thing to be truly feared is the morally shameful. To say, therefore, that the courageous person knows what is to be feared and what dared is simply to say that he knows what is morally noble and what shameful' (p. 101). And see in general Hobbs's discussion of Socrates' argument with Nicias (pp. 99–110).

195c *restricted to health and illness*: Nicias' point in this paragraph is obscure. He is saying that doctors (and all other experts) are limited in that they do not know what is threatening and reassuring outside their own area of expertise. In this case, a doctor does not know whether life or death is preferable for his patient: only the patient himself (or a prophet, Laches sneers) knows this. If this is the correct reading, it is the correct response to Laches' objection, in that Nicias qualifies his definition: courage is knowledge of what is threatening and reassuring *to oneself*.

195e *are you not courageous?*: the historical Nicias was famous for his over-reliance on diviners, which was partly responsible for the disastrous defeat of the Athenian army in Sicily in 413 BCE (see Thucydides, *The Peloponnesian War* 7.50). So there are some dark undertones to the sentences Plato here gives to Laches. It is also possible that Socrates' words at 193a contain a veiled allusion to Laches' behaviour at the battle of Mantinea, where he lost his life in 418.

196d *To paraphrase the proverb*: the original proverb was 'Something even a dog or a pig would know'—in modern slang, a 'no-brainer'.

196e *the Crommyonian sow*: one of the labours of the legendary Athenian king Theseus was to kill the savage sow of Crommyon (on the isthmus, near Corinth). Socrates has shoehorned in mention of animals in order to raise the question of whether or not they can properly be called courageous.

196e *too difficult for most human beings*: the debate triggered here by Plato, on whether animals are intelligent, or even can properly be said to experience emotions, engaged some of the best minds of antiquity, especially in the Stoic school, and culminated in Plutarch's light-hearted rhetorical essay 'On the Use of Reason by "Irrational" Animals' (late first century CE).

197b *too stupid to be afraid of anything?*: children—and women—were generally taken to be less rational than an adult male.

197c *a true man of Aexone!*: it's not entirely clear what this means. Aexone was Laches' deme (see the note on 180c), and one ancient commentator thought that people from this deme had a reputation for abusive wit, while another thought they were proud. The latter perhaps fits the context best: Laches does not want to look a gift horse in the mouth, as we would say.

197d *verbal distinctions*: as Laches has just distinguished 'courage' from 'daring', 'boldness', etc.

198a *a part of excellence*: 190c–d.

198b *the anticipation of future evil*: typically for Socrates, this is a rationalistic definition of fear, in that it focuses on the cognitive aspect of fear and ignores the emotional disturbance which is a necessary concomitant of it.

199a *not the other way round*: there is another snide reference to Nicias' over-reliance on divination during the Sicilian expedition (see the note on 195e). All armies were accompanied by diviners, who did in fact wield considerable power. Before any anticipated battle, the diviner sacrificed and judged from the victim's entrails whether or not the outcome of the battle would be favourable. If in his opinion the omens were not good, battle might well be delayed until favourable omens were obtained. But, as Plato says here, ultimate authority lay with the field commander.

199c *only about a third of courage*: the main weakness of this argument is the false analogy between courage (as a kind of knowledge) and other branches of knowledge. Even if we accept that courage is a kind of knowledge, we would still want to restrict it to knowledge of the present and the future, since past threats hold no fear. It is therefore illegitimate to infer that courage is the knowledge of all good and evil, not just future goods and evils. We should also query whether *all* goods and evils are the objects respectively of hope and fear: there are many things which are truly describable as good or bad which do not call for hope or fear. In other words, a person with knowledge of what is and is not to be feared does not have knowledge of *all* goods and evils, but only those that are relevant to her situation.

200d *refuses to help himself*: at *Theaetetus* 151b, Plato has Socrates say that when he is approached by someone who wants to study with him, but this person is not 'pregnant' with the potential for learning and advancement, he acts as a 'match-maker' and passes the person on to some other teacher. It looks as though Niceratus was a similarly unpromising student, at least for this line of work.

201b *'Modesty ill suits a man in need'*: *Odyssey* 17.347, also quoted at *Charmides* 161a.

LYSIS

203a *right under the wall*: the Academy and the Lyceum were two of the three major gymnasia of ancient Athens, the other being the

Cynosarges. Gymnasia were popular meeting-places for the leisured men of Athens. The Academy (later made even more famous by Plato's establishment of a philosophical school there) lay to the north-west of the city, and the Lyceum (later chosen by Aristotle and his followers as the site of their school) to the south-east, so Socrates was walking around the outside of the northern and eastern stretches of the defensive wall.

203a *the spring of Panops*: Panops was a local deity. The exact location of the spring is unknown, but to judge by what follows it had been built up (though presumably not on the grand scale of some of the urban springs).

203b *good-looking ones!*: see the first note on *Charmides* 154d, on the connection between gymnasia and homosexuality.

204c *the ability to recognize a lover and his beloved*: elsewhere in Plato (*Symposium* 177d, 198d, 212b; *Phaedrus* 257a; see also ps.-Plato, *Theages* 128b), Socrates makes the wider claim that he is an expert only in love, meaning, at the least, that he knows how to make himself attractive to the young men who formed the core of his circle of followers. In both *Symposium* and *Phaedrus*, love is portrayed as a kind of need or lack, which impels one to search for beauty and ultimately for knowledge. So here Socrates may be saying that he can recognize when someone is dimly aware that he lacks knowledge— i.e. has the potential to be a philosopher (literally, a 'lover of knowledge').

205c *the four-horse-chariot events and the horse-races*: horse-breeding was always a sign of wealth: there was little good ground available, especially around Athens, for the high-grade fodder required for race-horses; such land was usually given over to human staples. Apart from the Olympic games, the other three 'crown' contests (so called because victors won wreaths and prestige, not cash or other valuable prizes) were at Delphi (the Pythian games), Corinth (the Isthmian), and Nemea (not far south-west of Corinth on the Peloponnese).

205d *the founder of the deme*: on demes, see the note on *Laches* 180c. Lysis' deme was Aexone (204e). The details of the story are unknown beyond this reference. Heracles was also a son of Zeus, hence the kinship.

205d *won the victory*: it was common for wealthy men to pay a poet (such as Pindar, most famously) to compose an ode to celebrate their victory at one of the major games (on which see the note on 205c). Socrates is using this as a metaphor for Hippothales' conquest of Lysis. Reflections on Socrates' mockery of Hippothales can be found in A. Wilson Nightingale, 'The Folly of Praise: Plato's Critique of Encomiastic Discourse in *Lysis* and *Symposium*', *Classical Quarterly*, 43 (1993), 112–30.

206d *Hermaea . . . so he'll come and join you*: the Hermaea was a festival in honour of Hermes (one of the patron deities of gymnasia—see the second note on *Charmides* 154d). Details of the festival are obscure, but it would have involved athletic contests, and it was restricted to young men and boys—an exception to the law forbidding boys from mingling with their elders in gymnasia, to prevent pederasty (Aeschines, *Against Timarchus* 12). Perhaps this is why Hippothales suggests that Lysis will be anxious to get away from the others and join Socrates, to avoid unwelcome homoerotic attention from the young men present. As boys, aged about 12, Lysis and Menexenus are the youngest interlocutors to be found in Plato's dialogues (though Charmides may not be much older).

206e *dressed in their finery*: they would have been naked for the athletic contests (see the previous note), but by now had got dressed up for the festivities that would follow; as religious tradition dictated, some were also wearing wreaths. Knucklebones from small animals were used as dice, and can still be seen in the showcases of museums around the world. In the game of 'odd-or-even', shortly to be mentioned, two players faced off, each with a number of bones in their closed hands. A asked B whether he (A) had an even or odd number of bones in his hand. If B guessed correctly, he won a bone; if he guessed incorrectly, he lost a bone. Next it was B's turn, and play continued until one player had captured all the other's bones.

208a *Wouldn't they let you do that?*: chariot-racing was notoriously dangerous, and was usually entrusted to slaves, who were considered expendable.

208c *'My attendant here,' he said*: 'attendant' is a rough translation of the Greek *paidagōgos*, literally 'child-guide'. The *paidagōgos* was a trusted slave whose job involved looking after the young master, especially when he was out and about, and educating him in manners and etiquette.

208d *the blade or the shuttle*: the blade was a flat implement used for packing the threads tight on an upright loom; the shuttle was used to weave the thread of the woof between that of the warp. Notice the typical assumption that a woman's place was in the home, and that one of her primary jobs was weaving the household's clothing.

209d *what about the Great King, then?*: the Great King was the king of Persia, a byword for power and wealth.

210a *knew exactly what we were doing*: ash was used as a salve or, dissolved in various liquids, as a potion, for various medical purposes; medical writers even argued about the virtues of different kinds of ash. But ash was not good for eyes, and that is Plato's point (parallel to cooks putting too much salt in the food): people have that much trust in expertise. The last three cases—the neighbour, the Athenian state, the Great King—ascend a scale of exaggeration and humour. Why? Some think that Plato intends a *reductio ad absurdum* of utilitarian friendship (you will be loved as long as you are useful), or at least of the idea that utility is sufficient for friendship, but this seems unlikely given that utilitarian principles guide several arguments in the dialogue. I think we need only remember that Lysis is 12 years old: Socrates is keeping the discussion light at the moment.

210b *authority over others*: the idea that knowledge gives one or should give one authority over others is a familiar Socratic refrain (e.g. Plato, *Euthydemus* 291b ff.; Xenophon, *Memoirs of Socrates* 3.9.10), which culminated in *Republic* in Plato's dream that philosophers might be kings. But such authority is not used for selfish reasons: a Socratic ruler uses his wisdom to benefit his subjects (Plato, *Republic* 342e, *Euthydemus* 292b–c, *Gorgias* 515a; Xenophon, *Memoirs of Socrates* 3.2.4).

211e *by the Dog*: see the note on *Charmides* 172e.

211e *Darius as a friend*: see the Index of Names. Plato has Socrates speak about Darius in the present tense, as if he were still alive, so this Darius is presumably Darius II, who came to the Persian throne in 424 and died in 405. There are no other indications which allow us to be more specific about the dramatic date of the dialogue.

212a *so far from getting what I want*: it seems odd that Socrates, who is constantly portrayed by both Plato and Xenophon as surrounded by friends and admirers, should suggest that he has no friends. Plato means us to reflect on the elusiveness—the snake-like elusiveness (216c)—of the concept of friendship: the more one thinks about it, the further its nature seems to recede into the distance. As a hero-worshipper of Socrates, Plato may also have something like the following (question-begging) thought in mind: Socrates has no friends, because true friendship is between similarly good people, and there is no one in the world quite as good as Socrates.

212d *quails*: a quail-lover was not a gourmet of some kind, as a modern reader might think. Quails (and cocks: 211e) were used for fighting. Ancient Greeks very rarely ate meat.

212e *and his guest-friend from abroad*: Solon, Fragment 13 (Diehl). But Solon certainly meant not 'Blessed is he whose children are fond of him' etc., but 'Blessed is the man whose children are dear to him' etc. (or even just 'Blessed is the man who has precious children' etc.). Plato's distortion of Solon's meaning anticipates the fun and games to follow with the ambiguity of the Greek word *philos*, which may mean (1) 'a friend', in the sense that A is a friend of B only if the feeling is mutual; (2) 'friendly towards' or 'fond of', in the active sense; (3) 'dear to' or 'beloved of', in the passive sense. Here, then, Plato alters Solon's (3) to (2)—but then immediately goes on to use *philos* in sense (3). At the moment, he is teasing his audience by confounding the active and passive senses, though later he will provide the means of distinguishing them. Guest-friendship was a specialized form of friendship, whereby aristocrats from all over the Greek world (and even beyond) maintained a network of their peers. See especially G. Herman, *Ritualised Friendship and the Greek City* (Cambridge: Cambridge University Press, 1987).

213c *I'm really stuck*: Socrates has unfairly compelled this *aporia* by moving from 'friends *may not* be those who love' and 'friends *may not* be those who are loved' to 'friends *are not* those who love' and 'friends *are not* those who are loved'. He has also played the Sophistic game (see Plato, *Euthydemus*) of tricking the interlocutor by changing the sense of a key term (here 'friend') in mid-argument. In general, the argument of this section is vitiated by the assumption that friendship is something single: why should there not be different kinds of friendship (as Aristotle argued)? But, however bad the arguments, they serve their moral purpose: by exploring the semantic range of the Greek term *philos*, they challenge the commonsensical assumption that friends are those who feel affection for each other, and so create space for further investigation: see D. K. Glidden, 'The Language of Love: *Lysis* 212a8–213c9', *Pacific Philosophical Quarterly*, 61 (1980), 276–90.

214b *'Ever the god draws like to like'*: Homer, *Odyssey* 17.218. Plato alludes to the principle also at *Gorgias* 510b and *Symposium* 195b.

214b *about the universe as a whole*: Plato is thinking above all of Empedocles (see the Index of Names), for whom the principle of 'like to like' was a universal law.

214c *as a result of the wrong he does the other person*: see also Plato, *Gorgias* 507e, *Republic* 351c–352d.

215a *Is there any way they could?*: this would be a better argument if Plato had been talking about things that are identical in all respects, not just 'similar': it is still open for similars to affect one another in the respects in which they are dissimilar, or (relevant to the next argument, from 215c–216b) for dissimilars to affect one another in the respects in which they are similar.

215a *in so far as he's good*: Plato is not denying that a good person may need someone to cook for him, make his shoes, and so on. Good people are good in so far as they have knowledge (the Socratic doctrine that excellence is knowledge), and this knowledge affords them self-sufficiency in respect of their excellence: their excellence will not be enhanced by anyone else. Self-sufficiency is easier for a Socratic sage because he reduces his needs until they are easier to fulfil (see T. Irwin, 'Socrates the Epicurean?', *Illinois Classical Studies*, 11 (1986), 85–112 (repr. in Benson (ed.), 198–219, and in Prior (ed.), vol. 4,

226–51)). For the self-sufficiency of good people in Plato, see also
Menexenus 247e–248a, *Republic* 387d.

215d *beggar with beggar*: Hesiod, *Works and Days* 25–6. Plato quoted from
memory, and often slightly misremembered, or deliberately altered
texts to suit his grammatical context or philosophical purpose. Here
the change is slight, with the original lines reading: 'Potter is piqued
with potter, joiner with joiner, beggar begrudges beggar, and singer
singer' (this translation, which captures Hesiod's alliterations, is by
M. L. West).

215e *similars don't derive any advantage from similars*: the terms are very
much those of the natural scientists known as the Presocratics or
their relatives, the medical writers of the Hippocratic corpus. For the
former, see my *The First Philosophers* (Oxford: Oxford University
Press, 2000); for the latter, the most accessible single-volume text is
G. E. R. Lloyd (ed.), *Hippocratic Writings* (Penguin, 1978).

216a *the ones who are good at contradicting what one says*: certain Sophists
(such as those parodied in Plato's *Euthydemus*) made a virtue out
of being able to contradict whatever one said—and then even
contradicting the original contradiction.

217a *the friend of what is good*: earlier, however, Plato drove a wedge
between the concepts of goodness and friendship (215a–b); but
earlier he was (*a*) talking about friendship as a relationship between
human beings; (*b*) drawing on the reciprocal sense of the Greek term
philos, not the passive sense as here.

217d *ceruse*: ceruse—white lead—was regularly used as a cosmetic, particularly on women's faces, since ancient Athenian society held up
the indoor life as an ideal for its women and so they made their faces
pale. Plenty of other cosmetics were available too.

218a *be they gods or men*: this qualification is due to Plato's doubt that any
human being could actually attain such a state of perfect learning
that his life would be complete and he would stop wanting it.
The Greek for 'love of learning' is *philosophia*: no one can be a
consummate philosopher in this sense; it is a lifelong quest.

218a *no one who is bad and empty-headed loves learning*: compare Plato,
Symposium 204a.

218b *remain aware of the extent of their ignorance*: this intermediate condition is described in a stunning allegory or myth, in the context of
Plato's middle-period metaphysical views, at *Phaedrus* 248a–e.

218c *fool's gold*: the Greek expression is 'dreamt wealth'. A moment's
thought will reveal why Plato so quickly qualifies the definition of
friendship he has reached by this point. The idea that 'what is neither
good nor bad is a friend of the good because of the presence of
badness' implies that friendship begins and ends with selfish need.

But this cannot be the full story: need may be the basis of friendship, but I am not friends with everybody who does me good (doctors, dentists, garage mechanics, the boss at work), just because I need the goods they can offer.

219b *which we said was impossible*: 215a. It is highly cavalier of Plato to ignore here a proposition which is elsewhere taken to be a knock-down argument (216e).

219d *the final end which makes everything else that is lovable lovable*: quite a bit of ink has been expended on wondering what this primary lovable object might be. It is clearly inappropriate to import Plato's theory of Forms from later dialogues, because there is no hint of such metaphysical baggage here. It would be more Socratic to think that it is excellence (see e.g. Plato, *Gorgias* 467a–475e, with the same means–end distinction, establishing a hierarchy of desires, that we find here in *Lysis*) or knowledge (see Plato, *Euthydemus* 278e–282a, *Meno* 87d–89a), or perhaps just happiness (see *Euthydemus* 278e). Given the vagueness of Plato's description, a broad psychological characterization is probably best: the primary lovable object is *whatever* subliminally structures a person's desires and attractions into a coherent pattern. (This is Glidden's suggestion; further reasons for leaving things indeterminate can be found in D. Robinson, 'Is There a πρωτον αγαθόν in Socratic Philosophy?', in Boudouris, (ed.), vol. 1, 285–91.) Plato, or Plato's Socrates, may think that in actual fact there is only one such final goal, but that is not stated in the text or warranted by the argument (which, logically, can establish only that there is at least one such goal). At any rate, the possibility is raised that we need self-knowledge in order to consciously arrange our lives so that we aim at our true goal. It may also be the case that Plato thinks this final goal to be unobtainable—an ideal in the sense Tolstoy uses the word in the appendix to *The Kreutzer Sonata*—in that (see 218a), if we could obtain the object of all our desires, we would no longer be capable of feeling desire or love.

219e *three kotylai of wine*: a *kotylē* ('cup') was a liquid measure of about 0.48 pint (270 ml.).

221a *it's possible for hunger to harm a person, though it can also help him*: the good aspect of hunger is that it impels one to eat and stay healthy, the bad aspect is starvation; or (see Plato, *Gorgias* 499d) hunger is good if we eat healthy food, bad if we eat unhealthy food.

221d *as we were saying a moment ago*: Plato has hardly proved that desire is the cause of love; he has suggested no more than that they are closely related concepts.

221e *close to each other*: my translation of the Greek term *oikeios* as 'close' is an attempt to find a single term to cover all its occurrences here. The reason this is difficult is that Plato equivocates on both *philos* and *oikeios*: he moves from 'something *philon* (dear) is *oikeion* (one's own)' to '*philoi* (friends) are *oikeioi* (close, congenial)'. The passive sense of *philos* changes to the reciprocal sense, and a non-symmetrical meaning of *oikeiotēs* is shoved aside in favour of a symmetrical one. I think that this is why Lysis is said to keep quiet at 222a: we were told at 213d that he is capable of spotting mistakes in the argument. For a defence of the argument, see G. Rudebusch, 'True Love is Requited: The Argument of *Lysis* 221d–222a', *Ancient Philosophy*, 24 (2004), 67–80.

222b *the variety of colours he turned*: notice the contrast with Hippothales' reaction at 210e. At that point, Socrates had humiliated Lysis with the suggestion that no one could love him, but now he has implied that Lysis must love Hippothales.

222b *our earlier position*: see 214e ff.

222d *if we say instead that goodness and closeness are identical*: as they would have to be, in order to avoid the unwelcome conclusion that bad people can be friends, which was rejected at 214b–c.

222d *only good people can be friends*: which was rejected at 215c.

223a *like supernatural beings*: the intervention of gods often brought things to an end.

223a *displaying traces of their foreign accents*: slaves did of course have to learn Greek, but originally they were likely to come from further afield—from Scythia, Thrace, or Illyria, or from countries such as Caria and Phrygia in Asia Minor, and Syria in the Middle East. The slaves haul Lysis and Menexenus home: they are still not free (though Lysis' name could be translated 'release'); they still lack the knowledge which would gain them their freedom (209c–210c). The slaves are drunk with wine—as opposed to the interlocutors, who are drunk with words (222c). Rowdy slaves were a comic stereotype.

MENO

70a *how do people become good?*: The abrupt start to the dialogue, with no preliminary scene-setting, is unusual, but not unique. The irony of having the non-virtuous Meno ask about virtue is presumably the same as that of having the cowardly Nicias discourse about courage in *Laches*, or the tyrant Critias about self-control in *Charmides*. Meno's abruptness may be an attempt at characterization, but I cannot see much characterization in this dialogue; others disagree (see especially J. Gordon, *Turning toward Philosophy: Literary Device and Dramatic Structure in Plato's Dialogues* (University Park, Pa.: Pennsylvania State University Press, 1999), ch. 4).

The question whether excellence was teachable or a natural endowment was a topic of debate at the end of the fifth century and beginning of the fourth. We find traces of the debate in a number of places, but few sustained and dedicated discussions survive. Apart from those of Plato (not just *Meno*, but also *Protagoras*), there is the third-rate anonymous treatise *Double Arguments*, which cautiously comes down on the side of teachability, and Isocrates, *Antidosis* 186–92, who prefers a combination of teaching and natural ability. The discussion of the topic in *Double Arguments* makes it clear that several of the angles Plato employs to approach the question had become commonplaces.

70a   *and for their wealth*: the fertile plains of Thessaly, in northern Greece, were more suitable for horse-breeding than most parts of Greece, and the Thessalians profited from exporting grain too.

70c   *to provide them with answers*: that this was a feature of a Gorgianic display is attested by Plato also at *Gorgias* 447c. Other Sophists made the same claim: see e.g. Plato, *Hippias Minor* 363d. The ability to answer any and every question seems incredible, but worked because the Sophists discoursed at a high level of generality.

71b   *Do you think that's possible?*: the analogy between knowing Meno and knowing excellence is not very sound: in order to know whether Meno is rich etc., I do not need the kind of deep or thorough knowledge that Plato seems to require for something like excellence; an individual such as Meno does not harbour the kinds of necessary truths that Plato wants to see in a definition of something like excellence. But these differences need not worry us too much: Plato is just using a simple example.

71c   *Yes, I did*: one of the few internal references by Plato to another dialogue, in this instance *Gorgias* (unless this was still an unwritten project in Plato's mind).

71e   *and avoid suffering any harm himself*: the political conception of manly excellence outlined here had become accepted particularly as a result of the Sophists, since that was exactly the kind of 'excellence' they offered to teach. It may strike a modern reader as corrupt for a politician to use his influence to help his friends and harm his enemies, but in fact it was perfectly acceptable. See W. R. Connor, *The New Politicians of Fifth-Century Athens* (Indianapolis: Hackett, 1992). The idea that it was all right, even one's duty, to harm one's enemies, though disputed by Socrates (in Plato's *Crito*), was standard pre-Christian ethics.

72a   *a great many other excellences too*: like other interlocutors in the Socratic dialogues, Meno has given examples of types of excellence rather than trying to find what is common to all instances of excellence; he seems to believe that 'excellence' means different things in different contexts. The problem with this is that manly excellence cannot be responsible for other kinds of excellence, and so cannot tell us how to recognize excellence elsewhere. Moreover (though Plato does not have Socrates develop this point here), particular kinds of excellence are socially or contextually determined, but Socrates is looking for something that just is excellence, whatever determinants may contingently accrue to it. Aristotle, however, agrees with Meno at *Politics* 1260a: the virtues are different for a man and for a woman.

72c *Yes, I would*: 'Plato spares us Meno's attempt at defining a bee. It would have been interesting to see what Plato's own would have been' (E. S. Thompson, *Plato: Meno* (London: Macmillan, 1901), ad loc.).

72e *the same for a man and for a woman*: actually, the analogy with health is rather specious, because one could easily argue that health is different for a man and for a woman, because their physical requirements are so different. On the other hand, if one relied on a vague formula such as 'a state of appropriate well-being' as a definition of health, which is what Socrates appears to be pushing for, one could equally rely on a formula such as 'being well able to perform one's role in society' (Sharples, ad loc.) as a definition of excellence, and that is not far from what Meno is saying.

73b *If they're to be good*: notice the typical Socratic slide from being good *at* something (here, management) to being good *simpliciter*, i.e. virtuous or morally good. It was Socrates' influence that gained moral virtue a permanent place in discussions of excellence, which in itself is a wider concept. If excellence is what it is to be good at something, Socrates argued that what it is to fulfil one's function as a human being is to be moral.

73c *unless they had the same excellence*: the argument is circular. Why does Plato not have Socrates or Meno say, 'All right, then: excellence is single because it always consists of self-control and honesty'? That would be a legitimate conclusion to draw from the argument. Plato wants the constant presence of self-control and honesty to imply that excellence has a single nature. But the point is convincing only if self-control and honesty *are* the underlying single nature, otherwise their presence is not significant; but if self-control and honesty are the underlying nature of excellence, the argument concludes the search and is not just suggestive.

73d *justice is excellence*: there is in fact a sense of 'justice' in both English and ancient Greek whereby it is equivalent to 'morality', or excellence as a whole. We describe someone as just if she has moral integrity.

75c *as he was about shape*: Why does Meno claim that Socrates' 'definition' of shape defines one unknown by means of another unknown? Colour is hardly something unknown. And why did he call it 'simplistic'? We are meant to contrast 'simplistic' with 'grandiose' in 76e:

Meno is looking for quasi-scientific definitions. If so, colour may count as an unknown until it receives a scientific analysis. In any case, Socrates' definition here is not very informative: it could help us to identify any instance of shape, but it does not tell us what it is to be shape. I take it that Socrates' definition here means that there is nothing coloured which is not also shaped.

76b *in bloom*: see the note on *Charmides* 154a.

76c *certain emanations from things*: Empedocles explained sense perception (and certain other phenomena) as the accommodation by the sense organs of emanations given off by things: see especially Theophrastus, *On the Senses* 7–11. Plato moves naturally from Gorgias to Empedocles, because the former was said to have studied with the latter.

76d *'mark well what I say'*: a popular quotation from a lost poem by Pindar (Fragment 105 Bergk).

76e *and so on and so forth*: it is not quite clear why Socrates is not satisfied with the definition. He cannot mean that exactly the same formula could be used for scent and so on, because the definition mentions 'sight', and it is not clear why changing 'sight' to 'smell' or whatever would not do as a definition of scent. He may be concerned that the formula answers the question 'What are the conditions of sight?' rather than 'What is sight?'—that it names the material conditions for sight rather than its essence.

In a moment Plato will describe the definition as 'grandiose'. The word used is literally 'tragic', i.e. 'in the manner of a tragic poet'. It has been suggested that Plato so described it with reference to a lost play of Euripides, in which a character propounded some such theory (D. Sansone, 'Socrates' "Tragic" Definition of Colour (Plato, *Meno* 76d–e)', *Classical Philology*, 91 (1996), 339–45). Alternatively, the adjective may refer to the style of the passage, which has a certain 'lapidary urgency' (T. G. Rosenmeyer, 'Styles and Performances, and Plato's *Meno*', in G. W. Most *et al.* (eds.), *Philanthropia kai Eusebeia: Festschrift für Albrecht Dihle* (Göttingen: Vandenhoeck & Ruprecht, 1993), 404–25.

76e *the previous one was*: presumably the second definition of shape is meant (76a), since Plato himself criticized the first one: see the note on 75c.

76e *stay and be initiated*: elsewhere too Plato compares initiation into the Eleusinian Mysteries (for a brief account of which, see my *Athens: A History* (Macmillan, 2004), 134–7) with 'initiation' into philosophy: *Gorgias* 497c, *Symposium* 209e–210a, *Phaedrus* 250b–c, *Theaetetus* 155e. The reference to the Mysteries also allows us to pinpoint the dramatic date of the dialogue: Meno was about 20 or 21 years old when he died in 400; at the time of our dialogue he was old enough to have left Thessaly and have visited Athens on his own; he was presumably on his way to join the mercenary army of Cyrus in Asia Minor, which set off east towards Persia in 401; it is early in the year (the first initiation into the Mysteries took place in February); Meno is presumably staying with his guest-friend Anytus, who as a democratic politician was unlikely to have been in the city during the oligarchy which fell late in 403. All this suggests a date of January 402.

77b *'to enjoy fine things and to have power'*: a tag from an unknown poet. Once again, Meno has relied on an external authority, rather than his own thinking, for his view.

77e *desiring something good, aren't they?*: a problematic paragraph, especially because there is an apparent contradiction between claiming that people do not want something bad, and claiming that what they want is in fact bad. The solution is to realize that people want things *under a certain description*: Oedipus did not want to marry his mother; he wanted to marry a beautiful and powerful older woman. The idea that everyone always wants what is or what they at least take to be good for them is at the heart of the paradoxical Socratic denial of weakness of the will (see pp. xx–xxi): there are no irrational desires (or no overwhelming irrational desires). This proposition (found especially in *Protagoras*) has generated a huge amount of controversy, from Aristotle onwards. See, in general, W. Charlton, *Weakness of the Will: A Philosophical Introduction* (Oxford: Basil Blackwell, 1988). Additional bibliography on this passage of *Meno* in particular, and its consequences: D. Devereux, 'Socrates' Kantian Conception of Virtue', *Journal of the History of Philosophy*, 33 (1995), 381–408; N. Reshotko, 'The Socratic Theory of Motivation', *Apeiron*, 25 (1992), 145–70; T. Penner and C. J. Rowe, 'The Desire for Good: Is the *Meno* Inconsistent with the *Gorgias*?', *Phronesis*, 39 (1994), 1–25; M. Anagnostopoulos, 'Desire for the Good in the *Meno*', in N. Reshotko (ed.), *Desire, Identity and Existence: Essays in Honour of T. M. Penner* (Kelowna, BC: Academic Printing & Publishing, n.d. [2004]), 171–91. Further relevant reading can be found in footnote 13 on p. xx.

78a *desiring bad things and getting them*: Socrates is teasing Meno with a perversion of his claim that excellence is 'desiring fine things and having the ability to procure them for oneself' (77b). But he has got carried away, or he is resorting to common parlance or ellipsis: he has just devoted a careful argument to claiming that no one desires bad things, yet here he says that people who are in a bad way desire bad things. 'Desiring bad things' must be short for 'desiring what they take to be good things, but are in fact bad things'.

78d *the hereditary guest-friend of the Great King*: the 'Great King' was the king of Persia; on guest-friendship, see the note on *Lysis* 212e; on Meno's relations with the Persian royal family (if not the king, exactly), see Xenophon, *The Expedition of Cyrus* 2 *passim*, with T. S. Brown, 'Menon of Thessaly', *Historia*, 35 (1986), 387–404.

79d *not yet agreed upon*: see 75d. Plato is obviously right here: no valid definition can name the thing to be defined as part of the definition.

79e *your friend*: Gorgias (71c, 76b).

80a *in appearance*: Socrates had flat, snub-nosed features.

80b *arrested as a magician*: this is not to say that magicians were acceptable in Athens, but that in Athens, as a citizen, Socrates was not liable to summary arrest; at worst, a citizen could be summoned to face trial. In any other city, Socrates would not have this legal protection.

80d *the unknown thing you're looking for*: the background to 'Meno's paradox' is both general and specific. Specifically, Socrates himself had come up with a version of it at 71b, and Meno is remembering that; generally, certain Sophists had used this tactic to demolish the arguments of opponents. For discussion, see the following notes and pp. xxxviii–xli.

80e *going to search for*: there are subtle differences between Socrates' formulation of the paradox and Meno's original a few lines earlier. Socrates' version uses the third person, rather than Meno's pointed 'you', in order to frame the paradox as a genuine philosophical problem, not just an *ad hominem* outburst by Meno, and Socrates' version is more elegant. But most importantly, (1) Socrates omits Meno's 'at all', because he will claim, in effect, that even something unknown is in another sense known; (2) Socrates omits the second part of Meno's statement—how will you know that a search has been successfully concluded? Nevertheless, he does implicitly cover this aspect of the paradox in what follows. (3) He makes Meno's original far more of a paradox than it was. Additional bibliography: B. Calvert, 'Meno's Paradox Reconsidered', *Journal of the History of Philosophy*, 12 (1974), 143–52; J. Moline, 'Meno's Paradox?', *Phronesis*, 14 (1969), 153–61; M. Welbourne, 'Meno's Paradox', *Philosophy*, 61 (1986), 229–43.

81a *Who are they?*: we cannot now make a safe identification, though Pythagoreans seem to be the best bet: see P. Kingsley, *Ancient Philosophy, Mystery, and Magic: Empedocles and Pythagorean Tradition* (Oxford: Oxford University Press, 1995), 160–5.

81b *it never perishes*: for Plato's commitment to the immortality and transmigration of the soul, see *Phaedo* 81c–82d, 107c–108c, *Republic* 608d–611a, *Phaedrus* 245c–246a, 248c–249c, *Timaeus* 41d–42d, 90e–92c.

81b–c *In the ninth year . . . holy heroes*: Pindar, Fragment 133 (Bergk). Her 'ancient woe' was occasioned by the murder of her son by the Titans, who were seen as the progenitors of the human race. We human beings pay off this debt not just by undergoing a certain number of incarnations (otherwise Persephone would automatically 'accept the requital'), but also by moral behaviour during those incarnations. It is unclear whether 'in the ninth year' refers to normal years or to Great Years (large astronomical cycles) or to incarnations.

81d *about excellence and about everything else*: it is an implication of the idea that here on earth we only *recollect* knowledge that in our lifetimes we are less conscious than whenever it was that we knew things immediately: 'Our birth is but a sleep and a forgetting', as Wordsworth said in 'Intimations of Immortality'.

81d *all nature is akin*: Plato clearly means us to think that there are natural and necessary links between things, such that I can seamlessly move from one truth or idea or fact to another. Vlastos may well be right to say that 'what Plato means by "recollection" in the *Meno* is any advance in understanding which results from the perception of logical relationships' (p. 97 in Day (ed.)). Additional bibliography: S. Tigner, 'On the Kinship of All Nature in Plato's *Meno*', *Phronesis*, 15 (1970), 1–4.

81d *nothing but recollection*: the two most important questions (for a further list, see Weiss, pp. 70–1) are (1) if the soul knows 'everything', when did it learn it? And (2) how much is meant to be covered by 'everything'? If it did not learn things in this lifetime, could it have learnt things in previous lifetimes? After all, if *all* learning is recollection (81c), the soul can never have *learnt* anything; nevertheless, Plato uses the term 'learn' here and at 86a for the soul's acquisition of knowledge. Perhaps Plato might say that we have had infinite incarnations, and that over the course of these incarnations we have gradually built up our innate knowledge. (There may even be the possibility of learning something genuinely new even this late in our incarnations.) It is true that in a later dialogue, *Timaeus*, Plato seems to think that both the soul and the world are created, which would render the idea of infinite incarnations implausible; but elsewhere (e.g. *Phaedrus* 246a) he says that the soul is immortal, and that seems to be his position here in *Meno*. But if we take seriously the idea that *all* embodied learning is actually recollection, then perhaps the soul did its learning in its periods of disembodied existence, or in some indefinite (or even timeless) time before a first incarnation. When the doctrine of recollection recurs (especially in *Phaedo* and *Phaedrus*), the objects of recollection are Forms and they become known between incarnations, but it is far from clear that Plato had this metaphysical theory in mind when he wrote *Meno*. It is true that at 86a he has Socrates say that the slave first learnt his geometry when

he was not incarnated as a human being, but the slave recalls something considerably more complex than a Platonic Form (Forms are
characterized by singleness, simplicity, and eternally being just what
they are) and it is hard to see how anyone could learn geometry or
even the a priori principles of geometry (etc.) while disembodied.
The Gordian knot of these complexities is simply cut by saying that
'souls acquired or learnt their knowledge at the moment when time
began' (Bluck, p. 317), but there is no trace of this in our dialogue,
where Plato's main concern is just to argue that the soul did not
acquire its knowledge in *this* lifetime. It seems safest to think that for
the time being Plato is not restricting 'everything' to Forms and that
he is not prepared to take the theory further than the minimum
required to answer Meno's paradox (hence at 86b he has Socrates
decline to support every detail of the argument); all he needs for the
time being is the vague idea that the soul 'always' knew 'everything'
(81c, 86a). If pushed, he would surely have restricted 'everything' to
all general principles and timeless truths (especially the supposedly
objective truths of morals and mathematics), and would have eliminated empirical studies from the blanket assertion that *all* learning is
recollection (81d). Just conceivably, there is the beginning of such a
restriction at 85e, if we take 'subjects' there to mean propositional
subjects such as geometry, not e.g. learning *how* to do things. There
is certainly a restriction in that, as 84a shows, the slave has not by
then begun to recollect; he has, however, already come up with an
opinion or two; since they were false, falsehoods are excluded from
recollection. See also the end of the first note on 98a.

82b *born and bred at home*: it was felt to be somewhat improper to enslave
fellow Greeks (pan-hellenism infused the rival city-states of Greece
at least to that extent), and slaves generally came from abroad (see the
second note on *Lysis* 223a). The other main source, however, was
breeding slaves at home—and it looks as though they could be
referred to as 'Greek'. The best short introduction to Greek slavery is
N. R. E. Fisher, *Slavery in Classical Greece* (2nd edn., London:
Bristol Classical Press, 2001). It has been suggested (by D. Gera,
'Porters, *Paidagogoi*, Jailers, and Attendants: Some Slaves in Plato',
Scripta Classica Israelica, 15 (1996), 90–101) that Plato has Socrates
choose a slave for this demonstration not just because Socrates needs
someone uneducated, but also because he is not concerned with
the personal, probing aspect of the elenchus, but only with drily
demonstrating the process of recollection.

82b *boy*: the slave may be young—part of the point is that he should be
untutored—but the Greeks addressed slaves of any age as 'boy' (as in
the Southern States of America, or in South Africa, in the bad old
days).

82c   *equal in length as well*: some scholars take these two new lines to be diagonals rather than transversals. Nothing very substantial hinges on this, in terms of the slave's recollection or the geometrical problem involved. Transversals seem to me to fit the text better. The issues are debated between G. J. Boter (*Phronesis*, 33 (1988), 208–15) and R. W. Sharples (*Phronesis*, 34 (1989), 220–6), with a useful addendum by D. H. Fowler (*Phronesis*, 35 (1990), 175–81).

82c   *let this side be 2 feet long*: nothing significant hinges on the fact that Plato gives a value to the length of the side; it saves him having to talk in the abstract about equal lines, lines double in length, half as long, and so on. What follows is the earliest extended piece of evidence about Greek mathematics (the evidence for earlier mathematics comes from reports in later writers). Apart from anything else, it suggests (and other evidence proves) that at this stage Greek mathematics was geometrized rather than arithmetized: see D. H. Fowler, *The Mathematics of Plato's Academy* (2nd edn., Oxford: Oxford University Press, 1999).

82e   *just asking him questions*: Socrates' repeated insistence (here, and at 82b, 84c, and 85d) on his not teaching is due to the fact that Meno's paradox at 80d–e effectively denied that one could search for knowledge without the help of a teacher, as someone who already knows. Plato's reply comes in two stages: both the theory of recollection and the method of hypothesis are supposed to show, at the very least, that progress can be made even when both parties to the discussion are ignorant or at any rate are not making use of their knowledge.

82e   *the right way to go about remembering*: because memory works by association. Plato is claiming that Socratic argumentation follows natural chains of association. I take it that the talk of the kinship of all nature at 81d was just a high-falutin way of making the same point.

83a   *while this one is short*: this would of course produce a figure *AJMD* which would be double the area of the first square *ABCD*, but Socrates wants a *square* with double the area, not an oblong.

83e   *Three feet*: this is a guess, based on Socrates' pointing out that the line must be longer than 2 feet and shorter than 4 feet. It is wrong (because the square of 3 feet is 9 square feet), but it is less wrong than the previous guess (and not a stupid guess, given that, arithmetically speaking, we are in the realm of irrational numbers), so progress is being made. Socrates has led the slave towards this incorrect answer by means of his questions, but the whole process is constructive, not so much because the slave is now more nearly right than he was before, as because he has shed his false conceit of knowledge, and thereby created space for the 'recollection' of knowledge. As the image of the 'journey towards recollection' at 84a suggests, the false opinions that the slave has voiced so far do not count as recollection itself (except in the broader sense that recollection is a process), but as clearing the ground for recollection to take place. Moreover, the slave has been allowed to express his own opinions, rather than being merely spoon-fed someone else's ideas. Socratic questioning is educational in the literal sense: *educare* in Latin implies eliciting information, not putting information in.

84c   *double-length sides*: mimicking Meno's remarks about his fluency on excellence (80b). At the time, Meno thought that he had knowledge, which he could not express because he had been bewitched by Socrates; but, given the parallelism with the slave, Socrates is suggesting that Meno did not have knowledge, but a false belief. This is not the only parallel Socrates implicitly draws between Meno and the slave: the conversation with the slave passes through much the same stages as the earlier conversation with Meno, so that one could almost say that although at 80c Socrates refused to come up with a counter-image for Meno, in response to his simile of the torpedo, he has in effect likened Meno to an ignorant slave. See D. E. Anderson, 'The Theory of Recollection in Plato's *Meno*', *Southern Journal of Philosophy*, 9 (1971), 225–36. However, the reason the conversation with the slave parallels the conversation with Meno is simply that both follow the pattern of the elenchus: from conceit of knowledge, to *aporia*, to true belief—and maybe beyond, to knowledge.

85a   *cuts each of these figures in two*: it is hard to see how the slave could have come up with the diagonal on his own (even if it were already given: see the first note on 82c). This is where Socrates goes beyond eliciting replies and seeds new information. There is of course a large element of teaching in what Socrates does with the slave: his use of an interrogative tone of voice barely disguises this. But this is not enough to invalidate the whole lesson as an illustration of recollection, because (*a*) recollection is a process, not a flash of insight (85c with 98a), and (*b*) Plato insists that *all* learning is recollection (81d–82a), so that even straightforward geometry lessons are meant to be covered.

85c   *in a number of different ways*: since mere repetition of the same questions would hardly advance anyone towards understanding, Plato must mean this phrase 'in a number of different ways' to adumbrate the 'working out the reason' of 98a.

85d   *the knowledge he now has*: his latent knowledge of geometry.

85e   *all other subjects too*: there are of course enormous differences in the ways we learn different subjects, but at the moment Plato seems prepared to ignore the differences and allow his geometry lesson with the slave to stand as a model for how we acquire *any* knowledge.

86a   *for all time?*: no, it doesn't follow. Plato has not shown that there was not a time when the soul was ignorant (at best, he has shown only that it acquired knowledge some time in the past). And even apart from this mistake, all that could follow from the argument as it stands is that the soul is in a state of knowledge for as long as it exists; it does not follow that the soul has always existed.

86b *with particular vigour*: how much does Plato mean us to doubt? It is hard to see what elements of the story could be jettisoned without undermining the whole theory of recollection. In that case, he must mean that since there is no way to *prove* the immortality of the soul (a problem he thinks he has resolved by the time he wrote *Phaedrus*), there is no way to *prove* that the recovery of true beliefs is actually recollection. Nevertheless, he does believe that true beliefs *are* recoverable, and that we have within us a coherent system of beliefs corresponding to the objective matrix of concepts (81d). For reflections on this sentence, see R. Jenks, 'On the Sense of the Socratic Reply to Meno's Paradox', *Ancient Philosophy*, 12 (1992), 317–30.

86c *no point in even searching for it*: though the point about laziness is important, it is not clear that Socrates has overcome all of Meno's worries. Meno's question (80d) was raised in the context of a search where *neither* of them knew the answer: neither of them knows what excellence is. Socrates' leading (and sometimes deliberately misleading) questions to the slave, however, make it clear that he already knows the answer to the geometrical problem. But all Plato is trying to do at this point is have Socrates convince Meno of the reality of latent knowledge; he responds to the worry later (86d–87b), when he argues that where both or all interlocutors are ignorant, the way to proceed is to make an assumption. Another question that arises is whether Plato has resolved Meno's paradox at all, or just pushed it back. Could one not still ask how you can know that what you recollect is your quarry? But if recollection is seen specifically as a response to prompting (that is, to questions, whether asked by someone else or by oneself), you can know that you have found your quarry, because it was the specific result of specific questioning.

86d *or a natural endowment*: scholars complain that Meno has failed to notice that the question has already been answered, by implication: the experiment with the slave was meant to show that recollection is the way to find out what *everything* is, including excellence. Since 'teaching' has now been reformulated as 'recollection', we are surely entitled to say that excellence is teachable, in the sense of recollectable. But there is a gap: it is still relevant to ask how even someone who knows what it is gains it as a personal quality.

87b *inscribing the area inside a circle*: Plato has not given us enough information to securely identify the geometrical problem he has in mind, because that is not what is important to him: all that is important is that he should give a general illustration of arguing from an assumption or a hypothesis. But why use such a complex illustration, when simpler ones were available, and why leave things so obscure? Perhaps he wants us to work things out for ourselves. For identifying the problem, the starting-point is guessing what 'the given line' is: the diameter of the circle? The base of one of the figures involved? Some other line that helps solve the problem? For surveys of various suggestions and solutions, see G. E. R. Lloyd, 'The *Meno* and the Mysteries of Mathematics', *Phronesis*, 37 (1992), 166–83, and Sharples, 158–60; for the relation between Plato's 'method of hypothesis' and the practice of contemporary geometricians, see Bluck (pp. 76–85) and K. Seeskin, '*Meno* 86c–89a: A Mathematical Image of Philosophic Inquiry', in B. Hendley (ed.), *Plato, Time and Education: Essays in Honour of Robert S. Brumbaugh* (Albany: State University of New York Press, 1987), 25–41.

87b *let's not argue over which term to use*: Plato is not in any way abandoning his redescription of 'teaching' as 'reminding'; he is signalling the fact that, for ease of communication, he will continue to use the familiar term 'teaching', even though in actual fact all teaching is reminding, even when it is the kind of teaching that happens in schools or Sophistic seminars. If this is right, any interpretation that finds Plato tacitly reverting in what follows to 'orthodox' teaching and learning must be wrong.

87d *knowledge of some kind*: what follows is particularly critical for understanding Socratic ethics; Plato, *Euthydemus* 278e–282a is a parallel passage. The central issue is this: for Socrates, is virtue (excellence) the *only* good thing there is, or does he recognize other goods? There are passages in the dialogues which point in either direction, but here, at any rate, it seems clear that he is unequivocally calling health, wealth, strength, and good looks (and so on) goods. The most important passage is that from *Euthydemus*, but a careful reading of it shows that while Plato may be saying that excellence (virtue) is the only thing that is *always* good, other things are conditionally good, the condition being that they must be put to proper use by knowledge or intelligence (i.e. put to virtuous use, since knowledge is excellence on Socratic theory). This refutes Irwin's influential view that for Plato's Socrates excellence is the only thing that is good, and that it alone is instrumental in causing human happiness. By contrast, Vlastos has argued that while the contribution of excellence to human happiness vastly outweighs the contribution made by even the sum total of other things, health and wealth and so on can make a small difference.

89b *much more carefully than our gold*: state treasures were kept in temples on the Athenian Acropolis in rooms that were sealed with the city's seal. In *Republic* Plato makes provision for separating out the 'golden' class of potential philosopher-kings and educating them as rulers.

89e   *isn't teachable*: this obviously does not follow: something can be teach*able* without being taught (the situation is complicated by the fact that in Greek the same word can mean both 'teachable' and 'taught', but so far Plato has been talking about teachability). Nevertheless, it is plausible to think, in the case of excellence above all, that if it (as ordinarily understood) were teachable, there would be teachers of it. However, Plato really should not have made this logical blunder only shortly after arguing, in response to Meno's paradox, that the fact that something is not known does not mean that it cannot be known.

90a   *Polycrates' money*: I follow the interpretation of J. S. Morrison, 'Meno of Pharsalus, Polycrates and Ismenias', *Classical Quarterly*, 36 (1942), 57–78. This Polycrates is not the famous sixth-century tyrant of Samos, but the contemporary Athenian democratic politician; the reference is to an otherwise unknown incident when Polycrates tried to bribe Ismenias of Thebes to restore democracy in Athens during the regime of the oligarchic junta in 404–403 BCE.

91b   *generally called 'Sophists'*: see the note on *Laches* 178a.

91d   *get paid for this*: here and several more times in what follows Plato stresses that the Sophists charged for their teaching. To his mind, it was one of the distinguishing marks between Socrates and the Sophists that Socrates did not charge for his teaching. The Sophists were felt to prostitute themselves, in that they were obliged to accept anyone who came up with the money. See G. B. Kerferd, *The Sophistic Movement* (Cambridge: Cambridge University Press, 1981), 25–8, and A. Wilson Nightingale, *Genres in Dialogue: Plato and the Construct of Philosophy* (Cambridge: Cambridge University Press, 1995), 22–5.

91e   *his good reputation has not yet been dented*: important counter-evidence to the flimsy tradition that late in his life Protagoras was prosecuted in Athens for impiety.

92b   *hostile towards them*: hostility towards the Sophists and natural scientists—the new learning in general—was not uncommon in the last half of the fifth century (and was famously parodied in Aristophanes' *Clouds*). They were felt to be a subversive influence, to undermine traditional values. In our volume, there is another trace of this prejudice at *Laches* 197d.

92c   *no experience of it at all*: Anytus has no experience of the new learning, and yet he will be one of Socrates' accusers at his trial. More subtly, since Plato would agree with his condemnation of the Sophists, Anytus has the kind of lucky right opinion that Plato talks about at the end of the dialogue.

92d *a short while ago*: 91a.

93a *good at politics*: an admission which contradicts the denial of precisely
this point at *Gorgias* 516e–517a. The argument that follows is badly,
and obviously, flawed: it largely ignores the possibility that the sons
of the eminent Athenian statesmen Socrates singles out lacked natural aptitude (only one sentence in 93d glances in this direction), and
it totally ignores the possibility that people could be good at something, but bad teachers of it. At 93b Plato sets up a simple dichotomy:
either good men transmitted their excellence or it is not transmis-
sible; these are the terms of the discussion. Plato's failure to take into
account the issue of the aptitude of the sons is particularly odd
because he shows himself aware of this possibility at *Protagoras*
327b–c, which was almost certainly written before *Meno* (though this
could be used as evidence to argue the opposite case: S. Cahn, 'A
Puzzle Concerning the *Meno* and the *Protagoras*', *Journal of the History of Philosophy*, 11 (1973), 535–7). Bluck argues (pp. 27–8) that
the argument is purely *ad hominem*: Anytus' prejudices preclude
consideration of the sons' aptitude, and so Plato has Socrates omit it.

93d *could throw a javelin from horseback while remaining upright*: no mean
feat in the days before saddles and stirrups, and a standard part of an
Athenian cavalryman's training.

93e *certainly not*: Plato also draws attention to the apparent inability of
fathers to pass on their virtues to their sons at *Protagoras* 319e–320b
and *Alcibiades I* 118d–e (see also *Laches* 179b–180b). This is a pity,
because it is not a very strong argument. Anytus is more nearly right
(though he spoils the point with his snobbishness) at 92e: a great deal
of one's moral education comes not from individuals but from 'the
inherited conglomerate'. Interestingly, in *Republic* Plato allows that
the philosopher-kings could inculcate morality, based on true beliefs,
in the common run of humankind; the reason the fathers cited here
fail to do so is, then, presumably due to their lack of knowledge.

94d *among the allies abroad*: on the 'allies', see the note on *Laches* 179c.

94e *too busy looking after the city's affairs*: see *Laches* 179c.

95a *Anytus is angry*: it is not quite clear why, since Socrates has not been
particularly offensive. But Plato wants us to remember that Anytus
will be one of Socrates' prosecutors, and thereby to underline the
overriding pessimistic—even tragic—tone of the early dialogues.
Socrates was a good man, with a noble mission, yet all he really
succeeded in doing was irritating his fellow Athenians, who then
condemned him to death.

95d *where he says*: the two fragments that follow are lines 33–6 and 434–8.

96a *even though the issue is the same*: there is no real contradiction: in the
first four lines quoted, Theognis is taking 'wits' to be a natural

endowment which can be spoiled or enhanced by the company one keeps; in the second set of five lines, he says that, precisely because intelligence is a natural endowment and not teachable, it is possible for a good man to become bad, but not for a bad man to become good. Plato gives Socrates a long parody of Sophistic manipulation of the meaning of poems at *Protagoras* 339a–347a.

96c   *didn't we agree*: see 89d–e.

96d   *and Prodicus in mine*: for Prodicus, see the Index of Names. The sense in which Socrates ironically describes himself as Prodicus' student is that they were both in pursuit of definitions. Whereas the Sophist was after dictionary definitions, however, Socrates tried to find real definitions: see pp. xxxiii–xxxvii.

96e   *we were surely right to agree*: at 87e.

97b   *doesn't know it*: the contrast between someone who believes he knows the way to Larisa (presumably because he has been told by someone else) and someone with personal experience, and therefore knowledge, is telling. Plato means us to think that recollection, as access to knowledge, is just as vivid and immediate as firsthand experience, even though it is, after all, recollection. Apart from this point of minor interest, nothing should be built on the use here of a piece of factual knowledge: knowing the way to Larisa is simply an example of the reliability of knowledge; Plato is not restricting all knowledge to either factual information or firsthand acquaintance.

97d   *knowledge is so much more highly valued than true belief*: the distinction between knowledge and belief (if it is not merely commonsensical) goes back to the Presocratic thinkers Xenophanes and Parmenides, and the devaluation of belief was an element of that tradition (taken over by Plato himself in *Gorgias*). Plato is being radical here in pointing out that for practical purposes true belief was as effective as knowledge, and in later dialogues (where his emphasis is not on practical purposes, but on access to metaphysical reality) he reverts to the denigration of belief.

97d   *Perhaps there aren't any in Thessaly*: there were none anywhere, of course, but this is a little dig at Meno for coming from a cultural backwater. Plato also mentions the reputed mobility of Daedalus' statues at *Euthyphro* 11b–d.

98a   *by working out the reason*: if you work out *why* your true belief is true, if you 'have learned the axiomatic structure of the system in question and can prove any one of its elements' (A. Nehamas, p. 237, in Day (ed.)), you understand it and convert it into knowledge. You make it stable too, because your understanding makes it impossible for you to have your mind changed by someone else. Many modern philosophers too would agree that 'justified true belief' is a good working

definition of knowledge. It is very important to notice that the difference between knowledge and belief in *Meno* does not depend on their
objects (as in Plato's middle-period theory of Forms, in which Forms
are the only objects of knowledge), but on their degree of certainty.
The *same* thing—e.g. the road to Larisa or the slave's geometry—can
be the object of both knowledge and belief. But the fact that knowledge involves working out the reason has an important and often
overlooked implication: it is only topics where there are such chains
of proofs that can be the objects of knowledge. Plato is moving
towards his middle-period denial that the sensory world, which is
accessible to immediate acquaintance, can be an object of knowledge.
The best discussion of this much-discussed passage is G. Fine,
'Knowledge and True Belief in the *Meno*', *Oxford Studies in Ancient
Philosophy*, 27 (2004), 41–81.

98a *as we agreed earlier*: the reference must be to 85c–d, although Plato
did not talk about any such process there (a fact of which Tarrant
makes much, in 'By Calculation of Reason?', in P. Huby and G. Neal
(eds.), *The Criterion of Truth* (Liverpool: Liverpool University Press,
1989), 55–82). Plato is conflating 85c–d with the method of hypothesis of 86e ff., which has to do with chains of causal reasoning; for
reasons for thinking of the method of hypothesis as recollection, see
pp. xli–xliii. This sentence slightly modifies our understanding of
recollection. Earlier it seemed as though recollection was the initial
realization that, say, the square on the hypotenuse has double the area
of the square whose diagonal forms the hypotenuse. Now we see that
recollection is not just this initial realization, but the whole, perhaps
gradual, process of converting the initial realization (true belief) into
knowledge. See also 84a for recollection as a journey or process.

99c *anything they say*: an almost verbatim quotation from Plato, *Apology*
22c (about poets).

99c *despite the fact that they have no knowledge*: this is sophistic, of course,
and especially so under the circumstances, since Plato is ignoring any
tertium quid between knowledge and ignorance/inspiration, despite
the fact that he has just set up true belief as an intermediate. There is
a severe tension here, threatening to undermine the whole dialogue:
if what the slave has at the end of Socrates' questioning is true belief
(98a), then true belief is teachable (in the sense of 'recollectable'); but
then it makes no sense to claim that *only* knowledge is teachable, and
to dismiss true belief as available only by divine dispensation.

99e *may not like what you're saying*: because Socrates has denied
politicians such as Anytus any knowledge.

100a *dart around like shadows*: Homer, *Odyssey* 10.495.

100b *before asking how men come to get it*: see 71a–b, 86d.

TEXTUAL NOTES

Variations from the Oxford Classical Text:

Charmides 166b2: Reading ἐπιστήμη instead of στατική (van der Ben).
Charmides 167d4: ἀκοή (van der Ben).
Charmides 168b2: αὐτή (Shorey).
Charmides 170a10–b1: Retaining the nominatives found in the MSS.
Charmides 170e6: Reading [οὐ] (Schofield).
Charmides 171c8–9: Omitting ὥσπερ οἱ ἄλλοι δημιουργοί as a meaningless gloss.

Laches 184c9–d1: ὥσπερ ἔτι του διακρινουντος (Heindorf).
Laches 185d10–11: σκοπουμεν ὃ σκοπουμεν (Cron).
Laches 188d5: ζην [ἡρμοσμένος οὐ] (Schanz).
Laches 195c8: [εἰπειν οἰον] (Badham).
Laches 199c1: [καὶ πάντως ἐχόντων] (Stallbaum).
Laches 199d9–e1: [καὶ τὰ μή] (Badham).
Laches 201a3: λόγου (Heusde).

Lysis 211e8: [ἤ] (Watt).
Lysis 212c6: Reading μὴ instead of καὶ (Müller).
Lysis 212e7: <μὴ> (Schanz).
Lysis 214d2: <ἀεί> εἴη (Waterfield).
Lysis 216c7–d2: I have moved this sentence to c2, where it fits, punctuated with parenthetical dashes, as a long aside. The move also makes sense of the γάρ of d2.
Lysis 218b8: Reading οὐ instead of οὖ (Sedley).
Lysis 219b3: Omitting Burnet's added <του φίλου>.
Lysis 219c7: ἀλλὰ λήξει (Apelt) ἐπ' ἐκείνῳ (McTighe).

Meno 74b3: προσβιβάσαι (MSS).
Meno 75d7: ἐρωτων (Thompson).
Meno 76e7: comma after ἐκείνη (Thompson).
Meno 78b5: τούτου (MSS).
Meno 79b7: Giving τί οὖν δή to Meno (Stallbaum).
Meno 81a1: οὔκουν (Denniston).
Meno 83c5: τέταρτον (MSS).
Meno 87d5: comma after ἄλλο (Bluck).
Meno 88a2: Οὔκ (misprint in OCT).
Meno 89c6: punctuating without a question mark (Buttmann).
Meno 94e6: ῥᾴδιον (MSS).
Meno 96b3: punctuating with a dash, not a question mark (Bluck).

Meno 97a9: εἴ τις εἰδὼς (Venetus 189).
Meno 99a7: ἐπιστήμη (BTW).
Meno 99d9: Σειος (Maas, from Aristippus).

INDEX OF NAMES

Abaris the Hyperborean: a legendary shamanistic healer from the far north. The Hyperboreans were supposed to live 'beyond the north wind (Boreas)' in a kind of magical paradise sacred to Apollo.

Aeneas: a Trojan hero from the legendary Trojan War, later credited with the foundation of Rome.

Aleuadae: see ARISTIPPUS.

Anacreon: a famous sixth-century lyric poet, from the island of Teos. Over 150 fragments of his work survive, in various metres.

Anytus: a prominent democratic politician at the end of the fifth century, he is best known as one of the three prosecutors of Socrates at his trial in 399—so it is perhaps not surprising that Plato's portrait is barbed.

Aristeides: a famous Athenian statesman, prominent along with his political rival Themistocles in the second Persian invasion of 480–479, and called 'the Just' for his equitable treatment of Athenian allies.

Aristippus: from Larisa in Thessaly, a friend and the lover of Meno. He was due to join Cyrus on the ill-fated expedition to Persia, and so features briefly in Xenophon's *The Expedition of Cyrus*. He was a member of the Aleuadae clan, the leading family of Larisa.

Chaerephon: a constant friend and a disciple of Socrates whose devotion bordered on fanaticism (hence his 'madness'—*Charmides* 153b), best known for the story of his visit to the Delphic oracle to ask whether there was anyone wiser than Socrates (Plato, *Apology* 20e–21a). He was exiled during the junta of the Thirty Tyrants (404–403 BCE), returned to Athens after they had been driven out, and died in about 401.

Charmides: the uncle of Plato and a recurrent figure in his dialogues, he became a confirmed oligarch who died fighting against the democratic counter-revolution after the Thirty Tyrants had taken over the government of Athens in 404 BCE. During this brief period of oligarchy, Charmides was one of the ten-man committee which administered Athens' port, Piraeus.

Cleophantus: son of Themistocles, and famous for being a spoiled brat.

Critias: the leader of the Thirty Tyrants whose brutal oligarchic regime in Athens was a cacophonous coda at the end of the Peloponnesian War. He died during the democratic counter-revolution of 403, after only a few months in power. He was the uncle and guardian of Charmides, and a composer of tragedies.

Critias the son of Dropides: the great-great-grandfather of CRITIAS, and a contemporary of SOLON.

Ctesippus: a young Athenian, and part of the inner circle of Socrates' followers, if his presence at Socrates' death is anything to go by (Plato, *Phaedo* 59b). He also plays a part in Plato's dialogue *Euthydemus*.

Cydias: a little-known lyric poet. The lines paraphrased and partially quoted at *Charmides* 155d constitute his longest, and perhaps his only fragment. He may have come from the town of Hermione in the Argolis area of the Peloponnese.

Daedalus: a legendary sculptor, creator (most famously) of the labyrinth in Knossos, the wings on which he and his son Icarus flew from Crete, and numerous statues which were said to be so lifelike that they could move.

Damon: a prominent Athenian Sophist in the middle of the fifth century, and a personal friend and adviser of Pericles, the leading statesman of the era. He was particularly famous for his musical teaching (about which we can do little more than conjecture now), and had studied under the most famous teacher of the previous generation, Agathocles (also mentioned at *Protagoras* 316e).

Darius: the name of several Achaemenid rulers of the Persian empire. Before or during Socrates' time, there had been Darius I (522–486), the invader of Greece in 490, and Darius II (424–405).

Empedocles: from Acragas in Sicily, a prominent fifth-century philosopher, scientist, and shaman.

Eudorus: an otherwise unknown wrestling coach.

Gorgias: *c.*480–376 BCE, from Leontini in Sicily, one of the most prominent members of the Sophistic movement. He specialized in the budding art of rhetoric (*Meno* 95c), in which he was a great innovator. Although many elements of his style seem florid and artificial to us today, he appears to have dazzled his contemporaries.

Hera: the divine wife of Zeus, king of gods and men. Her chief provinces were royalty, childbirth, and marriage.

Heracles: the legendary son of Zeus, famous for his civilizing labours, who transcended his mortal nature to become a god.

Hesiod: fl. *c.*700 BCE; considered the second epic poet of Greece, after HOMER. His *Theogony* orders the gods into rationalistic genealogies and recounts stories about many of them, while *Works and Days* is full of practical and moral advice on daily life for the peasant farmer.

Hippothales: a youngish Athenian at the time of *Lysis*; nothing is known of him beyond his presence in this dialogue.

Homer: fl. *c.*750; the greatest epic poet of Greece. His *Iliad* sings of the death and glory of the legendary Trojan War, while his *Odyssey* recounts the fanciful and marvellous adventures of one Greek hero, Odysseus, returning from the war to his homeland.

Ismenias: a democrat and leader of Thebes at the end of the fifth and beginning of the fourth century BCE.

Laches: a prominent Athenian general and political conservative during the early part of the Peloponnesian War, he was killed at the Battle of Mantinea in 418.

Lamachus: one of the leading Athenian generals in the Peloponnesian War, and one of Nicias' colleagues on the expedition to Sicily, where he lost his life in 414.

Lysimachus: a wealthy but undistinguished Athenian nobleman. His son Aristeides was for a short while a member of Socrates' circle, but left (according to Plato, at *Theaetetus* 150e–151a, imitated by ps.-Plato, *Theages* 130a–e) before reaping the full benefits. Born about 480 BCE, Lysimachus was still alive in 402, the dramatic date of *Meno*: see *Meno* 94a.

Lysis: a young aristocratic Athenian boy, aged about 12 at the time of this conversation with Socrates. As was usual in Athenian society, he was named after his paternal grandfather.

Melesias: virtually unknown apart from his mentions in *Laches*. His son Thucydides may have been an associate of Socrates (ps.-Plato, *Theages* 130a–b). Melesias himself was one of the moderate oligarchs who seized power in Athens in 411 and ruled for a few months as a Council of 400 members.

Menexenus: a young aristocratic Athenian associate of Socrates, cousin of Ctesippus, and the chief interlocutor of the dialogue *Menexenus*.

Meno: a young Thessalian aristocrat from Pharsalus, whose family had long had ties to Athens. Xenophon gives him a savage obituary (*The Expedition of Cyrus* 2.6.21–9), after his death during the campaign of the Persian prince Cyrus to wrest the throne of the Persian empire from his brother, as avaricious, scheming, self-interested, and lacking any sense of justice.

Miccus: the owner of the wrestling-school where the conversation of *Lysis* takes place, and otherwise unknown.

Nicias: an Athenian nobleman who combined enormous wealth with political and military caution, and died partly as a result of the latter trait during the catastrophic Athenian attempt to conquer Sicily in 415–413. His son Niceratus (*Laches* 200d) was put to death by the oligarchs who were briefly in control of Athens in 404 and 403.

Paralus: along with Xanthippus, the two legitimate sons of PERICLES, who also had a son by his non-Greek mistress Aspasia, and adopted both Alcibiades and his brother Cleinias. Both Paralus and Xanthippus died of the plague in 429 BCE.

Pericles: c.495–429, an outstanding statesman and the virtual ruler of supposedly democratic Athens from about 450 until his death from the plague.

Persephone: legendary daughter of Demeter and, as wife of Hades, queen of the underworld.

Pheidias: the most famous sculptor of fifth-century Greece, famed for his statue of Zeus in Olympia (one of the wonders of the ancient world) and in Athens especially for the statue of Athena Promachos on the Acropolis and the cult statue of Athena in the Parthenon. He was a close associate of Pericles, at whose instigation the great temples and memorials of classical Athens were built, and was the supervisor of the construction of the Parthenon.

Pindar: 518–*c.*440, from Cynoscephalae in Boeotia, the most famous lyric poet of ancient Greece. Quite a few of his poems survive, particularly those he was commissioned to write in celebration of athletic victories.

Polycrates: an Athenian democrat at the end of the fifth and beginning of the fourth centuries BCE. Some time early in the fourth century, he wrote a pamphlet attacking Socrates on political grounds. The pamphlet forms the background to much of the defence of Socrates in the first two chapters of Xenophon's *Memoirs of Socrates*.

Prodicus: originally from the island of Ceos, Prodicus was one of the most famous of the itinerant Sophists who spent time in Athens. He was an atheist and a moralist, but was most famous for his work towards establishing what we might call the first Greek dictionary, especially by distinguishing near synonyms. Plato is generally more respectful of him than he is of most Sophists, though from time to time he gently mocks this aspect of his work—in this volume, at *Charmides* 163d and *Meno* 75e—and when he has Socrates claim to be the pupil of Prodicus (as at *Meno* 96d), this is certainly ironic.

Protagoras: from Abdera in northern Greece, the first and greatest Sophist (*c.*490–*c.*420 BCE). His views are extensively discussed by Plato in *Protagoras* and *Theaetetus*. An original thinker in many fields, he was a relativist, a humanist, a liberal political thinker, and an agnostic, but was most famous as a teacher of rhetoric.

Pyrilampes: a fifth-century Athenian aristocrat, famous for having introduced peacocks into Athens, which he brought back from a diplomatic mission to Persia. He became Plato's stepfather when he married his niece, Plato's mother Perictione.

Socrates: the constant protagonist of Plato's dialogues, witty, wise, merciless with his interlocutors' pretensions, and equipped with a devastating method for exposing flaws in their thinking. He was born in Athens in 469 BCE and was put to death by the restored democracy in 399 on the charges of irreligion and corrupting the young men of the city.

Solon: the Athenian lawgiver of the early sixth century, whom fourth-century Athenians looked back on as the founder of their democracy, though the system he established was actually a graduated timocracy: the wealthier one was, the more political power one could gain. Solon became one of the traditional Seven Sages of Greece, and many wise and pithy sayings were attributed to him. He was an excellent poet—poetry being in his day the only medium for didactic work—and he wrote poems to explain and justify his political policies as well as on lighter subjects. He was the remote ancestor of the family to which Critias, Charmides, and Plato himself belonged.

Stephanus: brother of Melesias, otherwise unknown.

Stesilaus: the teacher of the art of fighting in armour whose display occasions the conversation of *Laches*. He is otherwise unknown, but his subject was popular. At any rate, we know of others working in the same or similar fields at much the same time: the brothers Euthydemus and Dionysodorus (Plato, *Euthydemus* 271c–d; Xenophon, *Memorabilia* 3.1), and Phalinus (Xenophon, *The Expedition of Cyrus* 2.1.7).

Taureas: owner of a wrestling-ground, and wealthy enough to be required under Athenian law to finance the production of plays at a dramatic festival (Plutarch, *Life of Alcibiades* 16), but otherwise unknown. The wrestling-grounds and gymnasia of Athens were popular meeting-places for men of the leisured class.

Teiresias: legendary blind prophet, capable of understanding the language of birds and beasts as well as of predicting the future, whose adventures included a spell as a woman.

Themistocles: *c.*530–462 BCE. A great Athenian military commander during the second Persian War (490–489), and one of the statesmen chiefly responsible for establishing Athens' potential for greatness afterwards.

Theognis: elegiac poet of the later sixth century BCE, from Megara. A large number of short poems or couplets survive under his name, but not all are genuine.

Thucydides: not to be confused with the historian, this Thucydides was one of the most important conservative politicians in Athens in the 440s, during the inexorable rise to power of his rival, PERICLES. His son Melesias features in *Laches*.

Xanthias: an otherwise unknown wrestling coach.

Xanthippus: see PARALUS.

Zalmoxis: a god of the Getae (a tribe from Thrace – roughly, Bulgaria and the bit of northern Greece just south of Bulgaria), who was said by Herodotus to have been originally a slave of the mystic Greek philosopher Pythagoras, from whom he learnt his shamanistic powers. He returned to his people, used his knowledge to become their king, and was later deified.

Zeus: the divine lord and father of gods and men.

The Oxford World's Classics Website

www.worldsclassics.co.uk

- Browse the full range of Oxford World's Classics online

- Sign up for our monthly e-alert to receive information on new titles

- Read extracts from the Introductions

- Listen to our editors and translators talk about the world's greatest literature with our Oxford World's Classics audio guides

- Join the conversation, follow us on Twitter at OWC_Oxford

- Teachers and lecturers can order inspection copies quickly and simply via our website

www.worldsclassics.co.uk

American Literature

British and Irish Literature

Children's Literature

Classics and Ancient Literature

Colonial Literature

Eastern Literature

European Literature

Gothic Literature

History

Medieval Literature

Oxford English Drama

Poetry

Philosophy

Politics

Religion

The Oxford Shakespeare

A complete list of Oxford World's Classics, including Authors in Context, Oxford English Drama, and the Oxford Shakespeare, is available in the UK from the Marketing Services Department, Oxford University Press, Great Clarendon Street, Oxford OX2 6DP, or visit the website at www.oup.com/uk/worldsclassics.

In the USA, visit www.oup.com/us/owc for a complete title list.

Oxford World's Classics are available from all good bookshops. In case of difficulty, customers in the UK should contact Oxford University Press Bookshop, 116 High Street, Oxford OX1 4BR.

Bhagavad Gita

The Bible Authorized King James Version
  With Apocrypha

Dhammapada

Dharmasūtras

The Koran

The Pañcatantra

**The Sauptikaparvan (from the
  Mahabharata)**

**The Tale of Sinuhe and Other Ancient
  Egyptian Poems**

The Qur'an

Upaniṣads

ANSELM OF CANTERBURY   **The Major Works**

THOMAS AQUINAS   **Selected Philosophical Writings**

AUGUSTINE   **The Confessions
On Christian Teaching**

BEDE   **The Ecclesiastical History**

HEMACANDRA   **The Lives of the Jain Elders**

KĀLIDĀSA   **The Recognition of Śakuntalā**

MANJHAN   **Madhumalati**

ŚĀNTIDEVA   **The Bodhicaryàvatàra**